INDUSTRIALIZATION, TRADE AND
MARKET FAILURES

Industrialization, Trade and Market Failures

The Role of Government Intervention in Brazil and South Korea

Mauricio Mesquita Moreira

Senior Lecturer in Development Economics
University of Rio de Janeiro

Foreword by
Sanjaya Lall

St. Martin's Press

HD
3616
.B83
M67
1995

First published in Great Britain 1995 by
MACMILLAN PRESS LTD
Houndmills, Basingstoke, Hampshire RG21 2XS
and London
Companies and representatives
throughout the world

A catalogue record for this book is available
from the British Library.

ISBN 0–333–61891–2

10	9	8	7	6	5	4	3	2	1
04	03	02	01	00	99	98	97	96	95

Printed and bound in Great Britain by
Antony Rowe Ltd
Chippenham, Wiltshire

First published in the United States of America 1995 by
Scholarly and Reference Division,
ST. MARTIN'S PRESS, INC.,
175 Fifth Avenue,
New York, N.Y. 10010

ISBN 0–312–12223–3

Library of Congress Cataloging-in-Publication Data
Moreira, Mauricio Mesquita.
Industrialization, trade and market failures : the role of
government intervention in Brazil and South Korea / Mauricio
Mesquita Moreira ; foreword by Sanjaya Lall.
p. cm.
Includes bibliographical references and index.
ISBN 0–312–12223–3
1. Industrial policy—Brazil.   2. Industrial policy—Korea (South)
3. Brazil—Economic policy.   4. Korea (South)—Economic
policy—1960– I. Title.
HD3616.B83M67 1995
338.95195—dc20   94–18288
                                                        CIP

Contents

Contents

List of Tables

Foreword

The recent past has seen an explosion of interest in the development field on the subject of industrial policy and the role of the government in promoting industrialization. In part this reflected the natural swing of the pendulum from the extreme free-market ideology that pervaded most of the 1980s. In part it was driven by the growing evidence that the most successful industrializing countries in the developing world, the larger NIEs of East Asia, did not conform to the neoliberal image that had been painted of them at the height of the free market dogmatism. They were highly *dirigiste*, and their interventions were specifically targeted to 'picking winners' in industry. Their interventions were, moreover, not confined to promoting selected activities by offering infant industry protection. They covered domestic competition, foreign investment and the whole gamut of factor markets, from credit and labour to training and technology. The pattern of interventions varied, and these differences had clearly discernible effects on the industrial structures and patterns of specialization that resulted.

To put it simply, the most successful NIEs did practically everything wrong by the neoclassical book. The only exception was that their interventions were geared to succeeding in export markets rather than to achieving self-sufficiency in near isolationist conditions; this was the main ostensible difference between the NIEs and the host of less successful import-substituting countries. Yet being export-oriented is not to be non-interventionist. The exact relationship between export-orientation, interventions and industrial success remains an area that is not properly understood, and a great deal of the debate, especially from the neoclassical and neoliberal camps (the two are not always identical), remains dogged by ideology and obfuscation. The World Bank's recent study of the 'East Asian Miracle' is also unfortunately in this camp. The central issue, of market failures in industrialization, remains to be fully understood and its solutions appreciated. The theory and empirical evidence on these are still surprisingly weak. In the mainstream of development economics most investigation avoids the issue by making general assumptions about how efficient markets are rather than looking at the failures that exist. The way that some governments managed to overcome the constraints imposed by imperfect markets is thus relegated to the attic of non-issues. Yet it is crucial to policy-making, not only in establishing new industries but in re-structuring existing ones to cope with a more competitive and techno-logically challenging world.

This book by Mauricio Moreira is particularly welcome because it tackles market failures and the role of government in industrialization directly. In a provocative, perceptive and comprehensive comparison of trade and industrial strategies in South Korea and Brazil, Moreira takes to pieces the neoclassical characterization of industrial success and the theory that underlies it. He shows that it was not the existence of intervention *per se* that led to Brazil's relatively poor performance but the fact that its interventions were not properly designed to over-come market failures, and not disciplined by the objective of penetrat-ing world markets. South Korea intervened more comprehensively, but the nature of its interventions and their compelling objective of achieving export growth led to success unparalleled since Japan's.

The facts of the Korean case are now relatively well known, though the analysis of its interventions is still incomplete. The facts of the Brazilian case are far less understood, yet carry enormous interest for development economists. Its macroeconomic mismanagement is legen-dary and well understood, but the contribution of badly designed and implemented industrial strategy to holding back Brazil's export growth has been neglected. This book is the best account to date of the rea-sons why Brazil's import substitution policies failed. The reasons are not to do with the existence of interventions and the loss of static resource allocation benefits – they are to do with the failure to ad-dress the real market failures in becoming industrially efficient. The case is common to many import-substituting regimes, but this book provides new insights that should prove useful to all students of de-velopment and to policy makers. In the growing literature comparing Latin America and East Asia, Moreira's contribution stands out as one of the most interesting and valuable.

Queen Elizabeth House, Oxford   SANJAYA LALL

Acknowledgements

This book would not have been possible without the help of a group of people and institutions, to whom I wish to express my acknowledgements.

First, I thank Dr M. Pemberton of the University College London for his patient and effective supervision. Second, I would like to thank the following people for helping to clarify my arguments, and for giving me access to key information: Dr Brian Hindley of London School of Economics; Dr Paulo Tigre and Dr Rogerio Studart of the University of Rio de Janeiro; Dr Mike Hobday and Dr Hubert Schmitz of the University of Sussex; Dr Soogil Young and Dr Ji- Hong Kim of the Korea Development Institute; Dr Young-Suk Hyun of the Hannam University; Messrs Young Rak Choi, Jang-Jae Lee and Dr Taeyoung Shin, Dr Young-Sik Choi and Dr Wan-Min Kim of the Center for Science and Technology Policy; Mr Young-Chan Park of the Ministry of Trade and Industry; Mr Hank Sik Park of the Ministry of Science and Technology; and Ambassador Luis Amado.

Dr Sanjaya Lall of Oxford University deserves special mention as my main source of inspiration. His ideas and comments were crucial for my intellectual development, and for the development of this book.

I would like also to thank the financial support from the National Research Council (CNPQ) and from the Central Research Fund of the University of London. They were complemented by the priceless institutional support provided by the Korean Ministries of Trade and Industry, and of Science and Technology.

Finally, I wish to acknowledge the psychological and emotional support from my dearest friends, Heloisa Siffert and Maria do Carmo Moreira.

MAURICIO MESQUITA MOREIRA

List of Acronyms

AA	Automatic Approval
BEFIEX	Fiscal Incentives for Exports
BNDE	Banco Nacional de Desenvolvimento Econômico e Social
BOK	Bank of Korea
BP	Balance of Payments
CAPES	Campaign for the Improvement of the Higher Education Staff
CDI	Industrial Development Council
CNPQ	National Research Council
DC	Developed Countries
DRCs	Domestic Resource Costs
DUP	Directly Unproductive Activities
EP	Export Promotion
EPZ	Export Processing Zones
ERPs	Effective Rates of Protection
FCIL	Foreign Capital Investment Law
FDI	Foreign Direct Investment
FNDCT	National Fund of Scientific and Technological Development
GDI	Gross Domestic Investment
GDP	Gross Domestic Product
GNP	Gross National Product
HCI	Heavy and Chemical Industries
ICORs	Incremental Capital-Output Ratios
IMF	International Monetary Fund
INPI	National Institute of Industrial Property Rights
IS	Import Substitution
KAIS	Korea Advanced Institute of Science
KIST	Korea Institute of Science and Technology
LDCs	Less Developed Countries
LPF	Local Private Firm
MCT	Ministry for Science and Technology
MES	Minimum Efficient Scale
MOST	Ministry of Science and Technology
NAIs	Núcleos de Articulação com a Indústria
NBFI	Non banking Financial Institutions
NDP	National Development Plan
NICs	Newly Industrializing Countries

NIEs	Newly Industrializing Economies
NTBs	Non-Tariff Barriers
OECD	Organization for Economic Cooperation and Development
PPP	Purchase Power Parity
R&D	Research and Development
S&T	Science and Technology
SE	State Enterprises
SENAI	National Service for Industrial Apprenticeship
SMF	Small and Medium Firm
SNDCT	National System of Scientific and Technological Development
SUMOC	Superintendência de Moeda e Crédito
TNCs	Transnational Corporations
UN	United Nations
WPI	Wholesale Price Index

Introduction*

The outstanding industrial and macroeconomic performances of the East Asian newly industrialized countries (NICs) over the last three decades (Table 1), have deeply affected the debate over the best strategy for a successful industrialization. The structuralist thinking, which had originated and dominated development economics during the 1950s and 1960s, and which emphasized government intervention in the face of the LDCs' 'structural rigidities', was gradually replaced over the 1970s and 1980s by a new orthodoxy: the so-called neoclassical approach.[1]

Drawing on neoclassical growth (Solow 1957) and trade (Heckscher–Ohlin–Samuelson) models, where markets are assumed to be perfectly competitive, the new orthodoxy produced a very influential interpretation of the East Asian success, and of the relative failure of other LDCs. The key for this performance differential would have been, first, the extent of government intervention in the product and factor markets, and second, the trade-orientation of this intervention (trade and payment policies). Despite being quite distinct, these issues were combined in a new terminology, and given a 'one-to-one correspondence'. That is, heavy intervention was equated with inward-orientation and *laissez-faire* with outward-orientation, under the categories of import-substituting (IS) and export-promotion (EP) policy regimes. The former would have been adopted by the majority of the LDCs and the latter by the East Asian NICs.

This book aims to challenge this interpretation, by re-examining the role of government intervention in the industrialization of two countries, which, according to the neoclassical view, would have epitomised the differences between the IS and EP regimes. That is, Brazil and South Korea (hereafter Korea). The former is the largest country, in terms of GDP and manufacturing value-added, to have its policy regime classified as IS, and, for that matter, the largest NIC and LDC. The latter, by the same token, is the largest and arguably the most successful country, whose policy regime was labelled as EP.[2]

Drawing on Lall's (1991, 1992a,b) framework, which emphasises the role of government in overcoming market failures, we seek to show that even though trade orientation seemed to have been crucial to the differences in performance between these two countries, one cannot say the same about the extent of government intervention. Here, the

1

Table 1 Industrial and macroeconomic performance of selected NICs

| | Growth (%)[1] | | | | | | MVA capital goods (% GDP)[2] | External patent[3] | GDP deflator | | Inc. dist. top 20% | ICOR[4] | | Productivity (%)[5] | Debt/exp.[6] |
| | (a) GDP | | (b) Manufacturing output | | (c) Manufacturing exports | | | | | | | | | | |
	1965–80	1980–89	1965–80	1980–89	1965–80	1980–89	1987	1962–87	1965–80	1980–89	1987	1970–79	1980–88	1970–80	1989
Brazil	9.0	3.0	9.8	2.2	22.1	7.2	5.7	4.8	31.3	227.8	64.5 (0.59)	3.2	7.1	1.0	31.3
Mexico	6.5	0.7	7.4	0.7	9.4	24.3	2.9	27.7	13.0	78.7	n.a.	3.5	23.1	3.6	39.6
India	3.6	5.3	4.5	7.3	3.0	8.1*	2.9	6.1	7.5	7.7	41.4	7.4	3.9	0.1	26.4
Hong Kong	8.6	7.1	n.a.	6.0	17.2	15.0*	6.1	35.8	8.1	7.1	47.0	3.8	4.2	n.a.	n.a.
Singapore	10.0	6.1	13.2	6.0	21.7	11.0*	16.9	10.2	5.1	7.1	48.9	4.8	8.5	1.7	n.a.
Taiwan	9.0	8.4	12.4	8.3	35.1	17.2	10.3	56.9	7.0†	1.7†	38.0	3.9	4.1	11.9	11.4
Korea	9.9	9.7	16.0	12.0	31.2	16.2*	10.3	6.9	18.4	5.0	43.7 (0.36)	2.7	4.0	5.8	18.5
LDC[7]	5.8	3.8	7.8	6.0	n.a.	n.a.	n.a.	n.a.	16.7	53.7	n.a.	n.a.	n.a.	n.a.	n.a.

[1] (a) and (b) constant prices and (c) current US dollars. All rates calculated by the least square method except for 1965–80 Manufacturing exports for Hong Kong and Singapore which are simple compound average rates.
[2] Manufacturing value added as a percentage of GDP.
[3] External patenting accumulated in the US, normalized by manufacturing value added in 1988.
[4] Incremental capital output ratio.
[5] Value added per worker in the manufacturing sector.
[6] External debt service as a percentage of exports.
[7] Low-middle-income countries. World Bank definition.
*1980–88. † WPI

Note: Numbers in parentheses are Gini coefficients.

Source: IBGE (1990) and PCRER (1988) for Brazil's and Korea's data on income distribution, respectively. Data on productivity, MVA, ICOR and patenting from UNCTAD as quoted in Lall and Kell (1991:277). Data for Taiwan, CEPD (1992). The rest of the data is from World Development Report (1991) and World Tables.

key distinction appears to have been not between a hands-off and hands-on approach, but between a strategy where intervention was guided and disciplined by the aim of achieving international competitiveness – and therefore by the need to overcome key market failures – and another whereby intervention was largely driven by balance-of-payments (BP) considerations, and specially by the composition of the country's import bill.

The book is divided into four chapters. Chapter 1 lays down the groundwork for the analysis by presenting, first, the main points of the neoclassical view, and second the framework that has guided the search for an alternative explanation. Chapter 2 looks at the role of government intervention in Korea's industrialization, with particular emphasis to the post-1960 period, when the EP regime was adopted. It seeks to assess the results of the relevant government interventions in the product and factor markets. Chapter 3, in turn, deals with the government's role in Brazil's industrialization, focusing on the post-1950 period, when industrialization by IS became an explicit government policy. As in Chapter 2, it tries to cover the government policies that were pertinent to industrialization, in both product and factor markets. Finally, Chapter 4 compares the experience of the two countries and draws the relevant conclusions.

1 The Theoretical Background

1.1 THE NEOCLASSICAL VIEW

As suggested in the introduction, the concepts of IS and EP regimes –
which equate interventionism with inward-orientation and liberal policies with outward-orientation – are at the heart of the neoclassical answer
to the performance differentials between the NICs. Let us look then at
their meaning and at the sort of analysis that lies behind them.[3]

The IS Regime

Seen as a product of a mistaken structuralist scepticism about export-
led growth (e.g. Prebisch 1950 and Nurske 1962) and the functioning
of LDC markets (e.g. Rosenstein-Rodan 1943, Hirschman 1958), IS
would have prompted widespread and undue government intervention
in resource allocation. Protection and subsidies to the domestic industry would have led to a catalogue of problems related to industry and
trade biases, distortions in the factor markets and to rent-seeking.

Beginning with industry bias, Neoclassicals, backed by cross-coun-
try estimates of effective rates of protection – ERPs – (Little *et al.*
1970, Balassa 1971, 1982), argue that government intervention under
IS has led to a structure of incentives with a high inter-industry vari-
ance, which diverged sharply from what would have prevailed under
free trade. This would have resulted from the policy makers' neglect
of factor endowments, and from their failure to consider inter-industry
linkages. This 'perverse' combination would have led to the promotion of industries that reflected neither the countries' static comparative advantages, nor the policy makers' initial aims.

With regard to trade bias, it is considered the regime's hallmark. As
Krueger (1981:9) put it,

> An import-substitution regime can be defined as one where the overall
> bias of incentives favours production for sale in the home market,
> replacing imports ... Formally, bias is defined as the divergence

between the domestic price ratio of importables and exportables to the foreign price ratio.

As with industry, the trade bias claim is underpinned by the afore-mentioned ERPs estimates, which show that in IS regimes the value added for domestic sales was largely higher than that of exports. This bias is regarded as resulting from high and indiscriminate import pro-tection, which reduced the relative profitability of exports not only through tariffs and non-tariff barriers – NTBs (seen as particularly dam-aging because they were extended to raw material and intermediate goods used in exportables) – but also by an overvalued exchange rate (due to a demand for imports lower then it would have been under free trade).[4]

The deleterious effects of such a bias are reckoned to have been twofold. First, the de-linking of the domestic industry from international competition by both import protection and related export discrimina-tion, would have reduced the local firms' incentives to cut costs and increase productivity, compromising their profit maximising behaviour along the lines of Leibenstein's (1981) X-inefficiency. This would have been compounded by the limited size of the LDCs' markets, which curtailed the possibilities of domestic competition, and led to monopo-listic structures. In addition, the combination of restricted access to imports, exports disincentives and a limited domestic market, precluded firms from taking advantage of economies of scale and specialization. So, the standard production and consumption costs of protection would have been magnified by X-inefficiency, by the adverse impact of mo-nopolistic behaviour on prices and output, and by the economies of scale and specialization foregone.

Second, the conjunction of import-intensive IS industries, an increas-ingly incompressible import bill (reflecting IS progress towards down-stream industries) and sluggish exports, would have led to periodic BP crises, which damaged growth, and locked governments in a 'vicious' circle of ever stricter import controls, higher trade bias, sluggish ex-ports and BP crises.

To make things worse, policy makers, in the process of distorting incentives, would have also tampered with factor markets, particularly with the financial sector. Interest rates would have been held below the opportunity cost to promote capital-intensive, IS industries. This would have led, *inter alia*, to capital-intensive techniques, low sav-ings, financial disintermediation, capital flight, and credit rationing (McKinnon 1991). The overall result would have been a crippling resource misallocation, as evidenced by rising incremental capital-output ratios (ICORs), high domestic resource costs (DRCs) and by the high rates of unemployment and underemployment.

Finally, the new orthodoxy argues that the extensive government intervention, seen as inherent in IS regimes, would have been conducive to direct unproductive profit-seeking – DUP – (Bhagwati 1982) or rent-seeking behaviour (Krueger 1974). This criticism, initially directed at import controls, was soon extended to all forms of government intervention. As Krueger (1990b:17) put it

> When economic policies create something that is to be allocated at less than its [market] value by any sort of government process, resources will be used in an effort to capture the rights to the items of value.

As resources used to capture these 'items of value' did not expand the supply of goods and services, they would have been a 'deadweight loss', which added to the other costs related to the industry and trade biases. The DUP behaviour is seen to have affected both private and government sectors alike. With regard to the latter, structuralists are understood to have had a too naïve vision of the state, overlooking the fact that the proliferation of controls would be used by governments to pursue their own 'items of value'. Or in other words, the structuralists would have neglected the risk of 'government failure'. Krueger and Orsmond (1990:8), for instance, argue that,

> In the early development literature, it was implicitly assumed that governments would behave as benevolent social guardians. Experience has shown, however, that governments may instead behave either as 'autonomous bureaucratic states' or as 'predatory authoritarian states'. In the former, the bureaucracy in effect governs and behaves to maximise its power through increasing public employment and the activities undertaken by the state. In the latter, the dictator, or oligarchic ruling group has sufficient political power to extract resources from the economy either directly (through taxation) or indirectly through providing itself services at the expense of other sectors.

The EP Regime

Whereas the neoclassical view blames the IS regime for the poor industrial and macroeconomic performance of most LDCs, it argues, on the other hand, that the EP or outward-oriented regime was the commanding factor behind the East Asian success. As suggested before, the latter regime is painted as the perfect antithesis of the former. First, it would have been trade neutral, with some authors accepting the possibility of a slight bias towards exports. For instance, according to Balassa (1989:1667), outward-orientation is defined as,

> Neutrality in the system of incentives, with effective rates of protection being on the average, approximately equal in import substituting and in export activities.

But for Krueger (1985:197),

> It is a set of policies that leaves relative domestic rewards for exporting (compared to importing) at least equal to, and possibly greater than, the rewards that would exist under free trade.

This 'trade-neutrality', again backed by the ERP estimates mentioned earlier, would have been the result of low nominal import protection across the board, offset by export incentives or subsidies, and combined with a 'realistic' exchange rate. Among the incentives, emphasis is given to the exporters' freedom to choose between domestic and imported inputs, and to their access to inputs at international prices.

Second, incentives (notably export incentives) are believed to have been industry neutral, i.e., uniform among sectors and firms. They would have been provided 'automatically' (without discretion or long delays) and would have undergone few modifications over time.

Third, almost as a corollary of the other two characteristics, government intervention would have been minimal and in a functional fashion. That is, concentrated on widely accepted market failures – in markets for technology, human capital and infrastructure – without affecting the sectoral structure of the economy.[5] Extensive and selective government intervention is generally seen as incompatible with an EP regime, particularly if this affects trade,

> In general, an outward-oriented strategy is not consistent with detailed government quantitative intervention in any aspect of trade. (Krueger 1985:208) Trade controls are either non-existent or very low ... There is little or no use of direct controls and licensing arrangements ... (World Bank 1987b:82)

The causal mechanisms linking these characteristics with the performance of the East Asian NICs are mostly explained along the lines of the free-trade argument and its derivatives. This is based on the belief that the structure of incentives under the EP regime, for being industry and trade neutral, and because of the fiscal constraints (need for tariff revenue), would have been a sort of second-best solution to free trade, emulating its resource allocation. Its adoption, therefore, would have brought the Ricardian economies of specialization, the Heckscher–Olhin–Samuelson optimal resource allocation, and the higher incomes advocated since Smith's *Wealth of Nations*.

However, if one accepts Krueger's definition of the EP regime, the case for the free-trade argument looks muddled, since, as Findlay (1981) pointed out, there is no clear reason for a regime biased towards exports to have emulated the free-trade allocation. Moreover, even if we accept Balassa's definition, the question of how the 'once and for all' gains of a move towards a neutral regime were transformed into long term growth, is not properly answered. Balassa (1981b), for instance, suggests that the neutral character of the regime would have allowed resource allocation to be optimized throughout the process of industrialization. This, because prices would have been free to adjust to changes in factor endowment provoked by the accumulation of physical and human capital (the so-called 'stage approach'). This, however, does not explain how optimal resource allocation resulted in higher manufacturing investment, total factor productivity and growth.

More recently, the so-called 'new' growth theories have been trying to produce a more robust explanation. This is usually done by making technological change endogenous (traditionally an exogenous variable in neoclassical growth models) and by giving increasing returns a growth-enhancing role. The move, then, towards an open economy would have raised growth, first, by increasing access to embodied technology at world prices, and therefore by boosting the rate of technical progress; second, by raising productivity in sectors subjected to increasing returns due to the integration to the world market; and finally by optimizing allocation and therefore freeing resources to be allocated in research and development (Romer and Rivera-Batiz 1991). Despite being more robust, this explanation raises other difficulties related to the increasing returns assumption. As Helpman and Krugman (1985) pointed out, with increasing returns, free trade (or free trade allocation) might not be the first-best policy. Specialization might dislocate sectors with scale economies, and therefore reduce total income.

Apart from these growth-related allocational and technological arguments, the neutral regime is also said to have brought other less conventional behavioural, macroeconomic and 'policy' gains (Krueger 1984). The behavioural gains would have stemmed from the higher import competition brought by trade liberalization. This would have eliminated the losses related to X-inefficiency and monopolistic structures. The macroeconomic benefit, in turn, is explained by the removal of the BP constraints to growth, brought about by the end of export discrimination and by the realistic exchange rates. And finally, the 'policy' gain would have arisen from the fact that the reduced and neutral character of government intervention, would have minimized the deadweight loss associated with DUP activities.

1.2 THE BASIS FOR AN ALTERNATIVE VIEW

There seems to be no doubt that some of the neoclassical arguments have a great deal of validity. As the chapter on Brazil will show, export pessimism, combined with excessive mistrust of the market mechanism, produced wholesale government intervention and a costly industrialization, guided largely by the country's import composition. There was no regard for resource endowments or comparative advantages, and accordingly serious resource misallocations took place. The lack of international competition, either through exports or imports, left the domestic industry without enough incentives to go down the learning curve, and by looking inwards, the country forewent the potential specialization and scale economies that a more open economy could have brought. Moreover, periodic BP problems compromised long term growth, particularly in the 1980s.

Likewise, the chapter on Korea also supports the claim that outward-orientation brought, *inter alia*, better resource allocation, economies of scale and specialization, access to embodied technology at world prices, more competitive pressure on local firms to improve productivity, and a more stable BP and macroeconomic environment.

The problem with the neoclassical view, then, is not its assertion that trade orientation and relative prices matter, and that this explains a great deal of the performance differential between the East Asian NICs and the other LDCs. The trouble lies elsewhere. That is, in its attempt to equate trade orientation with government intervention, and to take the mixed results of inward-oriented countries as a clear indictment of any form of selective government intervention.

Again, as the chapter on Korea will show, and a number of other studies on Korea's industrialization has already suggested (e.g. Pack and Westphal 1986, Amsden 1989, Westphal 1990, Lall 1992a, and more recently, World Bank 1993), its policy regime was not firm, industry or trade neutral, and protection for the local industry was anything but low. In fact, government intervention in the product and factor markets, throughout every stage of its industrialization, seemed to have reached a scale that makes IS countries such as Brazil look like liberal economies. Studies of other East Asian NICs such as Wade's (1990) on Taiwan and Haggard's (1990) on Singapore also point in the same direction. The exception seems to be Hong Kong (Haggard 1990, Krueger 1985), but then, it is just the exception not the rule. In any event, the empirical case for the 'one-to-one' relationship between state intervention and trade orientation is at best weak.

When confronted with this evidence, Neoclassicals usually argue in two directions: fundamentalists contend that if selective intervention really existed, it was more of a hindrance than a help to industrial performance; moderates, in turn, – associated with the so-called market-friendly approach (World Bank 1993) – do not dispute the evidence but argue that the impact of intervention was minimal or irrelevant. The crucial factors would have been trade orientation and getting the fundamentals right (sound macroeconomic policies, investment in education, stable financial systems), as it would have been demonstrated by the case of Hong Kong.[6]

These arguments, however, neither answer the question of why generalizations were made on the basis of the exception and not the rule (Hong Kong can be a special case[7]), nor do they justify statements like 'outward-orientation is incompatible with selective intervention.' Moreover, the fact that they minimize any positive or relevant influence that selective intervention might have had, is mind-boggling, since it has affected the very variables that are dear to Neoclassicals. That is, relative prices, credit allocation, rates of return and market structures. On the other hand, one could not really expect something different of a framework where, as Shapiro and Taylor (1990) put it, the only thing not supposed to work properly is the state.

Given that, despite the neoclassical view, market imperfections and selective interventions seem to have been a fact, what this book suggests is that instead of being costly, counterproductive or ineffectual, selective interventions, at least in Korea's case, played a fundamental role in building an internationally competitive industry. Following Lall (1992a), this was so because interventions were factor-price conscious and were targeted at key market failures in the product and factor markets, which usually hinders industrialization in the third world. These interventions helped Korea to benefit from the advantages of an open economy, without having to face the drawbacks of a free-trade, hands-off regime, whose neglect of market imperfections compromises the acquisition of technological capabilities, and therefore, the exploitation of dynamic comparative advantages, and the achievement of international competitiveness.

This 'surgical' and selective approach to government intervention, contrasted sharply with that of Brazil. There, during the first stages of industrialization, the government adopted a hands-off approach, overlooking the obstacles to industrial development created by market imperfections. Later on, it gradually moved towards a IS strategy, which prompted wholesale intervention. Given the lack of selectivity, some market failures were tackled more by accident than design, but the remedies were often worse than the 'disease' (e.g. indiscriminate protection, negative interest rates). Moreover, indiscriminate intervention disrupted well-functioning areas of the market, damaging resource allocation and static comparative advantages.

So, what we are saying is: all right, we agree that government intervention, alongside trade orientation, was an important factor behind the performance differential between Brazil and Korea. Yet, not because it existed in the former and not in the latter, but because in the latter it was selective and fine-tuned to remedy important market failures, whereas in the former, it was indiscriminate (or perhaps we could say 'neutral'), and poorly designed. Why was that so? Certainly not because of the 'predatory' nature of the state, which would have been common to both countries. Leaving socio-political factors aside, a more plausible explanation seems to be related to – and in this point we have to agree with Krueger – the discipline imposed by the outward-oriented strategy, or in simpler terms, by the greater openness of the Korean economy. As she put it,

> Export orientation imposes a discipline and a set of constraints on all economic policies that prevent the adoption of very many measures severely antithetical to growth. (1990a:110)

There seems to be no doubt that in a more open economy, international prices cannot be ignored, and serve both as a constraint and as a guidance to government policy. In this sort of environment, the cost effectiveness (given the limitations and advantages of the country's factor endowment) of previous and future policies becomes more evident.

These policies, however, do not have to be of the functional kind advocated by Krueger and other adepts of the neoclassical view. Quite the contrary, the more open the economy is, the clearer are the relevant market failures, and accordingly, the easier it is to tackle them. And, as already noted, international prices and competition (not necessarily import competition) act as a safeguard against the risk of government failure.

So far we have talked a lot about market failures but have not specified them in any detail. As Lall points out, the requirements for efficient markets are very stringent,

> They include perfect competition (a large number of producers, with free entry and exit, operating under constant returns to scale and selling to a large number of buyers), full (and instant) diffusion and absorption of technology, perfect knowledge and foresight, no externalities, no missing or segmented markets, no transaction costs and no 'lumpy' (indivisible) factors ... If, however, some of these conditions do not obtain, and markets fail to operate efficiently, there is 'market failure' and optimality is not guaranteed. (1992a:3)

The neoclassical view accepts that these conditions are not met in the so-called 'public good' cases – for instance maintenance of law and order (including especially enforcement of contracts), infrastructure, certain forms of education and basic science – because 'collective consumption' and externalities prevent the market mechanism to produce optimal results (see, e.g. Krueger 1990b).

Apart from that, there would be the classical 'fair trade' (monopolies and anti-competitive behaviour), 'optimal tariff' (large countries) and *infant industry* arguments, with the latter being a case of heavily qualified acceptance. Neoclassicals concede that, in this case, intervention might be needed because of capital market failures, or because returns on technology and human capital investments are not totally 'appropriable', due to externalities transmitted through imitation and labour mobility (the 'appropriability' problem). Yet, they argue that the first best solution would be, in the former case, to develop the capital markets, and in the latter case, to subsidise investments in human capital and technology. In both cases, the second best solution would be production subsidies.

Protection would not be warranted because it would only mean trading one distortion (inequality between the shadow domestic and foreign trade marginal rates of transformation) by another (inequality between the foreign trade marginal rate of transformation and the domestic rate of substitution in consumption). Thus, there could be no way that protection would restore Pareto optimality (see Johnson 1965a, Baldwin 1969 and Corden 1974, chap. 9).

The 'market friendly' version of the neoclassical view admits that protection might be warranted because capital market imperfections in LDCs are rife, and budgetary considerations usually rule out the subsidy option. However, ERPs should be low (e.g. 10 to 15%), industry neutral and limited for a short period of time (e.g. five to eight years) because,

> Given our ignorance in regard to the extent of the additional social benefits particular manufacturing activities provide, it may be suggested to apply as a first approximation the 'market principle' in granting equal protection to all manufacturing industries and to let competition do the rest. (Balassa 1975:374)

But even so, they add,

> Trade policy is generally not a desirable instrument for encouraging domestic industry. Although protection may encourage learning by doing – by promoting production – and draw more workers to the protected sector, relative prices become distorted in favor of production for domestic markets. To offset the anti-export bias, additional measures are necessary, often resulting in a labyrinth of interventions. (World Bank 1991:103)

This 'labyrinth of interventions' is viewed as particularly damaging, given that most LDCs are assumed to lack the administrative capacity to ensure neutral incentives and to resist lobbies for long periods of protection.

Both the 'fundamentalist' and 'market friendly' versions of the neoclassical view, tend to grossly underestimate the market failures that are relevant to industrialization in LDCs. It is beyond the scope of this book to try to map out all of them. Instead, we will focus on those whose remedy by a selective and 'pro-market' government intervention, seemed to have played a key role in the performance differential between Brazil and Korea.

Market Failures in the Product Markets

Beginning with product markets, the relevant market failures seem to arise from the combination of externalities and dynamic and static factors. Let us take up each of these factors in turn.

Externalities

Externalities are actions of an individual or firm that affect another individual or firm but that are not reflected in the former's costs or benefits. As it is well known, if externalities are present, price-taking profit-maximizing behaviour (i.e., free market) is clearly not efficient.[8] Following Scitovsky's (1963) classical exposition, production externalities can be divided into two categories: technological and pecuniary.

Technological externalities are defined as external effects that are not transmitted through market transactions. With regard to industrial development, the most relevant case seems to stem from the diffusion of knowledge. That is, due to labour mobility or imitation, the benefits of innovating (or the benefits of generating knowledge) are not entirely captured by the innovator, favouring other firms or even industries. This situation drives a wedge between social and private returns, and accordingly, leads to underinvestment. Private investors only take into account the benefits that they can appropriate.

The generation of technological externalities is not 'industry neutral'. Industries where the competitive regime is 'science-based' (Nelson and Winter 1982) – i.e., where competition is closely linked to formal R&D and pure science – are more likely to generate externalities, and therefore to be affected by underinvestment.

The neoclassical answer to this imperfection is usually based on three types of argument: (a) that these externalities are irrelevant; (b) that the first best solution would be subsidies to knowledge-generation activities; and (c) that these externalities are not country specific, and therefore cannot be used as a justification for infant industry protection.[9]

Because of the obstacles involved in measuring these externalities, the first argument is not only an empirical but also a difficult question. Yet, most governments, particularly in the industrialized countries (notably the US and Japan), behave as if they were huge, distributing lavish incentives (e.g., domestic market protection, fiscal and credit subsidies and government procurement) to science-based sectors. The second argument does not allow for two vital considerations: the fiscal constraints that affect most LDCs; and the dynamic and static economies (see below) that heavily affect competition in science-based industries, making the subsidy option all the more unrealistic. And finally, the third argument is simply flawed since there is a crucial kind of knowledge – knowing how to innovate – that, due to a low inter-country-labour mobility, generates external effects that are mainly country specific. As Krugman (1984b:111), when referring to semiconductors, put it:

Knowing how to innovate, probably involves some things learned by word of mouth and some personal knowledge carried between firms by movement of individuals: the tendency of innovative firms to be founded by defectors from other firms is legendary. There is also probably an externality involved in the creation of a specialized labour market, which gives firms the needed flexibility. While the importance and nature of diffusion of this kind of knowledge cannot yet be directly measured, the economic geography of the U.S. high-technology sector, in which many firms are clustered near Boston and in California's Silicon Valley, seems to suggest that important externalities do not diffuse easily over long distances.

The second type of externality – pecuniary externalities – operates through the price system. In Scitovsky's formal definition, they arise whenever the profits of a firm are affected by the output and inputs levels of another firm. Since the latter's costs and benefits are not affected, this can result in over or underinvestment. Pecuniary externalities are particularly pertinent to industrial development when they are reciprocal and the industry is subjected to increasing returns. As a number of authors pointed out (e.g., Rosenstein-Rodan 1943, Corden 1974, and Krugman 1993), this can lead to the so-called coordination failure. That is, the price mechanism does not signal to socially profitable investments, because it does not reflect potential reciprocal externalities.[10]

Neoclassicals usually argue that this sort of market failure is irrelevant in the context of an open economy, given that the indivisibility problem virtually disappears. However, as Corden (1974:271) acknowledges, it remains likely to occur in the case of non-tradables, and, as demonstrated by Pack and Westphal (1986:111), it might be relevant even to tradables given the strong interdependence between the comparative advantages of upstream and downstream industries. Local production of inputs, for instance, might imply in domestic prices lower than import prices, because of transaction costs and a set of characteristics more appropriate to the local market. This price differential, in turn, might be a matter of 'life or death' to a downstream industry. Likewise, the establishment of a downstream industry might give a potential supplier the minimum efficient scale to break into the international market.

This sort of imperfection calls for a government role in diffusing information and in coordinating investment decisions by the private sector. This does not imply, as pointed out by World Bank (1993:92), that the government has to supplant the market as the key generator of information. Instead, it means that it has to act as an important complement. However, given that industrial development is affected by other market failures, particularly in industries with increasing returns (see below), the coordinator and information-diffusion roles might not be enough to preclude underinvestment and the associated welfare loss.

Dynamic Economies

Market failures in the product market might also stem from dynamic economies of scale in manufacturing, associated with learning and product differentiation. The former is the classical infant industry argument mentioned earlier, and following Posner (1961:330), it can be expressed formally as:

$$c = f\left(\int_0^t w_t Q_t \mathrm{d}t\right) \quad \text{for } \frac{\mathrm{d}c}{\mathrm{d}Q} < 0, \quad w_t = \varphi\,(t) > 0 \quad \text{and} \quad \varphi'(t) > 0;$$

where c is unit costs, Q the quantity produced, t the time and w the weights that are used to increase the relevancy of the recent past. This implies that first movers (fm) have a significant cost advantage over late comers (lc), and that for the latter to succeed, its learning curve has to be steeper (assuming it is linear) than the former by an amount that is an increasing function of the gap between t_0^{fm} and t_0^{lc}. The degree of difficulty involved in this task is also an increasing function of the industry's technological complexity.[11]

These dynamic economies of learning arise because, contrary to the neoclassical assumption, technology is not perfectly tradable. As Pack and Westphal (1986:108) put it

Knowledge in a communicable form is quite distinct from the capability to make effective use of that form of knowledge.

Likewise, Lall (1992b:166) draws attention to the fact that,

Technological knowledge is not shared equally among firms, nor is it easily imitated by or transferred across firms. Transfer necessarily requires learning because technologies are tacit, and their underlying principles are not always clearly understood. Thus, simply to gain mastery of a new technology requires skills, effort and investment by the receiving firm, and the extent of mastery achieved is uncertain and necessarily varies by firms according to this inputs.

Thus, latecomers in order to enter any industry have to gain technological capability (i.e. the ability to use and produce knowledge effectively)[12] which, in turn, implies investment in indigenous technological effort. This is a highly risky undertaking because:

(a) Productivity gaps are usually large, and to reduce losses, results have to be produced quickly;

(b) The lack of institutions to spread information, and the uncertainty inherent in a process of rapid development, aggravate the so-called informational imperfections (Stiglitz 1989);

(c) Investments in technology and human capital are affected by the 'appropriability' problem, noted earlier;

(d) Rapid results often require simultaneous investments by vertically linked firms (reciprocal pecuniary externalities), and as already mentioned, this is a piece of information not necessarily provided by the market;

(e) LDC firms, unlike their developed country counterparts, do no benefit from the externalities generated by a well-developed science and technology (S&T) infrastructure, or by a well-educated work force; and

(f) Constant flow of innovations by first movers, notably in 'science based' industries, can constantly shift the late comers' learning curve upwards, leading to prolonged and endless periods of losses.

The dynamic economies related to product differentiation arise from the fact that in the real world products are not homogeneous, and as Chamberlin (1933) and Joan Robinson (1933) have long pointed out, this leads to monopolistic powers. These economies were first discussed by Bain (1956), who stated that latecomers are disadvantaged because to make their product known and break the 'goodwill or preference barrier', they have either to offer their products at prices substantially lower than those of the incumbent firms, or expend heavily in advertising or both. In practice, this means that on top of the higher costs related to learning, latecomers or infant industries have to bear the financial burden of breaking the 'image' problem. As in the case of learning, these economies also depend on the technological characteristics of the industry, notably on the durability and complexity of the products.

Static Economies

On the static side, market failures arise basically from economies of scale, scope and internationalization. Again, contrary to neoclassical assumptions, increasing returns are not only a fact of life but also of theory. The literature on industrial organization has long ago (e.g., Bain *op. cit.*, Sylos-Labini 1962) incorporated the existence of economies of scale, and their implication for entry, pricing and market structure. Recently, even trade theorists have done the same (e.g. Helpman and Krugman 1985). Thus, instead of Marshallian firms with no market power, 'real' industry is dominated by large firms, which benefit from scale economies that are product (greater specialization of labour and machinery), plant (indivisibilities and the 'two-thirds rule' in continuous process industries) and firm specific (capital-raising economies, overheads, bulk-buying of inputs and scales economies in advertising and R&D).[13] Despite being a static concept, these economies have also a dynamic dimension for, as shown before, learning tends to increase both with scale and time (cumulative output).

The existence of scale economies (internal to the firm) also implies that incumbents are usually part of market structures, where marginal pricing means losses, and where scale related barriers to entry – e.g. high initial capital requirements and large (as a percentage of the market) minimal efficient scales (MES) – allow prices above average costs, i.e. long-term pure profits.[14]

The second static imperfection, called economies of scope by Baumol *et al.* (1982), make late comers often face not only large, but also diversified firms in the real world. This arises from,

> The possibility that cost savings may result from simultaneous production of several different outputs in a single enterprise, as contrasted with their production in isolation. (ibid. p.71)

That is, $C(y_1, y_2) < C(y_1, 0) + C(0, y_2)$, where C is the cost function and y_i the relevant products. Economies of scope are largely attributed to inputs that are readily shared in the production of different products. For instance, multiproduct firms can economize on management services by having a common pool of financial planners, accountants and market researchers, or they can optimize the use of machinery that is not product specific. Yet, there are also other multiproduct economies that are not linked to 'public inputs'. For instance, the economies of risk spreading, earnings stabilization, multibrand interaction (Scherer and Ross 1990:122), and the advantages of cross-subsidization or internal capital markets.

Finally, economies of internationalization imply that firms in the real world are often not only large and diversified, but also concurrently producing in several national markets. Even though it is difficult to distinguish these economies from those of scale and scope, there seems to be no doubt that internationalized firms have specific advantages stemming, *inter alia*, from: the ability to exploit factor price differences by spreading its manufacturing based among different countries; access to different capital markets; and intra-firm transfer of funds to minimize tax payments (see, e.g. Lall and Streeten 1977).

This all means that on top of cost disadvantages stemming from dynamic economies of learning and product differentiation, latecomers also have to come to terms with cost disadvantages and barriers associated with scale, conglomeration and internationalization. These are all imperfections that *do not depend on capital market failures*. They act by depressing the expected private returns and by magnifying the private investor's perception of risk. The 'shadow' rate of return and the 'shadow' risk, i.e., those that would prevail if dynamic and static economies were non-existent, would be certainly more attractive to latecomers. Accordingly, if allowed to operate freely, the market will, in all likelihood, lead to below-the-socially-optimum investment in industries where there might be dynamic comparative advantages,[15] or even in industries where changes in factor prices suggest static advantages. In short, they preclude the smooth 'stage approach' development suggested by the neoclassical view.

The Nature of the Intervention

These imperfections described above cannot be remedied by having the government acting only on the coordination failure. Nor are they likely to be remedied by subsidies or by short periods of low and neutral protection. Whereas subsidies to technology and human capital investments are likely to contribute to a steeper learning curve, this still leaves entrepreneurs with the prospect of a long period of losses, given that differences in productivity are normally far from marginal, and he still faces a series of other cost disadvantages related to product differentiation, size, conglomeration and internationalization. Moreover, since, as shown, learning is a function not only of R&D and human capital investments, but also of experience (cumulative output), if he cannot sell, the productivity gap is likely to increase instead of diminishing. As to production subsidies, even the moderate neoclassical view, as noted earlier, acknowledges that the combination of large cost disadvantages and budgetary restrictions makes the option unrealistic. The discussion of its effectiveness, therefore, seems pointless.

The option of short periods of low and neutral protection seems to be closer to a more effective intervention. Yet, it also underestimates the latecomer's cost disadvantages and overlooks the fact that the relevant market failures affect industries differently. The 'new theories of trade' have already demonstrated that under certain circumstances, protection can be a powerful instrument to allow latecomers to take advantage of dynamic and static economies of scale, and therefore reduce the productivity gap.[16] The argument is straightforward. Protection provides the two elements necessary to make it possible: scale and time. Not only does it make it easier for firms to enter with plants closer to the MES, but it also allows the cumulative output to grow faster. In addition, the 'new theories' have also drawn attention to the fact that the Mill-Bastable test, when applied to increasing return industries, should take into account the pure profits that might be shifted from foreign firms (Brander 1986).[17]

However, to be effective, protection might have to be neither brief nor neutral. Because the productivity gap can be large and the technology complex (making the learning curve flatter), a successful entry might require high levels of protection for periods longer than the, e.g., five years suggested by Balassa (1975). As Bell *et al.* (1984:115) put it,

> There is perhaps a fivefold to tenfold discrepancy between the duration of infancy commonly expected [by the neoclassical view] and the time that often appears to be needed to become internationally competitive.

Moreover, there are strong reasons to grant selective instead of neutral protection. For one thing, cost disadvantages, technology and competitive regimes (and accordingly externalities and market failures) vary among industries. For another, as already argued, factor endowments and static advantages have to be taken into account. Protection of a great number of industries that are not consistent with the country's factor endowment, can make static costs (resource misallocation and consumer loss) outweigh the dynamic benefits (exploitation of dynamic advantages, potential infant industry externalities, and profit shifting in oligopolistic industries). Moreover, when too many 'dynamic' industries are targeted at the same time, scarce resources (physical and human capital) might be spread too thinly, compromising the process of learning.

The question of which industry to protect is not necessarily a difficult one. Policymakers can follow both factor price trends and the experience of developed countries concerning industry-specific externalities. As Lall (1992a:14) pointed out,

> For most developing countries, it is not very hard to predict the next feasible stage of industrial development, at least in broad terms. The evolution of the existing industries is known from the experience of other countries, as is their requirements of skills, scales and technologies.

If, on the one hand, protection should be sector-specific or sector-selective, we agree, as suggested before, with the neoclassical proposition that it should be trade-neutral. In fact, we would go a bit further, and say that protection should not only be combined with export incentives, but also made conditional on export performance. The need to meet stringent international standards, makes export activity an effective substitute for import competition, avoiding a situation where protected firms lack incentives to go down the learning curve. Moreover, in cases where static economies of scale are relevant, the pressure to export rules out plants below the MES, and the export activity in itself, for going beyond the limits of the domestic market, gives greater scope for static and dynamic scale economies to be reaped.

It is also worth noting, that in the case of imperfect competition, economic theory has already shown that under a protected domestic market, firms will maximise profits if they price discriminate, and therefore export for a price that might be lower than their average costs.[18] Thus, in this context, protection can be a powerful incentive for late comers to move early into export markets, irrespective of export incentives or other forms of government persuasion. It is clear that in the short-term, this strategy will inevitably increase the cost of protection for consumers, since exports are cross-subsidised by higher domestic prices. In the long-run, though, as Westphal (1982) pointed out, the dynamic and static economies associated with greater export activity can lead to speedier reductions in unit costs and domestic prices, lowering the cumulative costs of protection, and increasing its cumulative benefits.

Besides being sector-selective and export-biased, protection should also be firm selective, in the sense that it should not benefit transnational company (TNC) affiliates. There seems to be a rare consensus in the literature, regarding the inapplicability of the infant industry argument to these firms.[19] Whereas there is no doubt that they also face a learning curve, and generate pecuniary and non-pecuniary externalities, their unrestricted access to capital, well-established brands and technology in the international market, does not make them legitimate candidates for protection. The more so because:

(a) Their access to parent company technology tends to exclude the 'know why' from their contribution to domestic technological capabilities. As Lall (1992b:179) put it,

> With few exceptions, the developing country affiliate receives the results of innovation, not the innovative process: it is not efficient for the enterprise concerned to invest in the skill and linkage creation in a new location. The affiliate, in consequence, develops efficient capabilities up to certain level but not beyond. . . . Such truncation [of technology transfer] can diminish not only the affiliate's own technological development, but also its linkages with the host country's technological and production infrastructure, and thus limit beneficial externalities.

(b) Their protection tends to harm those firms who really need to mature, i.e., the local private firms. TNC affiliates tend to share all the dynamic (learning and product differentiation) and static advantages (scale, scope and internationalization) of their parent companies, and therefore, as far as local firms go, the barriers to entry that they impose are not that different from those of free-trade; and

(c) Foreign ownership invalidates potential welfare gains related to the 'profit-shifting' argument.

Finally, protection alone is not likely to produce optimal results, because higher domestic prices might lead to excessive entry, the so-called 'crowding in' effect.[20] This means that even though domestic output expands, individual firms are forced to operate below the MES, and therefore prevented from taking full advantage of the dynamic and static economies of scale that protection could bring. Exports do not tend to mitigate this problem. With a fragmented and inefficient industrial structure, an early entry into the export market becomes less likely, because excessive domestic competition tends to restrain cross-subsidization, and marginal costs are bound to be higher than export prices.[21]

One could argue that as long as increasing returns are relevant, in the medium, long-term, restructuring will be inevitable, and the industry will assume a more sustainable configuration. This, however, would imply long and costlier periods of maturation, which could be avoided if a sustainable configuration were established right from the outset. The more so, because oligopolistic games are likely to produce drawn-out periods of restructuring, particularly if financially powerful firms, such as TNC affiliates, are major players.

This all suggests that, where increasing returns are relevant, protection should be accompanied by measures designed to promote sustainable configurations, preferably in the form of incentives to mergers and joint-ventures. Licensing might also be effective, but is more prone to DUP activities. Incentives to concentration are not only likely to speed up maturation, and reduce cost-disadvantages of size, but also form the basis for the establishment of local conglomerates. Large firms, given capital-raising economies, are better positioned to diversify, and therefore, capture the economies of scope, and eventually the economies of internationalization. The former economies are particularly valuable in the context of a developing economy, where managerial resources are scarce, and where missing capital markets put a high premium on the advantages of cross-subsidization (intra-firm capital markets).

Market Failures in the Factor Markets

So far we have assumed that factor markets work perfectly in LDCs. This, however, is a heroic assumption that often leads to the neglect of crucial obstacles to a successful late industrialization. These obstacles stem from major failures in the markets for finance, human capital and technology. These failures imply that intervention in the product markets is bound to have limited success, unless factor markets are also taken into account. Here, we agree with the neoclassical principle that, 'Interventions should attack the problem of market failure nearest to its source' (World Bank 1987a:70). For instance, the argument that protection is not likely to correct capital market failures seems to be indisputable. Protection has the specific function of helping the local private sector to overcome barriers created by the combination of dynamic and static economies. As will be shown, capital market failures in particular, and factor market failures in general, require specific measures.

The Financial Market

Beginning with the financial markets, it is well known that due to informational imperfections, they are likely to be imperfect even in developed countries, where problems such as adverse selection and moral hazard are common place. In LDCs, though, as Stiglitz (1989) rightly pointed out, these imperfections are severely aggravated,

> Because the process of change itself leads to greater informational problems; but more importantly, the institutional framework for dealing with these capital imperfections are probably less effective because of the small scale of the firms and because the institutions for collecting, evaluating and disseminating information are less likely to be developed (ibid. p.200).

This greater uncertainty leads to greater risks, which in turn, produce at least two undesirable effects. First, a strong bias towards short-term, liquid assets, and consequently to a shortage of long-term financing. And second, a market interest rate that tends to remain above the opportunity cost or its socially optimum level.

With inadequate and expensive finance, firms have to rely on internal earnings to finance not only learning and other entry related losses, but also capacity expansion. This increases their risk in an already risky environment, and compromises their growth and competitiveness. Needless to say that in this scenario, expected private returns tend to stay below the social desirable, particularly for investments and activities – such as technology intensive industries and exports – that are riskier anywhere in the world, but that are likely to generate higher pecuniary and non-pecuniary externalities.

True, at a purely static theoretical level, the first best solution would be to develop institutions to disseminate information, and to promote the capital markets. Yet, in the real world, things are not that simple. Efficient capital markets require elaborate and stable secondary markets to reduce the investor's perception of risk. Elaborate secondary markets, in turn, for requiring a large number of buyers and sellers, tend to be an increasing function of per capita income, and therefore, of the general process of economic development. Thus, LDC policy-makers who try to follow the 'first best' option are bound to find themselves in a quandary. They need to develop the capital markets to boost manufacturing investment and economic development. Yet, to have a well-functioning capital market, relatively high levels of per capita income are necessary. This problem was acknowledged even by Balassa (1975:375) who argued that, the development of capital markets is a function of the general process of economic development.

Thus, it is not surprising that late industrialized countries such as Germany and Japan, and NICs such as Korea and Taiwan, which for being late comers could not afford to wait for a gradual development of the capital markets, have turned to what Zysman (1983) called credit-based systems. That is, the banking system replaces the capital markets as the key agent in: a) providing long-term financing, b) centralising capital in the hands of Schumpeterian entrepreneurs, and c) divesting them of part of the risk involved in manufacturing investment.

This system would hardly develop by market forces alone. From the banks' viewpoint, as Zysman (ibid. p. 62) pointed out,

> Any loan is a gamble on the future solvency of the client, but a long-term loan involves a new kind of risk. Obviously, a long-term loan cannot in reality be secured by any physical assets. Moreover, a bank gets the bulk of the money it uses from funds deposited for a short-term at the going interest rate. If it lends a firm money for five-years, during the period depositors may withdraw their funds at which point the banks' reserves drop and it must reduce loans . . . Another, potentially more serious problem may occur should interest rates change in unexpected ways. If the short-term rates go down and the bank has lent long, its margin of profit increases, but if the rates go up, its profit margins are cut and it loses money.

This means that if *laissez-faire* prevails, banks would be hardly interested in granting long-term loans, particularly to investment in those manufacturing sectors where dynamic and static economies put late-comers in a very disadvantageous and risky position. From the firms' viewpoint, the fact that heavy reliance on long term borrowing makes them extremely vulnerable to economic downturns – debt is a 'fixed' cost – would in itself dampen their interest in this form of financing.

It follows, then, that credit-based systems are usually the product of government intervention, which, in order to promote the transformation of short-term savings in long-term loans, involves one or a combination of the following measures: (a) incentives to joint-ownership of banks and manufacturing companies, with the aim of reducing the banks' and firms' risks of engaging in long-term borrowing; (b) subsidised credit lines (rediscount facilities and preferential loans at below-market interest rates) to cushion the risk of interest-rate and macroeconomic fluctuations, and to encourage investment in imperfection and externality-prone industries; (c) interest rate ceilings (but with positive rates) to promote investment, reduce financial costs of highly indebted firms and to control monopolistic spreads of financial institutions and; (d) direct government ownership of segments or the whole financial system.

This credit-based system has a number of advantages over the traditional capital-market option. First, it allows firms to finance learning periods and growth rates, whose capital requirements might substantially exceed their usually meagre retained earnings and securities issues. Second, the high debt-equity ratios – which inevitably characterises the system – for making both firms and banks more responsive to interest rates and preferential credit, gives the government a powerful instrument to stimulate aggregate investment (along Keynesian lines) and to force allocation of resources to those sectors where dynamic and static economies drive a wedge between the expected private and social returns. Finally, as Wade (1988:134) pointed out, the credit-based system helps to avoid the 'short-termism' that affects decision-making in a stock market system.

On the minus side, there is no doubt that this system is more vulnerable to financial instability, DUP activities and government failure, due to the high debt-equity ratios and the usually prominent role of preferential credit. Yet, if, as in the case of product markets, government intervention is selective, factor-price conscious and made under the discipline of an outward-oriented regime, the advantages are likely to outweigh the benefits, as suggested by the cases of the countries mentioned above. Moreover, the alternative, as noted earlier, is not the 'textbook' capital market, but a tale of constant shortage of long-term financing, unduly high interest rates, undercapitalised firms and missed investment opportunities. Or even worse, the combination of an underdeveloped capital market with a traditional banking system (i.e. specialized in short-term lending) can produce, as the chapter on Brazil will show, uncontrollable inflationary pressures, given the firms excessive reliance on internal earnings.

It is also noteworthy that there is nothing inherent in a credit-based system, and in the greater government intervention that it normally requires, that necessarily leads to 'financial repression', i.e., to an atrophied financial system, incapable of performing properly the role of transferring savings to investors. The frequent occurrence of this problem among LDCs with interventionist regimes, led some authors (see, e.g. McKinnon 1991) to see it as a clear indictment of any form of intervention in the financial markets (except for the traditional regulatory role). Yet, a closer look at its causes shows that it arises mainly from negative interest rates and high inflation, normally a product of non-economic interventions (e.g. usury laws) and unsound monetary policies. They are not necessary conditions for the good-functioning of the credit-based system. The cases of Korea and Taiwan, which have undergone rapid financial deepening prove this point.[22]

Human Capital and Technology Markets

As suggested earlier, Neoclassicals admit that markets for human capital and technology are defective. Yet, until quite recently, the role of government in overcoming these 'functional' imperfections was hardly mentioned in their explanation of the East Asian NICs' success.[23] Even though a well-educated and trained work-force is not a sufficient condition for a successful industrialization, it provides, as Lall (1992a:28) put it, the 'absorptive base' on which industrial skills can be created. The larger and more qualified the absorptive base, the shorter will probably be the maturation period, and accordingly the lower the learning costs. Investments in education and training, however, are not efficiently allocated by the markets due to externalities and capital market failures.

From the labour's perspective, the rate at which future returns on education and training are discounted, tends to be higher than the social optimum, because the benefits they generate for the economy as a whole – for not being 'appropriable' – are not taken into account, and information imperfections can lead to ignorance, excessive risk aversion and, therefore, to myopic expectations. Moreover, even if there were perfect foresight and no externalities, labour would tend to under-invest, for capital markets, as an unsuspecting analyst admitted,

> Are not usually well organised for such purposes. In practice, if reliance were placed wholly on the capital market, under-investment in this form of invisible capital creation [education and training] would be likely, especially in less-developed countries. (Corden 1974:249)

From the firms' viewpoint, investments in training and formal education of their employees, as noted earlier, are hindered by the 'appropriability' problem. Labour mobility gives rise to externalities, and therefore to under-investment.

It is clear, then, that countries where the government intervenes and invests heavily in education and training are bound to have a better educated and trained work-force, and accordingly, their industry more likely to achieve international competitiveness faster and at lower costs.

Thus, the sharp contrast between Brazil's and Korea's experiences with education and training, with the former largely neglecting its relevance and the latter pouring significant resources, cannot be left out of the explanation of the performance differential. This contrast, as Lall (1992b) has shown, seems to be relevant not only for the cases of Brazil and Korea, but also for the whole group of East Asian and non-East Asian NICs.

On the technology market, we have already pointed out that, contrary to the neoclassical assumption, technology is not perfectly tradable. Whereas knowledge might be tradable, the capacity to make efficient use and to produce knowledge is not. Moreover, the market for the tradable elements of technology – via, e.g. licensing agreements and FDI – is far from perfectly competitive, due to asymmetric information between buyers and sellers (Arrow 1969), and to sellers' concentration. The latter results from the fact that technology is not always easily imitated, due to issues such as complexity and intellectual property laws. The overall result is that the trade of technology often involves prices above the marginal cost, and restrictive practices such as export restrictions.

It follows, then, that investments in domestic technological effort, as Pack and Westphal (1986:109) argued, are bound to generate 'surpluses for those undertaking the investments or for other beneficiaries'. The investors' surplus might stem from the acquisition of technological capability, which, in turn, might enhance their position in both product and technology markets. In the product markets, the acquisition of industrial skills is likely to speed up learning, reduce costs and improve quality, allowing greater market penetration, and even economic profits if investors manage to innovate. In the technology market, greater technological capability is likely to reduce informational asymmetries and therefore strengthen the investor's bargaining power over technology acquisitions. It might even allow investors to avoid the market altogether, and therefore avoid monopolistic prices. This last advantage is particularly relevant to science-based industries, where the key position of the technology in the competitive process, usually rules out the possibility of licensing technology altogether.

The other beneficiaries' surplus, i.e., externalities, can be pecuniary and non-pecuniary. The former includes easier and cheaper access to technology (via local transfer of technology or technical consultancy) and products with a set of characteristics more appropriate to the local factor endowment. At a macroeconomic level, greater technological capability might: reduce the BP costs of technological licensing (including restrictive practices); increase the private sector ability to respond to relative prices and explore dynamic advantages; reduce the cost of protecting infant industries due to speedier learning; and boost growth by speeding up technical progress. The non-pecuniary externalities consist mainly of the diffusion of knowledge through labour mobility and other channels.

The existence of these externalities implies that the private discount rate regarding investments in technological effort is bound to be higher than the social optimum, and therefore under-investment will follow. Moreover, as we stressed when discussing dynamic economies, the problems of imperfect information, precarious S&T infrastructure, R&D indivisibilities and the latecomer's dynamic disadvantages, all conspire to make domestic technological effort highly risky. The more so, because it tends to be seen as a dearer and riskier alternative to activities such as FDI and technology licensing, whose long-term and subtler disadvantages – e.g. truncation of technology transfer, monopolistic prices, restrictive practices – are usually overshadowed by short-term benefits such as reduced risk and quick results. In other words, the market underestimates not only the benefits of domestic technological effort, but also the social costs of the various forms of technology imports. The latter is wrongly presented as an alternative to the former, when the tacit nature of technology makes them, at best, a useful complement.

This all means that countries where the government, in the course of industrialization, intervenes to promote investment in domestic technological effort, and to redress the private sector's perception of the pros and cons of technology imports – via, e.g. fiscal incentives to R&D, investments in the S&T infrastructure, selective FDI and technology licensing restrictions – are likely to acquire technological capabilities faster, and therefore, to achieve and maintain international competitiveness quicker and at lower costs.

1.3 SUMMING UP

All things considered, it seems clear that even though Neoclassicals are correct about the role of trade orientation in the East Asian success, they are wrong to equate outward-orientation with a lack of state intervention. Without taking into account the role of the government in overcoming market failures, the success of outward-oriented countries, and accordingly the relative failure of those who looked inwards, cannot be properly understood. Both product and factor markets in LDCs are affected by important imperfections, which outward-orientation or 'keeping the fundamentals right', by themselves, are not likely to remedy, and that free-trade and inward-orientation are likely to aggravate. Outward-orientation, though, is important and necessary, not only because it brings the benefits of an open economy, but also because it guides and disciplines governments towards selective interventions, designed to remedy specific failures, or to make the best use of irreparable imperfections.

This alternative approach carries a view of the state that is neither the 'perfect state' of the structuralists, nor the 'predatory' state of the Neoclassicals. Here we cannot but agree with Pack and Westphal (1986:104),

> A government's ability to intervene selectively in pursuit of dynamic efficiency cannot be taken for granted. Indeed, most governments may lack this ability. But it appears to be a critical factor in using selective intervention to achieve faster and more successful industrialization. Hence, where this ability does not exist, the government is probably well advised to adhere rather closely to the strict neoclassical prescription for a neutral policy regime.

However, where the government's ability to intervene does exist, that is, where the state is not handicapped by widespread corruption and ill-qualified ministers and civil servants, the costs of non-intervention are likely to outweigh eventual government failures. In this case, the question to ask is not intervention or non-intervention, but how and where to intervene, and under what sort of incentive regime intervention is more likely to be successful. These are the issues that seem to provide the key to the performance differential not only between Brazil and South Korea, which we are going to look at closely, but also to the whole issue of the East Asian industrialization success.

2 South Korea[24]

As suggested in Chapter 1, Neoclassicals usually attribute the success of Korea's industrialization to the adoption, in the early 1960s, of a neutral, hands-off, outward-looking policy regime.[25] The essence of the argument is that the introduction of a low and uniform rate of protection, offset by equally low and uniform export subsidies, would have led the economy back to its shadow prices, guaranteeing allocative efficiency in line with the country's static comparative advantages. The speed, efficiency and international competitiveness of the industrialization that followed, would have been not more than an inexorable and theoretically predictable consequence. A more moderate version of this view (World Bank 1991, 1993) acknowledges that there were government interventions, but on the whole 'getting the fundamentals right' and the outward looking regime would have made the difference.

Following the lead given by authors such as Westphal (1982, 1990), Pack and Westphal (1986), Amsden (1989) and Lall (1992a), the purpose of this chapter is to question these interpretations through a careful investigation of the role of government in Korea's industrialization. It attempts to show, first, that even though outward-orientation was an important and necessary part of Korea's success, its policy regime was not firm, industry or market neutral, and overall protection was everything but low. Second, that high protection and non-uniform incentives were part of a set of measures designed to overcome specific market failures in the product and factor markets, which, constrained by the outward-orientation discipline, *effectively* paved the way to an internationally competitive industry.

This chapter is organized in four sections. The first sets a proper background for the discussion, reviewing the main characteristics of the pre-1960 industrialization and related policy regime. The following sections cover the government's policies during what is widely recognized as the three main stages of Korea's industrialization: the 'neutral' export-oriented regime of the 1960s, the heavy and chemical industry (HCI) drive of the 1970s, and the liberalization of the 1980s.

2.1 THE BACKGROUND: THE PRE-1960 PERIOD

The first significant spurt of manufacturing investment in Korea took place early this century under Japanese colonial rule (1910–1945). Until then, centuries of isolationism under the Yi dynasty (1392–1910) – only interrupted by the opening of the ports in 1876 – coupled with a feudal economy, had contributed very little to industrial development. When the Japanese took over, manufacturing accounted for only 3.3% of GDP.[26] Boosted, then, by political and institutional reforms that removed the last traces of the *ancien régime*, and supported by Japanese investments and skills, manufacturing growth eventually took off. It reached an annual compound rate of 10% over 1910-40, with the manufacturing share of GDP increasing to 21.9% in 1940.[27] Initially based on light industries, this manufacturing boom soon shifted to the heavy industry (mainly chemicals), following Korea's involvement in Japan's war preparations. As of 1940, heavy industry accounted for 50% of manufacturing output.

However, as Jones and Sakong (1980:23) pointed out, the contribution of these impressive developments to Korea's post-war industrialization was severely curtailed by three main factors. First, as Korea's industry was strictly built to complement the Japanese industrial structure, there were few backward and forward linkages, and sales were highly dependent on the Japanese market. As of 1940, two-thirds of the manufacturing output was exported to Japan. Needless to say that the Japanese withdrawal led to a severe market disruption.

Second, virtually all large manufacturing firms were owned by Japanese (as of 1941, they made up 91% of the total paid-in capital), who also held the overwhelming majority of the managerial and skilled jobs (81% in 1943). This fact greatly hindered the human capital build-up, and led to an acute shortage of qualified workers after the Japanese withdrawal. By 1946, 40% of the work force had no schooling and only 7.4% had secondary education (Table A.1). And third, the 1947 division of the country, left the South (which became Republic of Korea) without the bulk of the heavy industry and without 90% of the country's electric power supply.[28] Table A.2 shows that in 1953, the heavy industry's share of manufacturing output was less than half of that of the pre-war period.

Therefore, despite rapid progress under Japanese rule, Korea's industry in the wake of WWII was facing severe market disruption, an acute skill shortage and had lost most of its heavy industries and electric power supply. In 1948, manufacturing output was only 14% of the

1938 level. To add to the problems, the outbreak of the Korean war in 1950 led to the destruction of half of the remaining industrial struc- ture. By 1953, the manufacturing share of GDP had been reduced to 8% (Table A.5), and American consultants – hired by the UN to draw a reconstruction programme – were suggesting that Korea should con- centrate on exploiting its (far from abundant) agricultural and mineral resources (Krueger 1979:77).[29]

The chaotic state of the manufacturing sector was not, however, Korea's only problem in the early 1950s. In fact, it emerged from the Korean War unable to stand on its feet. Exports, mainly minerals (tungsten), were just a fraction of imports, which were mostly financed by foreign aid.[30] The financing of this huge foreign exchange gap soon became the main objective of the government's policies, which sought concur- rently to maximize foreign aid, carry out IS and boost exports, in this order of importance.

The IS strategy owed nothing to its Latin American counterparts. A complex multiple exchange rate system was introduced, used con- currently with high and escalating tariffs and comprehensive NTBs.[31] Unlike typical IS regimes, though, exports benefited from a range of export incentives, including preferential finance, and import licensing conditional on export performance (1957).[32] The results in terms of manufacturing growth were far from disastrous. Output grew at an annual average rate of 14.7% over 1954–59 (Table A.3), driven by a 'pre- emptive' IS in the light industry.[33] Yet, this figure looks less impres- sive if one takes into account the reduced size of the post-war manufacturing base.

In contrast, the results regarding overall economic and export growth were clearly disappointing. Given the industry's small share of GNP, its expansion failed to boost the rest of the economy, resulting in a lacklustre GNP growth of 4.6% p.a. over 1953–59. By 1960, Korea's GNP per capita was only $78, almost half of the LDCs' average.[34] As for exports, the figures were even more discouraging, doing nothing to alleviate the dire balance of payments (BP) problems.[35] Total ex- ports shrank in average by 3% p.a., and manufactured exports by 2.7%.[36] The latter accounted in 1960 for a meagre 13.5% of total exports (Table A.6) and for less than 1% of the total manufacturing output (Table A.4).

As one would expect, Neoclassicals blame the IS policies for these mixed results, particularly for the negligible manufactured exports.[37] The indiscriminate use of NTBs and high tariffs would have distorted relative prices, provoking a debilitating misallocation of resources; while their combination with multiple and overvalued exchange rates, would have biased incentives towards the domestic market, pulling resources away from exports. Furthermore, the attempt to 'buck the markets' with a plethora of regulations, viewed as intrinsic to IS regimes, would have stimulated rent-seeking at the expense of more productive activities.

Even though there is truth in these arguments, the emphasis on 'wrong' incentives seems to be unwarranted. To begin with, protection seems to have favoured labour-intensive sectors, which were very much in line with Korea's resource endowment.[38] This is confirmed by the evolution of the industrial structure over the period (Table A.2). Hence, there is little room to argue that resource allocation, from a static viewpoint, was disastrous.

Second, the extent of this incentive bias against exports also seems to have been overestimated. Table A.7 reveals that unlike typical IS regimes such as Brazil's (Table A.36), the purchasing-power-parity (PPP) exchange rate for exports was well above that of imports during the whole period. In addition, it was devalued by 45.5% over 1955–59. To be sure, it is true, as Krueger (1979) pointed out, that PPP exchange rates do not properly reflect the NTBs' impact on import premia. Yet, the same problem occurs with these indicators in other IS regimes, and they all tend to favour imports rather than exports. Moreover, whatever the relative level of the export and import exchange rates, one cannot dismiss the former's rapid devaluation as irrelevant.

So, if incentives were not that 'wrong', the explanation for the mixed industrial performance and negative export growth has at least to incorporate other factors. In this regard, there are two important variables that appears to be extremely relevant: the state of Korea's industry in the early 1950s, and the overall orientation of government policies. As to the former, we have already indicated the dire problems concerning the loss and destruction of industrial capacity and infrastructure, lack of qualified personnel and market disruption. These were problems that could not be solved overnight, least of all by market forces alone, and that were severely undermining the industry's performance and ability to respond to relative prices. So, even if prices were completely 'right' – and as shown they were not far from it – it seems unlikely that manufacturing growth would have been higher, or that exports would have promptly responded.

More to the point, without the protection given by the IS policies, the most probable result would have been a Korea along the lines suggested by the American consultants. That is, with no industry at all. Handicapped by the problems mentioned above and faced with a non-existent capital market, Korea's light industry would have been an easy prey for its international competitors, notably the Japanese. Protection gave this industry the necessary breathing space to deal with the problems of reconstruction, and most important, to build up human capital. Without it, the manufactured export boom of the 1960s, when prices were allegedly 'got right', would have been an impossibility.[39]

Turning now to the overall orientation of government policy, it seems to have been more of a hindrance than a help to industrial development. True, as just noted, IS policies were instrumental in rebuilding the industry, and had caused fewer price distortions than Neoclassicals want us to believe. Moreover, concerted action in the area of education helped to mitigate the industry's skill shortage (Table A.1). Yet, these benefits appear to have come more by accident than by design, in a government whose actions were dominated by,

> short-term objectives of reconstruction and maintenance of minimum consumption standards, both of which were to be achieved by aid maximization rather than investment and production. (Cole and Lyman, 1971:167)

This short-termism meant that the policies for industry were not more than a by-product of stopgap measures to finance the BP. Apart from education, protection was not accompanied by other measures geared to remedy or take advantage of market failures in the product (e.g. economies of scale, scope) and factor markets (e.g. lack of long-term financing, and S&T externalities). Nor was protection given according to a clear timetable, or made conditional on some sort of performance indicator.

In addition, and perhaps even more damaging, the government's overdeveloped instinct for political survival, led to a series of non-economic interventions,[40] which promoted widespread rent-seeking. Evidence that became available after the fall of the Rhee government (1947–60),[41] suggests that the principal origins of 'illicit wealth' were: (a) non-competitive allocation of import quotas and import licenses; (b) bargain price acquisition of former Japanese properties; (c) the selective allocation of aid funds and materials; (d) privileged access to cheap bank loans; (e) non-competitive award of government and US military contracts for reconstruction services.

Apart from the first, none of these activities can be said to have originated from IS policies, deemed by Neoclassicals as the main source of rent-seeking. Even in the case of NTBs, a competitive system for the allocation of quotas and licences could have avoided rent-seeking. As discussed later, the successful experience of the 1960s, where NTBs continued to be extensively used, tends to support this view. The problem of profiteering, then, was not so much in the type of policy pursued by the government, but in its objectives.

In short, Korea's industrialization took off early this century under Japanese colonial rule. Despite considerable development, the industry was in a very bad shape after WWII. The shortcomings of a 'colonial industrialization' became all too obvious when after the Japanese withdrawal, Koreans were left without the necessary skills to run the industry, with a poorly integrated industrial structure and without its main market. The North–South split made things worse, with the loss of most of heavy industry and power supply to the North. As if this were not enough, the Korea war destroyed half of the remaining industrial base. With the country living on foreign aid, the government turned to IS policies. These policies allowed the reconstruction of the (light) industrial sector and human capital to build-up, but failed to deliver high economic and export growth. This, however, had less to do with a disastrous industry and trade bias, than with the difficulties of learning and reconstruction, and with a government more interested in intervening to guarantee its political survival, than promote industrial and economic development.

2.2   THE 'NEUTRAL' OUTWARD-ORIENTED REGIME (1960–72)

The government's failure to deliver high growth and to reduce dependence on aid, compounded by widespread corruption, made its position by the end of the 1950s unsustainable. Internal and external pressure led eventually to a new civilian government in April 1960, quickly followed by a military *coup d'état* in 1961.[42] This political upheaval would have profound implications for Korea's industrialization. The military's commitment to growth and economic independence made a major overhaul of the policy regime inevitable. None of these objectives were likely to be achieved by the previous IS 'strategy', given the size of both the internal market and the foreign exchange gap.[43] An outward-oriented policy regime turned out be the answer.

The results were stunning. GNP growth more than doubled to 9.9% p.a. over 1960–72, boosted by a 20.1% annual growth of the manufacturing output (Table A.3). The latter, in turn, was led by exports that grew at an astonishing rate of 59.9% p.a., increasing its share of manufacturing output from 0.8 to 17.9%, and its share in total exports from 13.5 to 83.6% (Tables A.4 and A.6). Although there was a perceptible movement towards the heavy industry – both in terms of output and exports – the key force behind this performance was light industry, which by the end of the period still accounted for 76% of manufactured exports and 68% of manufacturing output (Table A.2).

As noted earlier, Neoclassicals were quick to attribute these remarkable results to the allegedly neutral and hands-off aspects of the new regime. This view, however, is both simplistic and misleading. First, it does not take into account that the new regime benefited from the manufacturing and human capital base built over the 1950s. And second, it overlooks the fact that government intervention under the new regime, rather than being neutral or non-existent, involved concerted action to remedy failures in the workings of product and factor markets. As the former argument was already outlined in the last section, the focus will now be on the latter, which seems crucial to explain not only the rapid and efficient industrialization of the 1960s, but also of the following decades.

We begin with the product markets, whose analysis, for the sake of clarity, was divided into trade and industrial organization policies. The former takes up the characteristics of the trade regime, which form the basis of the neoclassical version of the events, and the latter deals with the policies towards conglomeration and foreign direct investment (FDI). We then move on to the factor markets and cover the financial, human capital and science and technology (S&T) policies.

Intervention in the Product Markets

The Trade Regime

The first three years of the military government are usually seen as a transitional period, when moves to reform the trade regime would have been somewhat compromised by the macroeconomic imbalances provoked by an ill-advised expansionary policy.[44] In fact, a BP crisis precluded a more stable structure of incentives, with the government resorting to temporary and extreme measures to curb imports and boost exports.

Yet, despite the instability, the government's strategic option for an outward-oriented development was already clear – export growth was heralded as the only way to 'national salvation' – and the key instruments of the new regime were put in place. That is, a comprehensive import-control and incentive system that offered export and 'strategic' industries protection, access to producer goods at international prices, and a variety of financial and fiscal incentives.

In these 'transitional' years, the import side of the regime relied on controls inherited from the IS period. That is, imports continued to be subjected to licensing based on a 'positive-list' that had three categories: automatic approval (AA), restricted and prohibited.[45] The tariff structure and its rates also remained initially unchanged. The exchange rate, though, was unified through devaluations. These controls, however, were soon adjusted given the aforementioned BP problems that emerged in 1963. The number of AA items was, then, gradually reduced (Table A.9), tariffs were raised (Table A.10), and very restrictive measures were adopted, including an overall import quota and a full-scale export-import link, whereby only exporters were entitled to import. This last measure led to a highly profitable market for import rights, re-establishing in practice multiple exchange rates.[46]

On the export side, pre-existing incentives were reinforced and complemented by new ones. Exporters that already benefited, *inter alia*, from tariff-free access to imported inputs, preferential finance, and from the export-import link premium, were granted further fiscal incentives (exemption from business tax, and 50% reduction on income tax), lower preferential interest rates, direct cash subsidies (1961–64), and a trade promotion institution (KOTRA-1962) aimed at reducing export-related informational and transaction costs.[47] In addition, a full-scale annual export target (1962) was introduced, broken down by commodity, region and country of destination.[48]

These measures, reinforced by a maxidevaluation (98%) in May 1964, eventually improved the BP conditions (Table A.8), which in conjunction with a new, and this time, successful attempt to unifying the exchange rate (March 1965),[49] set the stage for a trade liberalization. This liberalization marked the beginning of what Neoclassicals believe to have been a fully fledged neutral, outward-looking regime, with a stable incentive structure that would last at least until 1972.

The liberalization consisted of a relaxation of the import controls imposed during 1961-64, coupled with an increase in the number and scale of the export incentives. As to import controls, (a) the full-scale export-import link was abolished and replaced by partial ones;[50] (b) import quotas were eliminated; (c) the number of AA items was significantly increased, and in 1967, the 'positive' list turned 'negative', with import categories remaining the same, but items not listed were allowed to be freely imported (Table A.9); and (d) the tariff structure was reformed in 1967, lowering the highest tariff from 250 to 150%. Yet, the weighted average tariff increased to from 49.2 to 56.7% (Table A.10).

On exports, the emphasis was on increasing credit and tax incentives. The preferential real rate on export credits turned clearly negative (Table A.13) and the types and volume of preferential loans for export increased significantly.[51] In addition, the government aiming at mitigating the perverse effect of duty-free inputs on intermediate goods producers, gave them access to export incentives through local letters of credit.[52] As for tax incentives, accelerated depreciation was granted to exporters in 1966 and in the early 1970s, two duty-free export zones were set up.[53]

This mere description of the reforms might have already raised doubts in the reader's mind about the possibility of describing the resulting trade regime as neutral or liberal. Yet before reaching any conclusion, one needs to examine the evidence supporting this claim. This appears to consist mainly of effective rates of protection (ERP) estimates, notably Westphal and Kim's (1982). The latter are shown in Table 2, and it seems clear that the figures for manufacturing and 'all industries' back allegations that the trade regime had low nominal and effective rates of protection, and was trade neutral insofar as effective subsidies did not significantly favour either exports or domestic sales.[54]

Although impressive, this evidence is misleading. A more careful examination of Table 2 and its methodology, suggests a regime that was industry and trade biased, with anything but low protection. Looking first at the issue of industry bias, Table 2 shows that sectors such as transport equipment, machinery, consumer durables and, to a certain extent, intermediate products II, had high rates of protection not only in comparison with other sectors of the industry, but also by Neoclassical standards.[55] This points to a bias towards capital-intensive sectors, suggesting that the promotion of infant industries or dynamic comparative advantages was not left to the market forces.

This last point is acknowledged by Westphal and Kim (1982:238) who reported the existence of significant incentives for selected IS industries, including indirect tax and tariff exemption on inputs and capital goods, preferential direct tax treatment and privileged access to subsidized credit. The government concern with IS is also revealed in the first two Five Year Plans (1962–71)[56] where the heavy industry, with the help of state enterprises,[57] was singled out for promotion. Although, as shown later, heavy industry targeting only entered full

Table 2   Korea's nominal, effective protection and
effective subsidy rates, 1968

Industry group (ISIC)	Legal[2] A	Nominal[3] A	Effective protection (ERP)[4] E			Effective subsidy E		(ES)[5]
			E	D	A	E	D	A
Primary activities	34	16	−16	18	17	−3	22	21
Processed foods	57	3	−3	−18	−17	2	−25	−23
Beverages and tobacco	135	2	−2	−19	−19	15	−26	−24
Construction material	31	4	−5	−11	−11	6	−17	−16
Intermediate products I[6]	31	2	31	−25	−19	43	−30	−22
Intermediate products II[6]	53	19	0	26	24	17	20	19
Consumer nondurables	68	9	−2	−11	−9	5	−21	−15
Consumer durables	78	31	−5	64	51	2	38	31
Machinery	49	28	−13	44	43	5	31	31
Transport equipment	62	54	−53	163	164	−23	159	159
Manufacturing	59	11	3	−1	−1	12	−9	−7
All industries	49	13	0	11	10	9	10	10

1, D and E stand for domestic and export sales and A is the average between them. 2, 1968
Sales at world prices as weights. Includes regular and special tariffs. 3, Direct price comparison.
Sales at world prices as weights. 4, Balassa method. 5, Effective subsidy rates are the percentage
excess of the domestic-producer-price value added, adjusted for credit and direct tax subsidies
over the world-price value added. Value added at world price as weights. 6, Intermediate products I and II correspond to intermediate products at lower and higher levels of fabrication, respectively.

Source: Westphal and Kim (1982:230)

swing after 1973, its impact could already be felt during 1960-73. Table
A.2 reveals a noticeable increase in the heavy industry's share of
output and exports over the period.

As for trade bias, despite the neutrality indicated by the aggregate
figures, most heavy industries had effective subsidies favouring the
domestic market, whereas in the rest of the industry they favoured
exports. Even for manufacturing as a whole, effective subsidies were
not well balanced, being biased towards export sales (Table 2). As
Findlay pointed out (Hong and Krause 1981:31), there is no theoretical reason, from a neoclassical and static point of view, to believe that
a trade bias, either in favour of exports or imports, is consistent with
the free trade optimal allocation of resources.

Moreover, not only incentives were not neutral, but the industry's
response was not always in accordance with then. As Westphal and
Kim (1982:222) somewhat reluctantly admitted:

For a significant number of products, including some of Korea's major textile exports, the import price substantially exceeded the export price. Export prices may have been set below average production costs and thus may not represent world prices at which sustained supplies would be forthcoming to the domestic market.

These authors also found out that major export sectors (accounting for 27% of manufactured exports in 1968) had higher effective subsidies and higher than average nominal protection to domestic sales. They were quick to suggest that in these cases, exports were inefficiently produced and subsidized by sales in the domestic market. This, in turn, would have been made possible by price discrimination and by institutional mechanisms linking incentives for domestic sales to satisfactory export performance. If so, it is completely at odds with the view that Korea's export composition was determined by a passive response to international relative prices.[58]

Finally, apart from the well-known drawbacks of the ERP concept,[59] the decision to use direct price comparisons on the grounds of widespread tariff 'redundancy' and NTBs, seems to have led to a gross underestimation of both the level and impact of the import controls. Theoretically, the procedure taken seems correct. As of 1968, actual tariff collection was just 36.2% of its potential value (Suh 1975:221). One has to be careful, though, not to write off tariffs as totally 'redundant'. As Luedde-Neurath (1986) pointed out, exemptions were granted on a highly selective basis, mainly for export and selected IS industries. Consumers and producers that catered to the domestic market did not benefit, and therefore had to face prohibitive tariffs in most sectors. This seems to be confirmed by the data available. In 1968, exemptions for export and selected IS industries accounted for 80% of the total, whereas commodities with prohibitive tariffs accounted for 70% of domestic sales of domestic production.[60]

There is also no doubt that NTBs were comprehensive. As of 1968, 60% of the manufactured imports and 42% of the importable items were subjected to NTBs (Table A.14). At the sectoral level, only raw material and food were relatively freely imported, whereas NTBs were particularly important in the consumer and intermediate goods sectors, which accounted for only 10% of AA imports.[61]

Yet, in practical terms, given the shortcomings involved in direct price comparisons, the results seem to have been as inaccurate as those derived from legal tariffs would have been. First, following again Luedde-Neurath (1986), direct price comparisons in LDCs tend to underestimate the impact of protection, given the differences in quality and product specification. This is particularly relevant to Westphal and Kim's estimates, since 45% of the products involved had prices below the international level. Although acknowledging that without effective market restrictions, these results could only be ascribed to quality and product specification differentials, they assumed zero nominal protection for most of these products.

Second, there was a number of factors in action during the period – e.g. government's direct control over key intermediate goods industries, constant monitoring of the private sector's prices, and fierce domestic competition –[62] that might have precluded local firms from taking full pecuniary advantage of import controls (i.e. to fix prices at the international level plus tariffs or equivalents), even though they still took full advantage of other non-pecuniary benefits such as the elimination of competition from well-established foreign firms.

These shortcomings appear to be behind the paradox of low nominal and effective protection despite high selective tariffs and widespread NTBs. The evolution of Korea's import composition (Table A.15) gives us a more realistic, if impressionistic, measure of the import controls' impact. For instance, the tiny share of consumer goods in 1969 (4.7%) smacks of a structure shaped not by international relative prices, but by stringent government controls.[63] It seems no coincidence that the import composition accurately reflects the structure of both tariffs (including exemptions) and NTBs, which virtually banned consumer goods imports, exempted raw materials, and had a more selective approach to capital and intermediate goods imports.

Taking all this into account, to equate Korea's move towards outward-orientation with the adoption of a neutral, low protection trade regime seems at best unsubstantiated. Accordingly, the same applies to explanations of Korea's manufacturing and export take-off based on this allegation. Moreover, even if the trade regime conformed with the Neoclassical description, supporters of this view would still have much explaining to do, since exports began to grow (1960) well before the fully fledged 'neutral' regime was in place (1967).[64]

If the rejection of the Neoclassical hypothesis does not constitute in itself an alternative explanation of the mechanics of the new trade regime and of its role in the 1960s boom, it gives us a stepping-stone. That is, the unmistakably selectivity of the new regime. As suggested by the description of the reforms, this selectivity was exercised through complex lines, at both market and industry levels. The industry's market was segmented into export and domestic sales. The former's regime was made liberal and industry neutral. The latter's, in turn, was made highly protectionist except for the upstream industries, whose protection was selective (in part an unavoidable consequence of the 'free trade' regime enjoyed by exporters) and accompanied by fiscal exemptions and long-term subsidized credit.

Despite pointing to opposing directions, the net effect of these incentives clearly favoured export-oriented growth. This, however, cannot be perceived by looking at cross-border relative prices alone, because there were other powerful forces dictating resource allocation (often, as shown by Westphal and Kim, in manifest conflict with price signals). It was these forces that reconciled the contradictory incentives and put them to good work. They emerged, first, from the government's decision to make protection, credit (thanks to its control over the financial market, examined later), and other non-pecuniary incentives, conditional on export performance.[65] And second, from a deliberate policy of conglomeration (also taken up later). The first policy made exports the main target of the private sector regardless of cross-border relative prices, and the second, by creating conditions for price discrimination, made exports profitable even when the international price was below average costs.[66]

The overall result was that Korea managed to boost its static comparative advantages beyond 'free-trade' limits, without giving up the policies that would bring dynamic benefits. On the static side, despite the already noted considerable development of the 1950s, the light industry in the early 1960s was still far from the international best practice. The combination of protection, conglomeration and subsidies, all under the stick of export performance, not only provided the industry with a safe haven for the catching-up, but also with the financial means and incentives (monopolistic profits at home plus subsidies) to promptly offer competitive prices abroad. If this policy makes little sense from a static viewpoint, in the long term it allowed industry to reap dynamic economies of scale and to reduce the productivity gap.[67]

On the dynamic side, the selective approach to heavy industry gave Korea the means to exploit dynamic comparative advantages and to respond quickly to changes in factor prices, without provoking any significant static misallocation of resources, or placing a too heavy burden in the country's limited capital and human capital resources. Moreover, it did not block the downstream industries' access to embodied technology and inputs at world prices. Korea, as will be shown, would fully benefit from this approach in the following decade.

Industrial Organization Policies

As noted earlier, there are two other government interventions in the product market, which, in conjunction with the trade regime, deeply affected the industrial structure, and played a key role in Korea's industrial success: the policies for conglomeration and foreign direct investment (FDI). Beginning with the former, there is enough evidence to show that the so-called 'big business' policy was not something that began with the 'HCI push' of the 1970s, as suggested by most of the literature, but with the 'neutral' regime of the 1960s. The main instruments of this policy appear to have been credit rationing, investment licensing, import and FDI protection.

The government's control over the financial sector (examined later) seems to have been deliberately used to increase concentration both at the industry and aggregate level. Hard facts are scarce, but this appears to be the only reasonable explanation of the extraordinary growth of the so-called *jaebols* (Korean word for conglomerates), and of their peculiar financial structure. For instance, Table 3 shows that over 1965–70, the share of small and medium firms (SMF) in total exports increased but remained quite marginal, and their shares of manufacturing output and domestic credit presented a marked decline, particularly the former. Moreover, in 1972, i.e. even before the start of the 'HCI push' (widely believed to have favoured large firms), SMFs had an access-to-borrowing ratio (27%) well below that of the large firms (46%).[68]

Even though these figures already point to a 'big business' policy, they underestimate its impact since small subsidiaries of the *jaebols* are included among the SMFs. The extent of this underestimation can

Table 3   Share of small and medium firms in exports, output and domestic credit, 1965–84 (%)

Shares of	1965	1970	1975	1980	1984
Exports	23	32.2	34.5	32.1	25.4
Manufacturing output	56.3	27.5	30.6	29.5	30.5
Domestic credit	32.6*	30.3	27.5	23.5**	n.a.

Note: Small and medium firm is defined as a firm with fewer than 300 employees. *1966, **1979.

Source: Michell (1988:84) for exports and manufactured output and Jones (1987:154) for credit. Both authors use data from the Small and Medium Business (SMB) Federation and SMB Industry Promotion Corporation.

be gauged by the fact in 1970 'competitive' markets amounted to only 36% of total shipments (Table A.16). Another strong indication of a credit bias towards the *jaebols* lies in the manufacturing debt-equity ratios. Over 1965–71, they rose from 104 to 345%, a level significantly higher than that of the US but similar to Japan's (Table A.25). Unlike the latter, though, the banks in Korea were in the government's hands and not in those of the conglomerates.[69]

The link between those high debt-ratios and the rise of the *jaebols* becomes amazingly clear in Jones and Sakong's (1980:273) account of the conglomerates' 'growth model':

One privately held company 'luckily' gets governmental approval for an industrial project. It will be typically financed by 1/5 equity and 4/5 foreign and domestic loans. The private firm may then grow rapidly if the project becomes successful. The firm then starts a new line of business with the profit accumulated from the first venture. Of course once again the firm will not usually put up much equity but will rely heavily on external debt.

As to investment licensing, a proper analysis of its role is virtually impossible, first because its existence was never officially acknowledged by the government, and second because it was hardly covered by the literature. It was very briefly mentioned by Kim, S. (1991:66), who maintained that over 1965–67, despite not being required to be formally licensed, investments had to be registered at the competent ministry, risking rejection or delay for various reasons.[70] Formally or not, though, the truth of the matter is that during the 'neutral' period, the government had enough power to 'kill' any business initiative by denying, for instance, access to credit, imports or technology licences (see later). The rapid increase in concentration suggests that this power was probably used.

In addition, any policy towards increasing concentration and forming local conglomerates would not have been effective without a protected domestic market and a restrictive FDI policy. The existence of the former was already discussed in the previous section, while the latter is going to be taken up next. First, though, we have to consider the benefits that a deliberate conglomeration policy has brought.

The advantages of size and conglomeration are controversial, and the literature on industrial organization emphasises the deleterious effects of monopolistic market structures on production, income and efficiency. Most of this discussion, though, assumes well functioning factor markets, constant returns, a closed economy and is done within a static context. In the dynamic and imperfect world of 1960s Korea, it is of limited use. In fact, the rise of the *jaebol* seems to have brought quite a few benefits, even allowing for the fact the light industry's scale economies at the plant level were limited (the most obvious benefit of size).

To begin with, given the scarcity of skilled labour and the amount of time involved in developing it, conglomeration allowed Korea to use more effectively its limited resources and therefore enter rapidly into a large number of industries. As Scherer and Ross (1990:122) pointed out, large diversified firms can 'economise' on skilled services by having a common central pool of managers and technicians whose skills are not product specific.[71]

Second, with respect to exports, conglomeration not only led to the economies of scope in marketing and distribution skills mentioned above (see Keesing and Lall, 1988), but also to scale economies that also characterize these activities and the importing of the necessary inputs.

Third, conglomeration gave local firms the opportunity to develop internal capital markets, whose importance cannot be underestimated given the then prevailing weakness of Korea's capital market. This seems to have been particularly instrumental in increasing the firms' capacity – via cross-subsidization and risk sharing – to sustain long period of losses associated with entry in infant industries.

Fourth, as noted earlier, the formation of monopolistic markets at home coupled with import protection, opened the way to price-discrimination, which, in turn, allowed firms to offer competitive prices abroad at the early stages of the learning curve.

Finally, the formation of local conglomerates made the transition to the heavy industry (see next section) smoother since local firms had the size and financial leverage necessary:

(a) To take advantage of the scale economies at plant and firm level (e.g. finance, marketing, R&D);
(b) To face the long-term maturation typical of investments in this industry; and therefore
(c) To fend off the imperfect competition of well-established foreign firms, which had the first-mover advantages of 'good-will' (Corden 1974) and static and dynamic economies of scale.

The drawbacks of monopolistic structures mentioned above appear to have been checked by the government's control over the *jaebols'* lifelines, i.e. credit and protection, whose maintenance was made conditional on export performance.

Table 4   Share of foreign firms in exports and manufacturing output in Korea, 1971–86 (%)

Share of	1971	1973	1975	1978	1984	1986
Exports	6.2	10.8	17.6	24.6**	25	18.3
Manufacturing output	n.a.	15.4*	17.0	19.3	18.3	20.2

* 1974 ** Manufacturing exports.

Source: Westphal *et al.* (1979:372) for 1971–75, Koo (1982:200) for 1978 and Bark (1989:23) for 1984–86

Turning now to the FDI policy, Korea managed to keep foreign firms at bay even though the letter of the law was indicating the contrary. At first sight the 1965–72 foreign capital legislation looks quite liberal.[72] Based on the 1960 Foreign Capital Inducement Law (FCIL), it granted lavish tax incentives for technology licensing and FDI.[73] Until 1965, there were some restrictions on foreign ownership (at least 25% of the capital had to be owned by local investors) and profit repatriation (maximum 20% of the invested capital), but they were completely removed in 1966. In 1970 and 1972, the government even established, as noted before, two free export zones where FDI incentives where even more generous.

The liberal impression, however, tends to fade away when FDI data are examined.[74] Table A.17 shows that loans were the bulk of foreign capital flows during 1966–72, and that in terms of FDI, Korea was at the bottom of the East Asian league by any indicator. The comparison with Latin American NICs is even more striking. During 1967–71, Korea's FDI share of net capital inflows was 3.7%, while Brazil's 33.8% and Mexico's 21.4%.[75]

These figures reflect the foreign firms' marginal share of exports and output. In 1971, they accounted for only 6.2% of total exports, and even though data for output is only available for 1974 (15.4%), that year's figure can be taken as evidence of how limited their share was in the previous decade, since the flow of FDI only became substantial (by Korean standards) after 1972 (Tables 4 and A.18). The foreign firms' role seems even more limited when we allow for the fact that up to 1972 only 36.1% of the FDIs had been majority or wholly owned by foreigners (Table A.19).

Moreover, evidence on FDI sectoral allocation suggests that the restrictions were sector specific. As Koo (1985:184) put it,

Throughout the sixties and seventies, very few DFI entrants were allowed to compete with domestic firms in the domestic consumer goods market. Relatively small investments were made in areas like food processing, pharmaceuticals, cosmetics and distribution services. With few exceptions, those foreign producers of consumer goods that were allowed entrance were asked to export their entire product or to substitute for imports.

This appears to square with the fact that FDI tended to be concentrated either on the intermediate goods sector (fertilizers, petrochemical) or on the leading export, labour-intensive industries such as electronics and textiles (Table A.20). Likewise, data for 1974 show that the foreign firms' export propensity (35.5%) was significantly higher than domestic firms' (21.0%).[76]

The assessment of the impact of this restrictive policy on manufacturing and export performance is far from straightforward, and like the general discussion on FDI costs and benefits, it is bound to be controversial.[77] Yet, one cannot help noticing that the FDI policy was remarkably consistent with the government's intervention in the other areas of the product and factor markets. It avoided the Latin American incongruity of offering local infant firms import protection, while at the same time inviting world class producers in, with its damaging effects on the former's growth and technological capabilities. This, in turn, had at least two important consequences. It helped to steer the country away from a truncated process of technological development, which, as with TNC affiliates in LDCs, was not likely to go beyond the adaptive and duplicative stages (Lall, 1992b); and, as noted earlier, it opened the way for the development of local conglomerates, whose benefits were already discussed above.

Moreover, it seems reasonable to assume that the TNCs' limited share of Korea's market and exports, also made resource allocation more responsive to the government's complex system of incentives, since local firms were not subjected to a global strategy devised elsewhere, and had their main source of capital controlled by the government.

Intervention in the Factor Markets

The Financial Market

To claim that Korea's manufacturing and export success during the 1960s was the result of 'neutral' incentives in the product markets,

Table 5 Flow of loans in Korea, 1965–72 (%)

Years	BOK loans	Bank loans[1]	Government loans	Foreign loans	Curb loans	Total	Total Government controlled[2]
1965	19	49	0	15	17	100	83
1966	6	44	0	48	2	100	98
1967	1	57	0	34	8	100	92
1968	2	51	0	35	12	100	88
1969	1	60	0	32	7	100	93
1970	0	52	2	32	15	100	86
1971	0	64	1	27	8	100	92
1972	0	82	0	21	–3	100	103

[1] Includes insurance and trust loans. [2] All less curb market loans. The curb market consists of credit transactions carried out outside the system of regulated financial institutions, not subject to control of either the monetary or the tax authorities (see Cole and Park 1983).

Source: Data from Hong (1979:164).

one has to implicitly assume that financial markets were complete, competitive and 'undistorted' by government intervention. That is not, however, what the evidence suggests. The capital market was virtually non-existent in the early 1960s,[78] and the government did not hesitate, for instance, to correct the bias towards short-term assets or to avoid interest rates above its socially optimum level.

Intervention in the financial markets began in 1961, with the nationalization of the commercial banks.[79] This move virtually gave the government total control of loanable funds. Table 5 shows that if one adds bank to foreign loans (the latter's overwhelming majority involved a governmental repayment guarantee)[80] the government's control amounted, in average, to 92% of the total credit.[81]

Despite the advice of people with untainted neoclassical credentials like Gurley, Patrick and Shaw,[82] state ownership of the financial sector was not combined with the textbook solution of market-led interest rates and credit allocation (which were in any event unlikely to solve the problems mentioned above). Instead, a rather heterodox approach was adopted. On the one hand, a misguided negative real interest policy, which until 1965 had largely prevailed (with the usual deleterious effects on financial intermediation), was dropped.[83] On the other hand, a discretionary loan policy coupled with multiple, subsidized interest rates was put in place (Table A.21).

The loan allocation policy was in principle based on a 'positive' list that' ranked industries and activities according to the government's priorities.[84] However, since these guidelines were usually far too general and comprehensive, and interest rates controlled, financial institutions could not meet the demand for credit. The government, therefore, had to step in to narrow down the number of sectors, activities or even firms, it was willing to favour. This was generally done by earmarking funds, by allocating them according to a financial and investment plan, or by 'direct guidance'. During 1963–73, 50 to 70% of domestic credit was officially classified as 'policy loans' and therefore allocated to targeted activities and sectors (Table A.13). This distinction between policy and non-policy loans, though, seems artificial since most of the analysts believe the latter were also subjected to 'direct guidance'.[85]

This overwhelming and discretionary control over credit was apparently used in the pursuance of four major aims: To boost manufacturing investment, to promote externality-prone activities such as exports, to foster dynamic comparative advantages in selected infant industries, and to promote conglomerates. With respect to manufacturing investment, in a bid to increase expected private returns, interest rates were held positive in real terms but well below the opportunity cost (Table A.13).[86] Though calling it 'mild financial repression', the market-friendly view (World Bank 1993:238) acknowledges that this policy:

> May actually have boosted aggregate investment and growth in the high-performing Asian economies [HPAEs] by transferring income from depositors, primarily households, to borrowers, primarily firms. Provided that the interest rate elasticity of household savings is sufficiently low and the corporate sector has a higher marginal propensity to invest than the household sector, the transfer may increase aggregate investment. Furthermore, the effective interest rate subsidy from households to firms increases the corporate profitability of investment reducing borrowing costs. Reinvested, these higher profits boost the equity of firms, enabling them to invest in riskier projects and borrow more to finance these projects. These may have partly offset the weakness of the equity markets during the HPAEs' economic take off periods by providing firms an alternative to equity financing.

Moreover, both commercial and development banks were forced to concentrate their resources on long-term loans,[87] and the former, with a few exceptions, were not allowed to provide consumer credit.[88] Short-term, working capital was supposed to come from the firm's internal earnings or from the unofficial curb market, which was also the only supplier of consumer credit.

Exports, as noted earlier, were the government's top priority, and not only benefited from unlimited short-term credit – coupled with a series of other preferential loans – but also had negative real interest rates over the whole period (Table A.13). Neoclassicals like to emphasize that the non-discretionary nature of the short-term export credit is an evidence of market-led resource allocation. This is, however, a mere drop of neutrality in an ocean of selectivity, since the export share of domestic credit was never more than 10% (Table A.21) and the short-term, non-discretionary part of it was even more diminished.[89]

The infant heavy industries, which under a deregulated financial market and free trade regime were not likely to see much of the banks' money, also benefited (selectively) from subsidized credit, particularly from the Korea Development Bank's equipment loans. Data on overall credit allocation shows that even though the light industry received the most,[90] more credit went to the heavy industry than would be justified by Korea's factor endowment. As illustrated by Chart 1, the gap between the heavy industry's share of output or value added and its share of incremental credit allocation over the 1960s, was comparable to that of the 'HCI push' (1973-79). As shown in the next section, the World

Chart 1   HCI's share of incremental credit allocation, manufacturing output and value-added, 1966–89

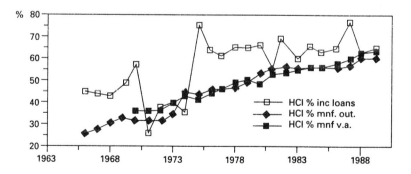

Note: 1, HCI% inc. loans is the heavy and chemical industry' share of the credit increase of the commercial and development banks. From 1984, it includes NBFI and Special banks' loans. 2, Share of manufacturing output is in current prices and share of value-added is in 1985 prices.
Source: BOK (a), EPB (a) and Suh (1975: 85)

Bank (1987a:41) drew attention to the latter gap, as evidence of significant 'distortions' in credit allocation (as opposed to a presumably 'neutral' 1960s).

Finally, the fact that credit allocation favoured large firms was already discussed in the previous section. We could just add that, beyond the benefits of intra-firm capital markets, by promoting conglomeration, the government also forced the banking system to perform the role that capital markets played in countries like England and the US, centralizing capital in the hands of the schumpeterian entrepreneurs, while at the same time divesting them of part of the risk involved in manufacturing investment. In other words, the banks (and ultimately the government) played the part of the shareholders, with the advantage that they were not seeking short-term profits. As noted earlier, Zysman (1983) called this type of arrangement, a 'credit-based financial system with administered prices' as opposed to the liberal capital-market based model.

Human Capital and S&T policies

Apart from intervention in the financial sector, there are two other government's moves in the factor markets that are overlooked by the 'neutral incentives' explanation, though not entirely by the market friendly view. The first concerns the strong commitment to education. Despite inheriting a population whose educational attainments in 1960 were already above the per capita GNP norm,[91] the military gave first priority to education, focusing on quantitative and qualitative improvements on the technical and primary levels. Even though not everything went as planned,[92] by the early 1970s the contrast between Korea's educational base and that of, e.g., the Latin American NICs was stark. For instance, Korea's illiteracy rate in 1970 had been reduced to 10.6% and the secondary enrolment ratio almost doubled to 41.3% (Table A.1). In Brazil, the same figures for the same year were 39.4% and 26%, respectively (UNESCO).

Heavy investment in the 'absorptive base' was accompanied by decisive measures that fostered investment in technological effort, and therefore led to the creation of industrial skills or technological capability. These measures are entirely overlooked by the two versions of the neoclassical view. That is, the Korean government:

(a) Restricted FDI and technology licensing;
(b) Promoted other less costly and more complementary forms of technology transfer, e.g. capital goods imports and turn-key plants;
(c) Fostered private conglomerates capable of overcoming imperfec-

tions related to R&D activities (economies of scale and scope, risk diversification, indivisibilities); and

(d) Invested in R&D and in the S&T infrastructure.

As FDI and conglomeration policies were already dealt with, let us look closer at the other measures. In the case of technology licensing, after a brief and costly period of *laissez-faire*,[93] it was formally restricted in 1969. The new regulation established that all technology contracts had to be approved by the Economic Planning Board, had a 3% royalty ceiling and could only last for a maximum three years. In addition, it banned clauses involving, e.g., export restrictions or input procurement (Kim and Lee 1990:88). The impact of this policy can be gauged by a comparison of Korea's data on technology licensing with those of other NICs. For instance, Westphal *et al.*'s (1985:190) estimates for 1970–71, put Korea's payments for disembodied technology at 0.04% of GNP, and Brazil's at 0.20%. On the other hand, thanks to the selective protection to the heavy industry, Korea had in the early 1970s one of the NICs' highest ratio of capital goods imports to investment (20%) (ibid.: 187).

As to investments in S&T and R&D, the first relevant moves seem to have been made in the second half of the 1960s, with the establishment of the Korea Institute of Science and Technology (KIST) in 1966, the Ministry for Science and Technology (MOST) in 1967 and the Korea Advanced Institute of Science (KAIS) in 1971. The first institution was aimed at industry related applied research, the second was supposed to co-ordinate the S&T policy, and the third had the task of supplying highly qualified scientists.[94] This institutional build-up was accompanied by a gradual increase of R&D outlays, funded primarily by the government (Table A.22). Given the light industry's weight during the period, the bulk of R&D outlays and institutional support were related to problems arising from the adaptation and use of imported embodied technology. Apart from this more practical and immediate benefit, these measures set the institutional and human capital stage for a decisive move into the technology-intensive heavy industries, whose advisability in the early 1970s was being suggested by a clear change in factor prices.[95]

Summing Up

Trying to summarize what has been said so far about Korea's 1960–72 policy regime, it seems clear that it was not market, industry or firm neutral, nor had low levels of protection for the domestic market. On the other hand, it appears evident as well that it allowed Korea to benefit from the advantages of an open economy (e.g. better resource allocation, scale and specialization economies, and access to frontier technology), without having to face the drawbacks of a free-trade, hands-off regime (i.e. inability to fully exploit dynamic comparative advantages due to market failures). How could it be?

It seems to have been the result of co-ordinated government action in the product and factor markets. A selective trade regime was set up, virtually segmenting export and domestic markets. The former was made liberal and industry neutral, while the second, protectionist and selective. This arrangement allowed exporters free access to producer goods at world prices, while offering the light industries and selected sectors of the heavy industry an exclusive domestic market where to reap static and dynamic economies. This, however, could not have worked without interventions in other areas of the product and factor markets, which not only reconciled the regime's contradictory incentives but also made sure that the local firms' response would be optimized.

That is, conglomeration gave local firms access to the economies of scope and scale particularly necessary to exploit dynamic advantages in the heavy industry, and set the conditions for price discrimination, which boosted static advantages. The FDI policy was instrumental in at least three ways: in preventing TNCs from taking advantage of the protection at the expense of the infant local firms; in precluding a truncated technological development; and in assuring a prompt private sector's response to incentives. In the factor market, the discretionary credit policy was used to: reconcile the contradictory incentives of the product market; to boost manufacturing investment via subsidized interest rates and long-term financing; to forge the aforementioned local conglomerates; and to increase the expected private returns of externality prone activities, and infant industries. Finally, the policies towards human capital and S&T assured that the process of acquiring technological capabilities would not be hampered by a poor stock of human capital, or by local firms' under-investment in indigenous technological effort.

It seems then that it would be a harsh understatement to affirm that interventions were a minor coadjutant, or that they did do changed the course of the events.

2.3 THE HEAVY AND CHEMICAL INDUSTRY (HCI) DRIVE (1973-79)

The 1973-79 period, together with the 1950s, is usually portrayed in the trade and development literature as the 'dark ages' of Korea's policy regime. The essence of the argument is that Korea, after seeing the light in the previous decade, inexplicably abandoned the outward-looking, hands-off strategy, to build its HCI. The argument goes on, saying that, fortunately, after having paid a *heavy price* in terms of misallocation of resources and (export) growth, Korea abandoned, in the early 1980s, this 'irrational' strategy and restored the quasi-free-trade regime.[96] Despite being dominant, this interpretation seems to be quite misleading. Even though the mid-1970s really seems to have marked a significant adjustment in the policy regime, its basic structure and orientation do not appear to have been altered. Secondly, even though there is evidence of misallocation of resources, the balance between cost and benefits does not seem to favour the former.

The first signs of adjustments in the regime came out with the third Five-Year Plan (1972-76), which unlike its predecessors, set specific investment and export targets for each of the selected HCIs.[97] The decision to target these industries is often explained on both economic and political grounds.[98] The economic justifications would have been, first, worries with the ever growing trade deficit – aggravated by the first oil shock – (Table A.8) viewed as a result of the industrial structure 'shallowness'; and second the perception that Korea's comparative advantages were changing and that the adjustment to these changes would not be secured by market forces.

In fact, although exports have grown faster than imports (at 41.2% p.a. over 1960-72 against 23.0% for imports), it was not enough to prevent the worsening of the trade balance due to the exports' very small initial base. The minus side of giving exporters access to inputs and capital goods at international prices, turned out be ever declining net foreign exchange earnings per dollar of export, reflecting not only Korea's poor natural resource endowment but also the size of the capital and intermediary goods industry.[99]

The shift in comparative advantage was being signalled by a rapid growth in labour costs (Table 6) *vis-à-vis* the so-called second tier NICs; a trend that was being compounded by rising protectionism in the developed countries towards labour-intensive goods.[100] The export prospects of HCI products, however, were perceived as being brighter not only because of the changes in factor prices but also due to an

Table 6   Growth rates in labour productivity, wages and unit labour costs in manufacturing, 1965–84

	1965–73*	1974	1975	1976	1977	1978	1979	1980	1982	1984
Wages, nominal	21.6	35.3	27.0	34.7	33.8	34.3	28.6	22.7	14.7	8.1
Wages, real^2	9.8	8.9	1.3	16.8	21.7	17.3	8.8	–4.6	7.1	5.7
Labour productivity	13.0	7.0	7.5	7.0	10.9	12.0	15.8	10.6	7.8	10.5
Unit labour costs^3	7.7	26.0	17.9	26.4	20.7	19.8	10.9	10.9	6.4	–2.2
Real unit labour costs^4	–2.8	1.8	–5.7	9.1	9.7	4.7	–6.0	–14.0	–0.6	–4.3

* Arithmetic average. ^{2} Nominal minus consumer price index. ^{3} Rate of change of nominal wage index/labour productivity index. ^{4} Rate of change of the real wage index adjusted by the rate of change of the labour productivity index.

Source: Data for 1965–73 from Amsden (1989:201) and for the rest of the period EPB (a).

alleged Japanese decision to move away from pollution-prone and natural-resource intensive industries (Enos and Park 1988:34).

As to the political motivation, it would have stemmed from apprehensions about national security. The Nixon administration decision to reduce US ground forces stationed in Korea and the opening of US relations with China would have persuaded the government to build its own defence industries.[101]

These economic and political aims prompted the government to adjust the policy regime, increasing protection to the HCIs, and channelling more resources in their direction. The objective of the adjustment, however, was not only to develop HCIs for 'domestic consumption', but also to make them leading exporters. The solution adopted was very similar to that successfully applied to the light industry. FDI was kept at bay, while high protection in a highly concentrated domestic market was combined with access to credit conditional on export performance, and subsidies for exports. The very nature of the HCIs, however, requiring capital and technology in a large scale, and its impact on the competitiveness of downstream sectors, demanded greater selectivity in protection and credit allocation, greater investment in human capital and indigenous technological effort, and greater emphasis on technology licensing.

Adjusting Intervention in the Product Markets

The Trade Regime

On the export side, the need to adjust incentives to achieve the HCI aims coincided with an unprecedented boom in exports. Boosted by the high growth of the world economy and international currency realignments (Table A.7), Korea's exports grew 50% in 1973, convincing the government that incentives could be streamlined and fiscal resources reallocated to the HCI programme.[102] Apart from reducing credit and interest subsidies,[103] export incentives accruing from import rights were reformed to increase protection for the HCIs. Tariff exemptions for capital goods were confined to selected export and import industries,[104] automatic exemptions for imported inputs were replaced by a 'drawback' system, and import-export links were phased out.

Although these changes led to a decline in export incentives (Table A.12), they should not be interpreted as a policy 'u-turn' towards an inward-looking strategy. It was more of a strategic adjustment to foster HCIs and eliminate excessive profits, than a change in direction. The key elements of an export-oriented growth were still there. For instance, even though the official exchange rate was held constant over 1974-79, the PPP exchange rate remained above its 1968 level, then considered 'realistic' (Table A.7).[105] Moreover, new export-promotion measures were introduced, offering fiscal and credit subsidies to trade companies (1975), and post-shipment financing for HCI exports, through the newly established Korea Export-Import Bank (1976).[106]

On the import side, the tariff structure was reformed and NTBs tightened. The former was adjusted to increase protection for the HCIs and reduce it for the rest of the industry. Overall the simple and weighted average rates declined slightly over the period (Table A.10).[107] As to NTBs, they were considerably tightened over 1968-78, notably to capital and consumer goods (Table A.14). These changes meant that import controls – until then confined to consumer goods and selected HCI goods not used in export production – were expanded to cover most of the HCI sectors, irrespective of the market of destination. This seems to be confirmed by the results of interviews conducted by the World Bank during 1975-76, reported by Westphal (1979:271):

it appears that competing imports of heavy industrial products have been effectively prohibited in numerous cases, even when the prospective importer is engaged in export activity. The products include

Table 7   Korea's effective protection rates[1] for the domestic market, 1968–82

Sector (ISIC)	1968	1978[2]	1978[3]	1982
Agriculture	19	57	77	74.
Mining	4	–1.5	–26	–2
Processed foods	–18	–44	–29	–48
Beverages and tobacco	–19	33	28	15
Construction material	–11	12	–15	51
Interm. products I	–25	37	–38	62
Interm. products II	26	21	8	40
Consumer nondurables	–11	67	31.5	43
Consumer durables	64	243	131	52.5
Machinery	44	44	47	32
Transport equipment	163	327	135	124
Manufacturing	–1	32	5	28
All industries	11	39.7	30.6	n.a.

[1] Direct price comparison, Balassa method. [2] Estimated by Young, S. (1984).
[3] Estimated by Nam (1984). *Note*: For definitions of Ind. groups see Table 2.

Source: Westphal and Kim (1982:230) for 1968; Young, S. (1984) *Trade Policy Reform in Korea: Background and Prospect*. KDI as quoted in World Bank (1987:35, vol. 1) for 1978 and 1982, and Nam 1981:201 for 1978.

basic chemicals and metals as well as mechanical engineering products. For the last group, the machinery producers' association determines eligibility for an import license, subject to arbitration by Ministry of Commerce and Industry, for items in the restricted list. The criterion used is that equipment with domestically produced similar cannot be imported unless the terms on which it can be purchased, including price, quality, and delivery date, are not competitive with those for the imported item.

The last part of Westphal's report draws attention to the fact that the additional protection given to HCIs was not unconditional. As with the light industry in the previous period, protection was linked to world prices, but this time not only through export performance but also by price controls.[108] Along with higher tariffs and tighter NTBs, the HCIs were also favoured by fiscal and other pecuniary incentives, based on sector-specific promotion laws, including tax holidays, special depreciation and purpose-built estates and infrastructure.[109]

ERP estimates for 1978, for what they are worth,[110] suggest that all these changes reinforced the selectivity implicit in the 1960-72 trade regime (Table 7). Effective protection rates for HC industries—transport equipment, durable goods, machinery and intermediate goods II—perhaps except for the last one, were either increased or remained relatively high. Furthermore, as in 1968, incentives in manufacturing continued to be biased towards exports.

Industrial Organization Policies

As noted in the previous section, right from the beginning of the outward-oriented regime, the government opted for promoting local conglomerates, apparently aware of their effectiveness in overcoming key market imperfections in the product and factor markets. This conviction seems to have become stronger with the decision to move into the HCI. Not surprisingly. Faced with an industry characterized by high risks, huge capital requirements, long investment maturation and significant economies of scale both at the plant and firm level, it would have been economic suicide to raise an infant industry based on Marshallian firms. Another option would have been the costly Latin American solution of 'protected' inward FDI. This, however, as shown later, was unequivocally ruled out by the government.

This renewed emphasis on the *jaebols* involved only marginal changes in the policy regime. After a decade of 'big business' policy, a hard core of large and highly diversified local firms was already in place. The main instruments continued to be credit and investment licensing. Tables 2 and 7 show that the SMFs' share of total credit and their access-to-borrowing ratio declined even further in the first half of the 1970s. The former continued to dwindle in the second half of the decade, whereas the latter remained below the large firms' ratio, notwithstanding a significant improvement.[111] Data on economic concentration also suggest that the 1960-72 trend was maintained, with the competitive markets' share of total shipments falling to 26% in 1977 (Table A.16). This development put Korea's levels of concentration well above those of Japan and others NICs such as Taiwan (Table A.23).

Like the conglomeration policy, the approach to FDI was not significantly changed but restrictions were made official and apparently reinforced, given the abrupt decline of investments after 1973 (Table A.18). These adjustments seem to have been triggered by a significant rise in FDI over 1972-73,[112] and tend to confirm the government's option to minimize its reliance on foreign firms. The 'officialization' of the restrictive policy came in the form of an amendment to the FCIL (1973), whereby a 'new' set of criteria for FDI approval was intro-

Table 8   Access to borrowing by each sector. Korea, 1972–84[1]

	1972	1974	1976	1978	1980	1982	1984
Total							
manufacturing	45.41	45.22	40.97	39.29	38.55	32.53	28.17
Large firm (a)	45.72	45.65	41.36	39.69	39.25	32.26	27.84
Small firm (b)[2]	27.27	24.44	34.98	37.02	33.79	33.87	30.40
(b)–(a)	–18.45	–21.20	–6.38	–2.67	–5.46	1.61	2.56

[1] Ratio of total bank loans and foreign loans over total assets of each sector.
[2] Small and medium business is defined as firms with fewer than 300 employees.
Source: Financial Statement Analysis, BOK, as quoted by Cole and Cho (1986:26).

duced. These criteria, which led to a FDI 'positive list' similar to that of pre-1967 for imports, consisted of a series of market, ownership, localization and scale restrictions that continued to virtually rule out projects that competed with domestic firms in the external and internal market, or projects where the majority of the capital was owned by foreign firms.[113]

Data on the foreign firms' sectoral distribution, ownership structure and share of output and exports, indicate the continuity of the FDI restrictive policy. The share of output and exports, for instance, increased significantly between 1973-78, but remained quite marginal by LDC standards (Table 4).[114] The sectoral distribution seems to have followed the move towards the HCI (Table A.20), with investment shifting from sectors such as textile and apparel to chemicals and electrical and electronic goods. Finally, the overwhelming majority of the projects continued to be majority owned or co-owned by local companies (Table A.19).

Adjusting Intervention in the Factor Markets

The Financial Markets

The adjustments in the policy towards the financial markets were confined mainly to the direction of credit allocation. The credit-based system remained in place, the banks remained in the government's hands, loan allocation continued to be discretionary, and interest rates remained subsidized. The bulk of the resources, though, was concentrated on the HCI targets and on the agents that would carry out these investments: the *jaebols*.

The changes in credit allocation can be said to have begun in 1972 with the Presidential Emergency Decree. This decree can be viewed both as a government response to the deleterious effects of an IMF sponsored stabilization (1970-71), and as a preparatory measure for the implementation of the HCI investments.[115] The combination of a restrictive monetary policy and a maxi-devaluation (1971), in an environment of highly leveraged conglomerates, led to a financial crisis that not only slowed the economy down but also put the HCI investments in danger. Keeping with tradition, the government avoided a market solution, and chose to bail out the debt-ridden conglomerates and to reduce interest rates even further (Table A.13).[116]

The reasoning behind these measures seems to have been, first, that without financially sound conglomerates, a move towards the HCIs, based in local private firms, would not be possible. And second, that widespread business failures would damage Korea's credit standing in the international market, and accordingly, deprive the HCI 'push' of an important source of capital.

Despite the drastic nature of the 1972 measures, the government's perception appears to have been that they would not be enough to carry out the industrial restructuring. They were, therefore, complemented by an increase in the *jaebol* and HCI biases of the loan allocation policy. As the former was already discussed in the previous subsection, let us concentrate on the latter. As can be seen in Chart 1, the HCI bias shot up to unprecedented levels, fuelled by a relative and absolute increase of the so-called 'policy loans' (Table A.21). These loans, which in their overwhelming majority were linked to HCI investments, received a boost with the establishment of the National Investment Fund, in 1974.[117]

It is also worth noting that despite the greater HCI and *jaebol* bias, credit allocation continued to favour exports. The share of preferential credits to exports in total domestic credits almost doubled during the period (Table A.21).

Human Capital and S&T Policies

Without neglecting the need to constantly improve the 'absorptive' base – illiteracy was virtually eradicated in the 1970s and all other human capital indicators showed enough improvement to keep Korea on the top of the NICs' league[118] – the government, with the HCI targets in mind, set out to strengthen engineering and technical education, and to improve the S&T infrastructure to boost domestic R&D

capability. A number of research institutes specialized in HCI sectors were then established, and the 'Technology Development Promotion Law', which included a series of fiscal incentives to private R&D, was introduced.[119] The results, at least quantitatively, seem impressive. The R&D share of GNP rose significantly reaching 0.86% in 1980, with the private sector accounting for a growing part of it. The R&D share of sales almost doubled over 1976-81, and the number of researchers per capita more than trebled over 1972-76 (Table A.22).[120]

This renewed emphasis on indigenous technological effort was accompanied by a substantial increase in technology licensing, reflecting the HCIs' higher imported technology requirements.[121] Yet, contracts continued to be carefully screened and approved according to a set of priorities,[122] in a continuous effort to overcome informational imperfections, and to strike the right balance between the various and complementary ways of achieving technological capability.

Success or Failure?

As stressed in the introduction to this section, the HCI period is often viewed as marking a shift towards a more selective and inward-looking strategy. However, as shown, not only the HCI policies were not inward-looking, but there was not such a thing as a neutral, hands-off policy in the 1960s. Therefore, far from representing a rupture, the HCI strategy can be interpreted as a continuation of an interventionist, selective and export-oriented policy regime. Its results, though, remain to be assessed.

As stated elsewhere, the task of assessing the outcome of a specific policy regime in a dynamic perspective is fraught with difficulties, not least because the counterfactual question cannot be properly answered.[123] Yet, most critics of the HCI strategy – usually looking from a neoclassical viewpoint – seem to be in no doubt about its negative results regarding resource allocation and export growth.

The World Bank (1987:45, vol. 1), for instance, agrees that the HCI policies were consistent with Korea's emerging comparative advantage but has 'mixed feelings' about the results. Changes in the industrial structure would have 'occurred too rapidly and at excessive cost' and the substitution of 'bureaucratic judgement for market tests' would have led to idle capacity and lower ICORs (incremental capital-output ratio). Likewise, Balassa (1985) argues that the bias of credit allocation towards the HCI, coupled with an overvalued exchange rate, would have resulted in overcapacity in the HCI and damaged light industry performance, adversely affecting economic and export growth. Along similar lines, Jung-ho (1990:99) maintains that, 'By employing the HCI policy, Korea has paid a high price in terms of the weakened export competitiveness of the light industry' and adds that, 'The net effect of the HCI policy on the export competitiveness of the HCI seems to have been nil or negative.'

The belief, though, that the government's handling of the HCI drive was problematic, is not a privilege of Neoclassicals. There seems to be a widespread consensus that the demand for some investments was overestimated, too many companies were licensed to enter particular industries and too many industries were targeted at the same time.[124] What generally distinguishes the neoclassical criticism is its rather gloomy picture of the HCI drive outcome, and its underlying assumption that the economy, particularly exports, would have performed better had the incentive regime been neutral and more outward-looking. Yet, if the aforementioned microeconomic misallocations of resources are viewed from a macroeconomic and dynamic perspective, the neoclassical negativism does not appear to be warranted.

First, the macroeconomic performance was quite impressive. GNP grew 9.6% p.a. whereas manufacturing output growth reached 17.2% p.a., roughly matching the previous period performance (Table A3). The fly in the ointment was inflation, whose annual average rose to 20.5%. Yet this figure was not that far from the 'neutral' period average (16%). The current account showed in 1977 the first surplus since 1965 and, despite heavy investment and foreign borrowing, the debt service ratios declined over 1972-79 (Table A.8).[125]

Second, HCI policies were remarkably successful in expanding the HCI's share, not only in manufacturing output but also in manufactured exports. During 1972-80, the former increased from 32 to 55%, whereas the latter rose from 24 to 46%. In 1984, HCI products were already accounting for more than half of Korea's exports (Table A.2). Moreover, the HCI import ratio fell from 39 to 24% over 1974-80 (Table A.4), suggesting, on the one hand, an irrefutable industrial deepening, and on the other, a considerable selectivity in this process, since the level of imports remained well above that of Latin American NICs.[126] Despite all this evidence, adepts of the market-friendly view (World Bank 1993:332), using a rather *gauche* measure of factor intensity,[127] insist in contesting the effectiveness of the HCI plan. According to their calculations, the industrial structure changes were at odds with the government's plan, since they favoured labour intensive sectors. This result, though, is not surprising since sectors such as machinery, electrical machinery and metals were classified as labour-intensive.

Third, when export performance is examined, the picture that emerges is far from disappointing. True enough, export growth declined. The annual average rate fell from 36.5 to 19.9% between the 1960-72 and 1973-79 periods. However, this does not seem to be related to the strategy adopted, whose often mentioned problems – lack of credit for the light industries and an overvalued exchange rate – appear to have been overestimated. As noted earlier, the PPP exchange rate remained at a level considered 'sufficient to sustain rapid export growth.'[128] As to the credit bias, it is true that most of the incremental credit went to the HCIs. However, it is also true that a similar situation occurred in the 'neutral' period and there was no talk of credit starvation. More-over, despite the obvious differences in capital intensity, the light industry's access-to-borrowing ratio during 1973-79, was on average higher than the HCIs'.[129]

The decline in export growth appears to be better explained by other supply and demand variables of the export equation. On the supply side, the growth of the real wages above labour productivity after 1976 (Table 6), might have squeezed profits, particularly in the labour-intensive light industries, discouraging exports.[130] To have devalued the exchange rate to make up for the higher labour cost, would have hindered the adjustment of the export composition to changes in the relative factor endowment. On the demand side, the sharp reduction in the world trade growth after the first oil shock, and the rise in protectionism that accompanied it, seem to have played a major role in reducing export growth. The growth of world exports fell from 8.7 to 4.6% p.a. be-tween the two periods, whereas the share of Korea's exports to devel-oped countries under-restriction rose from 26.7 to 32.2% over 1976-79.[131]

If the aforementioned factors are taken into account and if we allow for the fact that Korea's exports outperformed those of the developed countries and other Asian superexporters (Table 9), the portrayal of the HCI policies as a disaster for exports is unwarranted. In fact, the export performance was quite remarkable, particularly that of the HCIs, which, despite their infant condition, outperformed the light industries, significantly increasing their share of total exports (Table A.2).[132]

As in the 1960-72 period, the implausible combination of high pro-tection and export growth was made possible by linking the latter and access to credit to the former, by fostering conglomeration, and by selective protection. Protection gave the HCIs guaranteed access to static (production and R&D) and dynamic economies in the domestic mar-

Table 9   Export performance of the East Asian NICs, 1974–79[1]

Countries	Export value (US$)	Export quantum
Korea	29.4	16.1
Taiwan	23.8	14.1
Singapore	27.0	11.4
Hong Kong	17.6	11.7
Developed market economies	16.4*	n.a.

[1] Arithmetic averages of annual growth rates. * Average annual growth rate: 1975–79.

Source: Data from IMF and World Bank as cited by Balassa (1985:166) and UN (ITSY).

ket.[133] Conglomeration made sure that these economies would be optimized at the firm level, and that an early entry to the export market was possible through cross-subsidization and price discrimination. Selectivity gave infant exporters access to producer goods, while avoiding a too heavy burden to upstream industries and to the country's limited capital and human capital resources. As before, this arrangement was complemented by FDI protection, subsidized and discretionary credit for exports and manufacturing investment, and government direct intervention and incentives for indigenous technological effort.

When looked from a static viewpoint, this export-cum-protection strategy does not appear to be economically sound. Resource allocation is distorted and a heavy burden is imposed on domestic consumers. However, as Westphal (1982: 273) pointed out, if the usual assumptions of constant static and dynamic returns are dropped, the results can be welfare improving. Higher export growth can lead to dynamic and static economies that, in turn, would reduce unit costs and ultimately lead to lower domestic prices. Moreover, as HCIs are largely characterized by oligopolistic structures, the strategy of forcing the entry of local firms into the domestic and international markets might also shift profits from foreign to local producers.[134]

The third relevant point about the HCI policy assessment concerns the declining ICORs (Table 10). As the standard Heckscher–Ohlin model shows, a declining productivity of capital does not necessarily mean inefficiency. Any economy whose relative factor endowments are changing is bound to present a long term increase in the productivity of the 'ex-abundant' factor, matched by a less productive 'ex-scarce' factor. However, due to short-term macroeconomic fluctuations and market failures, this is not a smooth and inexorable process. For instance, due

Table 10   Korea's average incremental capital output ratios, 1970–88*

	1971–73	*1974–77*	*1978–81*	*1982–84*	*1984–88*
All industries	2.26	2.70	6.54	4.41	2.76
Manufacturing	1.37	1.40	2.63	1.61	n.a.

* Changes in output are lagged by one year. Both output and fixed investment are in 1980 constant prices.

Source: World Bank (1987:152, vol. 1) for 1971–84 and Lall (1992b:16) for 1984–88

to static and dynamic increasing returns, a LDC moving into the heavy industry (despite comparative advantages in the technologically mature sectors) will probably have the productivity of its capital stock sharply diminished, insofar as the MES will be larger than the initial market, and because of teething problems.

Korea's option for an outward-oriented strategy made this fall particularly acute, since scale economies and the pressure to be competitive led to HCI plants whose capacities were well beyond what the domestic demand could absorb.[135] On the other hand, the data available shows that, by acting this way, it avoided the experience of inward-oriented NICs, where the temporary fall in productivity was seldom overcome because of the size of the domestic market and the lack of international competition. For instance, Table 10 reveals that after rising sharply over 1978-81 – reflecting also the 1979-80 recession – ICORs declined steadily during the 1980s, to levels close to those of the 'neutral' period. Data on the HCIs' capacity utilization show a similar trend (Table A.24), and it is noteworthy that for the manufacturing sector as a whole, rates appear to have been very close to the international norm despite the peculiarities of the HCI strategy and the teething problems.[136]

The fourth relevant point concerns the indicators of total factor productivity (TFP). The adepts of the market-friendly view (World Bank 1993:315) argue that TFP growth in some of the targeted sectors was below the light industry's average. In fact, calculations carried out by Dollar (1991) show that over 1966-78, TFP growth in the heavy industry (0.2%) was below that of the light industry (2.2%). Apart from the difficulties and heroic assumptions involved in measuring TFP, these figures seem to reflect two facts: first, that the light industry was further behind the international best practice than the heavy industry. Dollar's calculations show that the HCIs' TFP in 1968 was 82% of the West German level, whereas that of the light industry was 64%. Second, the complexity and difficult access of the HCI technology, which tended to prolong the learning period. Moreover, it is noteworthy that despite these considerations, HCIs' TFP converged on the West German levels, reaching 85% of its value in 1978, reflecting the exceptional performances of the chemical and transport equipment sectors.

Finally, a few words about the so-called counter-factual case. As noted earlier, there is no doubt that policy mistakes happened and that HCI drive successes could have been achieved at lesser cost. Given that a Pareto-optimum situation is only a theoretical possibility, one can always argue that it could have been better. However, there is little evidence to support the hypothesis that Korea could have exploited its dynamic HCI advantages, or even that it could have had a better economic and export performance, had it pursued a neutral regime.

First, to assume that a smooth, 'stage approach' development would have been possible, one has to overlook the market imperfections stemming from the dynamic and static economies of scale, and non-homogeneous products that characterize the HCIs, which, in turn, are compounded by imperfect markets for capital and technology. This means that barriers to entry were high, and that without government intervention Korean firms' chances to succeed would have been slim. In fact, despite all government support and the rise in labour costs, the HCI average rate of return over 1973-80 (5.1%) was very close to the light industry's (4.2%), reflecting the difficulties in entering the industry.[137] This point is acknowledged by the World Bank (1987:47, vol. 1), which argues that,

Without the virtually unlimited government support that was offered to the HCI investments, no private agent would have been willing to bear the obvious risks.

Yet, in a recent report, the same World Bank (1993:314), using a simple two factor Heckscher–Olhin model and data on industrial structure international norms, suggests that the HCI plan was not effective, because the evolution of Korea's industrial structure conformed with the international norm and with the model predictions. As Lall (forthcoming) pointed out, the two factor approach cannot capture appropriately the impact of government intervention in the process of learning and industrial deepening; and international norms may be misleading because they reflect the promotion efforts of other countries in the sample.

Table 11   Korea and second tier NICs' average wage rate, 1975–87*

	1975	1980	1985	1987
Korea	100	100	100	100
Indonesia	47	26	27	19
Thailand	83	49	55	50

* US dollars, Korea = 100

Source: UNIDO.

Table 12 East Asia's unit labour cost index, 1976–79

Annual change (%)	1976–79*
Korea	27.5
Taiwan	9.4
Singapore	3.9

* 1975 prices.

Source: Kim, J.H. (1990b:36)

However, even if we accept those evidences, they, by themselves, do not prove that a hands-off policy would have produced the same results. As argued before, the government's plan was to remedy failures that were impeding the market to operate efficiently. If the resulting industrial structure conformed with the one that would have prevailed in the case of perfect markets, this seems to be evidence of the success of the plan and not of its failure or ineffectiveness.

Second, given that the market was not perfect, it seems reasonable to assume that, had the government adopted a hands-off policy, the transition to a more capital-intensive industrial and export structure would have been not only delayed but also reduced in scope. This, in turn, given the conditions of the labour market during the period, would have been more of a hindrance than a help to the light industries. As pointed out by Bai (1982), Korea's Lewisian turning point seems to have occurred in the mid-seventies when real wages started to grow consistently above productivity (Table 6).[138] *Ceteris paribus*, a delay in the HCI drive would have put even more pressure on the labour market, eroding even further Korea's comparative advantage in labour intensive goods *vis-à-vis* second-tier NICs, while investment in HCI sectors, giving the market failures, would have been slow to respond to factor prices. The overall result, then, would have been a poorer export and growth performance than the one that actually happened.

Two pieces of evidence seem to support this hypothesis. First, data in Tables 11 and 12 show that notwithstanding a near three-fold increase in Korea's capital-labour ratio in manufacturing over 1966-80 (Hong 1987:314), its unit labour cost grew well ahead those of Taiwan and Singapore and the wage rate gap with the second tier NICs rose sharply during the second half of the 1970s.[139] Second, even though incentives favouring HCIs were dropped in the early 1980s (see next section), HCI outperfomed light exports by a large margin. The former grew 17.4% p.a. during 1980-88, while for the latter, 9.6% p.a.[140] In this context, it does not seem to be hard to predict what would have happened with the overall export performance, had exports remained concentrated on labour-intensive goods.

All in all, by targeting the HCIs, the government prevented an even steeper rise in labour costs than the one occurred during the 1970s, which would have compromised even further the export performance of the light industry. Moreover, by pre-empting a move in factor prices, helping the private sector to bridge the financial and technological gaps between the light and heavy industry, the government opened the way for Korea's swift adjustment to its changing comparative advantage, placing the country in a better position to exploit it.

2.4 THE LIBERALIZATION (1980-90)

In the early 1980s, puzzlement would have been the probable state of mind of an occasional observer of the Korean economy, versed only on its neoclassical description, on being informed of the government intentions to liberalize the economy. In fact, it would have been no easy matter to grasp the purpose of the liberalization in an economy that was portrayed as one of the best examples of an outward-looking, neutral and free trade-like regime. The neoclassical answer to this paradox was to blame the HCI period. The liberalization would have been, then, a response to the policy mistakes of the 1970s and not to those of the 1960s. Not surprisingly, as will be shown, the government's official explanation also followed along these lines.

The last year of the HCI period was marked by a serious political and economic crisis. Fuelled by the hectic pace of investments, wage increases above productivity (Table 6) and by the building up of foreign reserves, inflation (WPI) jumped from 9 to 18.6% over 1977-79 forcing the government to act. In April 1979, a stabilization plan was announced, but was compromised by the second oil shock and by the president's assassination in October. The ensuing political and economic turmoil was aggravated in 1980 by the perverse combination of a poor harvest and an international interest rate shock, which were the last straws that pushed the economy into stagflation and BP problems. In this year, GNP fell by 3.7%, WPI growth shot up to 39%, and the current account deficit reached 8.8% of GNP.[141]

When the new administration took over in May 1980, it was keen to distance itself from the political and economic difficulties inherited from its predecessor. The blame for the economic crisis was then conveniently laid at the door of a policy that tried to 'pick winners' and to substitute 'bureaucratic judgements for market tests', even though the political and international elements of the crisis were also quite obvious. A draft of the Fifth Five-Year Plan (1982-6) issued in 1981 stated that Korea would 'return' to a fully fledged outward-looking policy. This would mean that,

> Investment choices will be left to the initiative of the private sector and the government will provide only the general framework in which such choices will be made by private entrepreneurs in co-operation with their bankers and financiers.[142]

An ambitious programme of reforms was then launched that would limit government intervention in the product and factor markets to 'functional' failures (e.g. R&D and unfair competition).

Liberalizing the Product Markets

Trade Reforms

Trade liberalization began in earnest in 1983,[143] after the government had successfully tackled the macroeconomic crisis.[144] The programme consisted basically of two five-year advanced liberalization schedules, one for NTBs, and one for tariffs. The former envisioned the import liberalization ratio, on an item basis, increasing from 80.4% in 1983 to 87.7% by 1985 and to 95.4% by 1988. In sectoral terms, light and intermediate product industries were to be the first to be liberalized (Nam 1985:25). Tables 13 and A.9 show that both macro and sectoral targets were virtually attained, except, perhaps for primary goods.

As for tariffs, the average rate was to be reduced from 23.7% in 1983, to 20.6% by 1984 and 16.9% by 1988.[145] As shown in Table 14,

Table 13   Korea's import liberalization ratio by industry (1983–89) (%)[1]

Industry	1983	1985	1988	1989
Primary goods	73.2	78.2 (77.8)	75.3 (80.5)	74.2
Chemicals	94.4	95.6 (95.7)	100 (99.6)	100
Textiles	80.4	93.1 (90.4)	98.8 (97.8)	99.5
Steel and metal	90.9	95.6 (94.9)	100 (100)	100
Machinery	68.7	83.0 (83.2)	100 (100)	100
Electric and electronic	53.6	73.8 (73.9)	100 (100)	100
Others	81.2	82.8 (83.7)	94.9 (88.2)	94.9
Total	80.4	87.7 (87.7)	94.7 (95.4)	95.5

[1] Total restricted items divided by total importable items (CCCN 8 digit). Numbers in parentheses are planned.

Source: Young (1988:27), Koo (1984:24), World Bank (1987, vol. 1:61), KFTA (1988:4) and Kim, J.H. (1990:10).

Table 14   Korea's legal tariff rates by sector, 1979–93

	1979	1983	1984	1988	1989	1993
Agricultural products	n.a.	31.4	29.6	25.2	20.6	(16.6)
Non-agricultural goods	n.a.	22.6	20.6	16.9	11.2	(6.2)
Raw material	n.a.	11.9	n.a.	9.5	n.a.	n.a.
Intermediate goods	n.a.	21.5	n.a.	17.1	n.a.	n.a.
Finished goods	n.a.	26.4	n.a.	18.9	n.a.	n.a.
All products	24.7	23.7	21.9 (20.6)	18.1 (16.9)	12.7	(7.9)
Coeff. of variation[1]	0.69	n.a.	0.61	0.64	n.a.	(0.75)

Note: Numbers in parentheses are planned. [1] Standard deviation divided by the mean.

Source: Young (1988:30), KFTA (1988b), EPB (1989), IMF (1984) and Table A.10.

tariff rates in 1988 were a bit off target, particularly given the increase in the coefficient of variation that was supposed to go down. Yet, it can be said that, overall, the changes in tariff protection were very much in line with what was planned. The announcement of the tariff schedule coincided with the reform of the tariff deduction scheme, which aimed at attenuating its industry-specific character. Except for the export drawback, deductions were then limited to 55-65% of the tariff rate and restricted to facility equipment and machines. In addition, the list of sectors entitled to these incentives was shortened, with the narrower category of 'new technology' industries replacing the 'strategic' one.[146]

On the export side, the aim was to limit the amount of subsidy to match the decline in protection. This was done mainly by raising, in 1982, interest rates on export loans to the level of the general rate (Tables A.13 and A.12).[147] Yet, exporters continued to benefit, *inter alia*, from preferential access to short (until 1988 and in the SMF's case up to now) and long-term loans, and from tax-free reserves.[148]

The cut in subsidies was accompanied by the introduction of a 'dirty-floating' exchange rate, linked to a multicurrency basket. This system led the PPP exchange rate to rise during 1984–85, probably offsetting the reduction on export subsidies (Table A7). From 1986, though, given the diplomatic pressures caused by a huge commercial surplus with the US, the government was forced to appreciate the won, even though, on a PPP basis, it remained below its historical average. In March 1990, after being identified under the US trade act as 'currency manipulator' (MTI 1990b:18), the Korean government adopted the so-called 'market middle rate system' that was supposed to be intervention-free.[149]

Industrial Organization Reforms

The government's long-standing 'interference' with the development of the industrial structure was also to be abandoned or 'neutralized'. That is, the anti-FDI, pro-*jaebol* and sectoral biases that until then had marked the government industrial policy were no longer desirable.

The reforms began with FDI policy. In 1980, new sectors were opened to foreign firms and restrictions on projects wholly owned by foreigners were relaxed (Koo 1985:179). In 1984 the positive list turned negative. As with import controls, all the sectors not in the 'negative list' were to be 'fully' open to FDI, although not necessarily automatically approved.[150] The negative list was to be phased out by the early 1990s. As of 1989, the government was claiming that 97.5% of the manufacturing sectors was open to FDI. In addition, the restrictions on capital repatriation and on foreign ownership ratios were also abolished, and the range of tax incentives available expanded (Bark 1989:15).[151]

The next in line was the conglomeration policy. In 1981, the government passed a new law – the Anti-Monopoly and Fair Trade Act – devised to tackle market imperfections impeding trade and fair competition. It was supposed to mark the end of decades of tacit support to the *jaebols*, either through the financial market or by investment licensing. This act was followed later on by other anti-*jaebol* measures concerning: finance (in 1984, the top thirty conglomerates' share of total bank credit was frozen, and groups whose debt-equity ratio exceeded 500% had their access to new credit blocked); diversification (from 1985); and cross-investments (investments in affiliated companies were limited to 40% of a corporation's net assets in 1987). Moreover, from 1985, a number of sectors were reserved exclusively to SMF, mainly among suppliers of small parts and components to the machinery sector.[152]

Apart from the financial sector reforms (taken up later), the sectoral bias of government policy was to be tackled mainly through changes in fiscal incentives, which were to be reduced and made sector neutral. At first, direct tax incentives (e.g. tax deductions) were phased out and replaced by indirect ones (e.g. preferential depreciation). These, in turn, were concentrated on 'functional' activities, notably R&D, with industry-specific incentives being restricted to fewer 'strategic' sectors (Rhee 1987).[153] In 1986, the search for neutrality went further with the seven existing industry-specific promotion laws being replaced by the Industry Development Law. This law, instead of naming 'strategic' industries, only specified two broad categories entitled for government support, i.e., sectors where it 'would be difficult to attain international competitiveness despite a comparative advantage for the Korean economy' and 'structurally inefficient declining industries in which Korea is gradually losing competitiveness.' Government intervention in these categories was limited to 3 years.[154]

Liberalizing the Factor Markets

Financial Sector

On the financial market, liberalization began with a package of measures aimed at minimizing government controls over credit allocation, and at reducing its *jaebol* and HCI biases. This package included the privatization of the commercial banks (1981-83), the relaxation of the requirements for establishing non-banking financial institutions (NBFI), and the unification and overall increase of the interest rates (Table A.13). These measures were complemented by the decision to earmark 35% or commercial bank credit and 55% of local bank loans to SMFs, and to phase out the policy loans (including short-term export loans), which, as a result, had their share of domestic credit reduced from around 60 to 45% over 1979-86 (Table A.21).[155] These measures were apparently successful in reducing the HCI and large firm biases in credit allocation (Chart 1 and Table 8).

In a second stage, the government sought to reduce the firms' 'excessive' dependence on credit by complementing the initial package with incentives and restrictions to expand equity financing. This was done mainly by the enforcement of lower debt-equity ratios and by the introduction of tax breaks for stock ownership. This drive towards equity financing affected particularly the *jaebols*, which, as said before, had a freeze imposed on new loans since 1984. These measures led to an immediate reduction on the firms' debt-equity ratio, but despite the stock market boom in 1987, the ratios remained well above those of the OECD (Table A.25).[156]

Human Capital and S&T

The government conversion to liberal economics did not go far enough to negate the existence of market failures in human capital formation and S&T. Adopting the 'weaker version' of the neoclassical approach (Lall 1991), the rhetoric was that interventions in these areas were 'functional' or sector neutral, and accordingly, did not distort relative prices. Predicting, then, a further shift in comparative advantage towards technology-intensive sectors, the government stepped up investments in engineering and scientific education, R&D and S&T infrastructure. Both the R&D share of GNP and the number of researchers per capita more than doubled over the period (Table A.22).

There were, though, important changes in the implementation of this policy. In a bid to increase private R&D outlays, financial and fiscal incentives were greatly increased, which undoubtedly contributed to the rise in the private sector's share of total R&D from 32 to 81% over 1980-88.[157] There were also institutional changes, with state research institutes being merged for the sake of greater efficiency in R&D management, and the division of labour between these institutes, universities and the private sector were more clearly defined. Universities were to concentrate on basic science; government institutes were to provide a link between the universities and the private sector, while focusing on the development of 'core and original' technology of 'national interest'; and private firms were to undertake 'commercial' R&D (MOST 1988 and Lee *et al.* 1991).[158]

Alongside the drive to promote indigenous technological effort, restrictions on technology licensing were eased, with the government

Table 15   Korea's import penetration ratios, 1980–87

Sectors	Imports / domestic production				Imports / domestic supply			
	1980	1983	1986	1987	1980	1983	1986	1987
Agriculture and forestry	21.9	17.4	14.5	15.7	18.8	15.5	13.2	14.2
Mining	536.9	517.8	324.6	330.9	85.0	83.4	77.0	77.5
Food, beverages and tobacco	7.5	5.6	5.7	6.6	7.1	5.4	5.6	6.5
Textile and leather	5.4	7.3	7.7	8.4	7.9	11.5	12.4	13.6
Lumber and wood	2.3	4.8	8.5	8.8	3.1	5.2	8.9	9.4
Paper, printing	16.9	12.1	14.6	14.8	15.3	11.2	13.3	13.6
Chemicals	15.6	17.2	20.1	21.9	14.9	16.4	19.6	21.1
Nonmetallic minerals	4.4	7.0	8.5	8.3	4.9	7.3	8.6	8.5
Basic metals	21.8	18.7	22.6	22.7	21.6	19.0	21.3	21.1
Metal products and machinery	50.3	37.3	35.2	34.9	42.4	36.5	36.0	36.5
Other manufacturing	7.5	7.4	5.5	5.6	13.8	13.8	12.6	14.5

Source: Bank of Korea, Korea's Input-Output Tables.

raising the ceiling on the value of contracts needing approval, and exempting an increasing number of industries from the restrictions (Enos and Park 1988:37). As a result, and given the changes in the industrial structure, royalty payments more than doubled between 1977-81 and 1982-86.[159]

Assessing the Results

Overall Performance

Considering the evidence above, it seems undeniable that Korea has moved into a policy regime closer to the neoclassical ideal. The burning questions, though, are to what extent and under what circumstances. To answer these questions becomes particularly important given Korea's impressive export, BP and overall macroeconomic performance during the liberalization.

Exports grew 12.2% p.a. over 1980-89, outperforming those of the 'world' (4.1%) and middle-income countries (5.4%).[160] On the import side, despite the liberalization, Korea was not flooded by imports, nor suffered any significant industrial dislocation. Table 15 shows that after seven years of liberalization, imports had not made any substantial gain on the domestic market, except for lumber and wood, non-metallic, chemicals and textile and leather. Even in these sectors, the rise in import penetration appears to have been more related with Korea's lack of natural resources and the move towards resource-intensive sectors, than with the dislocation of local producers.[161]

The dislocation-free hypothesis seems to be further confirmed by three other pieces of evidence. First, by the data on sectoral production and employment, shown in Table 16. The picture that emerges from this table – with all sectors presenting significant growth in output, employment and establishments – is in sharp contrast, e.g., to Chile's experience of the 1970s.[162] There, the liberalization programme led to a radical change in the industrial structure, with seven out of 20 manufacturing sectors having lower levels of production in 1980 than in 1970 (Edwards 1985:232). Second, by the stability of Korea's import composition, which in 1989 was still dominated by capital and intermediate goods (Table A.15). Finally, by the estimates for the income elasticity of imports, which reveal that both the elasticity range and its average declined between the 1970-79 and 1980-88 periods.[163]

If Korea was not flooded by imports, it was not swamped by FDI either. Table 17 shows that, despite the more liberal legislation, by the end of the 1980s, its FDI indicators continued to trail badly those of the other NICs and second-tier NICs. Figures for the foreign firms' shares of each industrial sector were not available, but if we take into account that the FDI share of gross domestic capital formation during 1979-85, was below that of the 1966-78 period, an educated guess would be that Korea's industry has not suffered from denationalization either (Table A.17).

The overall result of these trends, limited inflow of FDI notwithstanding, was a dramatically improved BP, with Korea having in 1986, not only its first trade balance surplus since the Korea war, but also a current account surplus. As both surpluses persisted for four years, Korea was able to reduce considerably the burden of its foreign debt (Table A.8). To complete the rosy picture, the external balance improvement took place in a high-growth (10% p.a.) and low-inflation environment (5.2% p.a.), with the economy roughly matching the growth performance of the previous periods, while presenting a superior inflation record (Table A.3).

If the neoclassical assessment of the HCI drive is accepted, the rational follow-up would be to attribute all this remarkable economic performance to the efficiency gains produced by the liberalization. One could say that the reinstatement of a neutral, outward-looking incentive regime led the economy back to the right relative prices, and the

Table 16   Korea's rate of growth in production, employment and number of establishments by industry, 1980–89 (%)[1]

Industry	Production (1985 Won)	Employment	No. of establishments	Change in the share of total Mnf. value added (%)[2]
Food, beverages and tobacco	7.7	2.3	0.2	−5.2
Textile and leather	6.4	2.4	7.6	−4.2
Lumber and wood	8.8	4.8	4.3	−0.2
Paper, printing	8.9	6.9	4.2	0.0
Chemicals	9.1	5.1	8.4	−3.0
Nonmetalic minerals	9.0	2.7	3.3	−1.4
Basic metals	11.5	3.0	5.4	2.0
Metal products and machinery	18.7	8.2	11.2	14.1
Other manufacturing	7.4	5.9	1.1	0.4
Total manufacturing	11.6	4.8	7.3	−

[1] Annual compound average rate. [2] 1980–1988. Total does not add to zero due to rounding.

Source: EPB (a) and EPB (b).

Table 17   Foreign direct investment stocks: values and relative to GDP

Country	Year	Stock[1]	% of GDP
Korea	1987	2.8	2.3
Taiwan	1988	8.5	8.1
Hong Kong	1985 (est.)	6.0–8.0	20–26
Singapore	1986	9.4	53.8
Brazil	1987	28.8	9.6
Mexico	1987	19.3	13.6
India	1984 (est.)	1.1–1.5	0.6–0.7
Thailand	1986 (est.)	4.0–5.0	10.5–13.1
Indonesia	1987	7.9	11.3
Kenya	1984	0.6	12.0

[1] US$ 10^9

Source: Lall (1990, table 4).

rapid export and overall growth that followed were its logical consequence.[164] The trouble with this interpretation, though, is that it has both empirical and logical problems.

First, as the previous sections have shown, one could not talk of a return to an outward-looking, hands-off policy since the HCI strategy was solidly committed to export growth, and Korea had never had a neutral incentive regime.[165] Second, despite the 'distortions', the performance of Korea exports and economy during the 1960s and 70s was as good as that of the 1980s, except perhaps for inflation. And third, if it is assumed that Korea's policy regime really shifted to a neutral mode during the 1980s, and that is the reason the Korean economy performed so well, why, then, was there no major structural adjustment? Or to put it differently, if Korea's experience with intervention during the HCI drive was a complete failure, why was the transition to a market-led economy virtually dislocation-free?

A more consistent explanation, capable of dealing with these points raised above, has to take into account both the efficiency of the past government interventions, and the timid character of the liberal reforms.

The Efficiency of Previous Interventions

It can be said that the government intervention, not only in the 1970s, but also in the 1960s, prepared the way for the 1980s liberalization. By using financial, fiscal and trade instruments to overcome market failures in the product and factor markets, the government created the conditions by which a transition to a more liberal economy would be particularly beneficial. Without strong local firms – nurtured by decades of protection, abundant long-term credit, export-orientation discipline, and supported by an increasingly sophisticated human capital stock and S&T infrastructure – liberal reforms would have played havoc in the Korean manufacturing sector, hampering the economy's ability to adjust to changes in comparative advantages. On the other hand, after achieving a competitive and diversified industrial structure, continuation of widespread intervention would be ill-advised because key market failures had already been overcome, and because of the danger of 'government failure' in administering an increasingly complex economy.

The lack of major dislocations during the 1980s liberal reforms comes as an important evidence to support this interpretation. As Chile's experience has shown, had government intervention not been efficient and market-failure oriented, Korea would have found it difficult to maintain a virtually uninterrupted two-digit export growth for another decade, let alone its overall growth and inflation record. The limited adjustment costs, however, cannot be entirely ascribed to the efficiency of the government's past policies. It has also a bearing on the gradualist approach of the reforms, and on the government's persisting determination to intervene, both functionally and selectively, wherever market failures were still relevant despite the liberalism of its rhetoric.

How Gradual and Liberal were the Reforms?

The Product Markets Beginning with trade reforms, Korea took more than a decade to do less than Chile did in five years. While the latter removed all the NTBs and reduced all tariffs to a uniform 10% in a 5-year period (Edwards 1985:231), the former, as late as 1987, had close to 30% (in value terms) of manufactured imports still under NTBs, and at least 27% of the importable items under some sort of contingency measures (Tables A.14 and A.26). In 1988, its average tariff was still 18%, and the tariff structure was anything but uniform (Table 14).

Behind these figures seems to have been a strategy that was both cautious and selective. Cautious because local firms were not only given plenty of time to adjust to competition in their home market, but were also assured by safeguards in the trade legislation that any major dislocation would be avoided.[166] Selective because industries where the static and dynamic advantages of a protected domestic market were substantial were the last to be liberalized, and in some cases only partially. The 'new technology' industries are a case in point. They were favoured with special laws that effectively barred imports of items like computers, telecommunication equipment, semiconductors, machine tools and electronic consumer goods.[167]

After 1987, the prudence and selectivity of the government's strategy was somewhat compromised by heavy pressure from Korea's biggest trade partner – the US – which forced a swift removal of NTBs and contingency safeguards (Tables A.14, A.9 and A.26).[168] Yet, in 1990, the government showed that it was not prepared to live passively with the vagaries of a free trade regime, particularly when this means competing with foreign firms, which have time, scale, technology, a well functioning capital market and a developed S&T infrastructure on their side (and not seldom their own governments). Therefore, amid a return to a trade and current-account deficit caused by the combined action of speedier liberalization, currency appreciation, and higher labour unit costs, Korea resorted again to NTBs to stop imports, particularly of consumer goods.[169] The NTBs took the form of a tacit anti-import campaign, which used the *jaebols'* tight control over distribution to curb imports.[170]

On the industrial organization side, the reforms could not be more pragmatic. Despite all the talk about enhancing the role of the price mechanism, the government continued to play a key role in shaping Korea's industrial structure and controlling the influx of FDI. This was already evident at the beginning of the decade, when the government decided to bypass a market solution to correct the HCI drive excesses. Commercial banks were 'persuaded' to support mergers and capacity reduction programmes in the distressed sectors, whatever their expected returns. The underlying reasoning, as Young (1986:52) put it, seems to have been that industrial adjustment had to precede import liberalization and not vice versa. As in its 'damned' past, the government was again trying to prevent that the weakness of the capital markets and their short-termism put years of capability building in danger.[171]

The government determination to continue to intervene was also written 'all over' the 1986 Industrial Development Law (IDL), despite assurances to the contrary.[172] The use of loose categories such as 'sunrise' and 'sunset' industries, left plenty of room for the government to intervene to avoid the occasional socially damaging market solution. That is what happened for instance, between July 1986 and December 1987, when no fewer than eight industrial sectors were designated for a three-year rationalization programme under the IDL provisions, with the government bailing out financially distressed firms, and defining the sectors' number of competitors and overall capacity.[173] Again, in a context of imperfect capital markets, the government seems to have had no anxieties to avoid the risks of a long-drawn-out market solution, with its potentially disruptive effects in terms of bankruptcies, asset-stripping and denationalization.

On the issue of conglomeration, the same pragmatism seems to have prevailed. With the *jaebols* being the backbone of Korea's economy and with market imperfections such as economies of scale and scope being neither temporary nor 'reparable', it is not surprising that the government actions fell well short of its rhetoric. To begin with, the Fair Trade Act did not restrict conglomeration (Lee 1986). Second, the majority of the credit and diversification restrictions were either relaxed by the government or skirted by the *jaebols*. In the case of the former both things apply, since they were periodically relaxed according to the economy's performance and the industry's restructuring needs, and the *jaebols* used the financial liberalization to diversify into the financial sector. As to diversification, restrictions were apparently sidestepped by starting-up nominally independent companies using 'retired' senior executives (FEER 1988, Sept. 29). More to the point, as noted earlier, the government's own restructuring exercises continued to promote concentration as a means to achieve efficient market structures.[174]

No wonder economic concentration continued to rise. Both the top 5 and 30 *jaebols* increased their share in total shipments during 1977– 85.[175] In 1985, the competitive markets' share of the total shipments still amounted to only 37.8%, slightly better than in 1977, but still lower than in 1970 (Table A.16). In addition, the ratio of the top 10 *jaebols'* sales to GNP climbed from 48.1 to 68.3% over 1980-89.[176]

Finally, on FDI deregulation, the government did not take the naive view that Korean firms were prepared to face the imperfect TNCs' competition in its own market, without any sort of safeguard. Despite the changeover to the negative list and the increase in the number of deregulated sectors, when one takes into account other scant but telling evidence, the general impression is that the government continued to be very much in control, deciding when, where and in what terms FDI would take place.

For instance, investments in sectors not listed were still subject to screening, unless they were majority-owned by local firms, and relatively small (under $3 million). Investments would not be allowed to go forward if the sector in question was under 'rationalization requirements', which, as of January 1989, included key sectors such as textiles, ferro alloy, fertilizers, automobiles, diesel engines, heavy electrical equipment and heavy construction equipment (MTI 1990b). Still depending on the sector aimed, investments could also face export, local content and local equity participation requirements.[177] Lastly, at least until 1987, foreign investors had to live without effective protection for intellectual property. It was only in 1987 that Korea enacted a series of basic intellectual property laws, but even then problems of enforcement led the government to establish the Intellectual Property Rights Task Force in December 1988.[178]

Factor Markets   In the financial markets, as the above analysis might have already suggested, the government continued to have a strong influence in credit conditions and allocation, despite the commercial banks privatization and other deregulating measures. Behind this apparent contradiction lies what can be called a two-track financial deregulation. Whereas the NBFIs had establishment requirements, loan allocation policy and interest rates semi-deregulated in 1985, the commercial banks, as late as 1990, still had to cope up with Ministry of Finance suggestions concerning their officers, loans and interest rates.[179]

Even though this asymmetry of the financial reforms can be justified on the grounds of the banks' high proportion of non-performing loans (mainly for shipbuilding and construction), there is no doubt that it also allowed the government to maintain control, directly or indirectly, over the majority of the loanable funds.[180] In fact, some of the key 1960s' and 1970s' characteristics of the financial system were well and alive during the 1980s.

For instance, credit allocation continued to be highly selective. Resources continued to be channelled into manufacturing investment, 'strategic' sectors and activities, at rates still below the private opportunity cost. As noted earlier, banks were forced, their financial health notwithstanding, into a virtually permanent industrial 'restructuring' programme. The 'new' technology sectors were particularly favoured, and exporters continued to have preferential access to credit. Moreover, as the unification of interest rates was not accompanied by their deregulation, bank credit continued to carry a reduced but still significant financial subsidy. As of 1989, the difference between the general loan and the deregulated corporate bond rates ranged from 2.7 to 5.7% depending on the client's credit-worthiness.[181]

Moreover, there are signs that credit allocation continued to favour large firms. Even though, as noted earlier, the anti-*jaebol* and pro-SMF measures seem to have had some success in reducing this bias until 1984 (Table 8), we have already given two good reasons to believe that this tendency was reversed after 1985: the periodical relaxation of the credit controls, and the *jaebols'* diversification into the financial sector. The first reason is particularly relevant after 1985, when credit controls were significantly relaxed because of the collapse of one major conglomerate. This seems to be confirmed by the data available, which show that the top ten *jaebols'* share of total borrowing jumped from 25 to 53% over 1986-89 [FEER (1988, 29 Sept.) and (1990, 1 March)].

The second reason was very much a result of the government two-track liberalization. The NBFIs not only were deregulated faster, but were also freed of the ownership limitations imposed on banks. Therefore, the conglomerates had the opportunity to diversify into a segment of the financial sector, which, given their relatively freer asset management and interest-rate policies, increased their share on total deposits from 10 to 18% over 1980-89 (BOK 1990c, Feb.). It was not possible to find reliable data on the NBFIs' ownership structure, but even government officials agree that they are entirely dominated by the *jaebols*.[182]

These characteristics of the financial reforms seem to indicate that despite suggestions that their final objective was a financial system based on the liberal, capital-market based model of the US and UK, in practice though, they have moved in the direction of a credit-based financial system along the Japanese lines, where the short-termism and myopic behaviour of the capital-markets are compensate by heavy involvement of the banks in the financing of manufacturing investment, forced by strong government 'guidance' and conglomerate ownership.[183]

The last point on the factor market liberalization concerns the 'functional' S&T policy. Even though, in theory, the government's higher investments and incentives could have benefited all firms in all sectors, in practice, 'strategic' technology-intensive industries were the main beneficiaries. For instance, on top of import protection noted earlier, industries such as computers, semiconductors, telecommunications and machine-tools were particularly favoured by government procurement, and by direct subsidies coming from special government funds, set up to develop 'key technologies'. Most of these funds were linked to the so-called 'National R&D Projects', where the developing costs were usually split between the government and hand-picked private firms, with the former typically bearing most of the expenses.[184] So, under the guise of 'functional' S&T policies, the government not only continued to intervene to prop up local technology effort, but it did so by clearly targeting industries seen as having the potential to bring externalities and dynamic comparative advantages.

Summing Up

From the arguments outlined above, it seems quite clear that, despite the official rhetoric, the Korean government conversion to the liberal cause was far from dogmatic. For all the advances towards a more liberal regime, one cannot help noticing that far from becoming an anathema, government intervention continued to be used selectively, and to be largely driven by the aim of giving local firms the best possible chance of succeeding in the domestic and international markets. Market solutions or liberal models were only adopted when the government was sure that, instead of letting local firms disadvantaged because of imperfections in both local and international markets, it would increase their competitiveness.

In the product markets, the government continued to seek protection, within the trade relations constraints, for those industries where dynamic and static economies of scale were relevant, and this included not only trade barriers but also FDI protection. Likewise, it did not hesitate to intervene to reshape the industrial structure towards more efficient and sustainable configurations, avoiding the risks of a protracted and costly market-led solution. In the factor markets, equity financing and private ownership of the financial system were encouraged, but on the other hand, in order to protect the industry from the short-termism and myopic behaviour of the capital markets, the bank's commitment to long-term financing was promoted by the governments' heavy hand and by conglomeration ownership. Finally, indigenous technological effort was encouraged not only by functional measures but also by targeting the technology-intensive industries where the existence of externalities was expected to promote the technological capabilities of the whole industry.

2.5   THE OVERALL PICTURE

The analysis of the trajectory of Korea's industrialization, and of the role played by the government, has shown that the established, neoclassical view of Korea's success does not bear close scrutiny. The tale of a country that was highly rewarded for 'keeping the fundamentals right' and renouncing an interventionist, inward-oriented regime in favour of a liberal, neutral and outward-oriented strategy is, to say the least, misleading.

To begin with, the IS period of the 1950s, rather than being a total disaster, was instrumental in rebuilding the light industry and in raising the educational standards of Korea's work force. Without the capacity and capabilities built during this period, it is hard to envisage the export take-off of the 1960s.

The regime adopted in the early 1960s represented, no doubt, a significant change in trade orientation. It is also indisputable that this new orientation played a major role in improving Korea's industrial and overall economic performance. Yet, the new regime was far from liberal, hands-off or neutral. Rather than representing the end of government intervention, it meant its reform. The wholesale, politically-motivated and cost-blind pattern of intervention was replaced by one disciplined and guided by international prices, and by the need to remedy market failures. It is only by taking this fact into account that the policy regime of the 1960s, and the success it has achieved, can be fully understood.

This new regime involved in the product markets, a selective system of incentives, which granted exporters free access to producer goods at world prices, while offering – under strict performance conditions – the light industries and selected heavy industries an exclusive domestic market, where to reap static and dynamic economies. This was complemented, first, by a conglomeration policy that optimized these economies at firm level, and that allowed an early entry to the export market via cross-subsidization and price discrimination. And second, by a restrictive FDI policy, which protected local firms from the imperfect competition of TNCs, and secured a prompt private sector's response to local incentives. In the factor markets, it ensured that manufacturing investment and exports did not suffer from the lack of proper financing, while favouring conglomeration by concentrating resources in local 'winners'. Finally, it also made sure, via direct government investment or incentives, that the acquisition of technological capabilities would not be hampered by a poor stock of human capital, poor S&T infrastructure or by local-firms' under-investment in indigenous technological effort. In short, hardly what one would call a liberal regime.

In the early 1970s, prompted mainly by evidence of factor price changes and industrial restructuring by developed countries, the government promoted a move towards the heavy industry. Contrary to the established view, though, this move neither broke with the previous strategy, nor resulted in disaster. No doubt, there were adjustments in the policy regime. The HCI market imperfections, and related entry barriers, required modifications to give local firms a fair chance to win. Hence, HCIs were granted greater access to credit (still concentrated on the local winners), and were provided with higher, but still selective, import and FDI protection. Moreover, to meet the HCI technological requirements, government investment in human capital and S&T was stepped up. These changes, however, did not alter either the previous pattern of government intervention or the trade orientation of the regime. The ultimate aim remained to build an internationally competitive industry and to remove the market failures that blocked the way. The ever increasing share of HCI exports throughout the 1970s and 1980s, and the fact that a two-digit export performance was sustained, speaks against any negative assessment of the HCI drive.

Lastly, in the 1980s, the government, under a new administration, moved to liberalize the regime. Painted as if it were a return to the good old liberal days of the 1960s (which in fact never existed), the liberalization was nothing more than a logical follow-up to two decades of heavy government intervention. This intervention for overcoming key market failures, opened the way for a strong and internationally competitive local industry, and therefore, for a future and wise reduction of the government role. This reduction, however, despite the rhetoric was far from dogmatic. Our analysis has shown that the state continued to intervene in those areas where market failures are beyond repair. and therefore intervention can lead to a better solution. It is this context, and not of a dogmatic, without antecedents, liberalization, that the impressive industrial and overall economic performance of the 1980s has to be assessed.

3 Brazil[185]

Unlike Korea's, Brazil's centenarian industrialization has produced mixed results. On the plus side, it has led to an exceptional growth record, which until the 1980s compared favourably with most LDCs (Table 1). It has also produced a large and diversified manufacturing sector, whose value-added ranked seventh in the world in 1988; and whose export performance over 1965-80, reached East Asian standards. Yet, on the minus side, industrialization was accompanied by rising inflation, by the build-up of the external debt and by the worsening of the income distribution (Table 1). By 1980, the signs of serious resource misallocation were all too obvious, with 35.4% of the economically active population estimated to be under-employed.[186] The indicators of productivity and technological activity do not point to an encouraging performance either, with Brazil lagging behind countries like Korea and Mexico. To complete the picture, in the 1980s, output and manufactured export growth fell sharply to well below the LDC average.

These sort of disparate results have been generally associated in the trade and development literature, with an inward-oriented policy regime with lapses of outward orientation. Rather unsurprisingly, Neoclassicals credit the good results to the allegedly export-oriented, hands-off periods of government policy, and the bad ones to those when IS and selective intervention prevailed. The arguments are well known and were already taken up in the introduction. Outward-orientation, equated with a neutral incentive regime, would have led, *inter alia*, to better resource allocation, economies of scale and technological dynamism. Conversely, IS and its selective policies would have, *inter alia*, distorted resource allocation, hampered exports, and promoted oligopolistic markets, rent-seeking behaviour and technological backwardness.

Authors closer to the structuralist tradition, in turn, emphasize the role of IS policies in building a diversified industrial structure, in overcoming supply inelasticities, and in boosting growth. It is acknowledged that the IS strategy has hurt exports, but the bad results, particularly of the 1980s, would have *come from the side of macroeconomic failure, not a debilitating sectoral misallocation*, as Fishlow (1990: 66) put it. Sceptical of export-promotion strategies, they argue that the

87

state has failed to back up IS with sound fiscal and monetary policies.

Although there are merits in these two interpretations, they both have important drawbacks. The neoclassical view correctly draws attention to the benefits of a more open economy, but, given its assumptions that product and factor markets are generally efficient in LDCs, they tend to underestimate the market failures facing the Brazilian government, and therefore, fail to consider the dynamic interaction between the IS and export promotion periods. On the other hand, the structuralist view rightly points out that, given the nature of the market failures, government intervention was vital. However, it does not address the point that under an inward-oriented incentive regime, the diagnosing and correction of market failures was far from satisfactory, leading to often misguided and wholesale interventions. These, in turn, set the stage for much of the 'macroeconomic failures'.

All these things considered, this chapter seeks to show that as in the case of Korea's success, the mixed results of Brazil's industrialization can be better understood if we focus on the role of government in overcoming market failures. The analysis is divided into five sections, broadly reflecting the evolution of the government policy towards industrialization in general, and market failures in particular. That is, the minimalist government of the pre-1956 period, the 1956-63 import-substitution strategy; the pseudo-neoclassical revolution of 1964-73; the half-hearted attempt to reform the IS regime during 1974-79; and the complete lack of direction of the 1980s.

3.1 THE 'UNINTENTIONAL' INDUSTRIALIZATION: THE PRE-1956 PERIOD

When the first significant surge of manufacturing investment took place in the 1890s, Brazil could be described as an open, export-oriented and agriculture-based economy, with its trade-GDP ratio standing roughly at 28% (Table A.27). At that time, agriculture accounted for 56% of GDP (Table A.28), with more than half of the agricultural output (mainly coffee) being exported. Industry accounted for only 12% of GDP and consisted mostly of small establishments in the textile and food sectors.[187] Manufactured exports were virtually inexistent, with coffee accounting for as much as 60% of total exports.

Half a century later, though, the picture was somewhat different. Notwithstanding the low (by subsequent standards) levels of FDI, the nearly uninterrupted growth experienced during this period had increased

Chart 2 Brazil's manufacturing import ratio, 1907–55 (1939 prices)

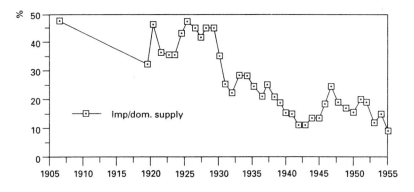

Note: 1907 and 1919 in current prices.
Source: Villela and Suzigan (1977:39) for 1907 and 1919 Malan *et al.* (1980:207)

the industry's share of GDP to 30% and the manufacturing import-ratio had dropped to an amazing 10% (see Chart 2). Yet, Brazil's industrial structure was still 'shallow' and lacking diversification. The share of the so-called heavy industries was only 35% (Table A.29), and despite considerable development, both the capital and durable consumer good sectors were still incipient, accounting for not more than 11% of total manufacturing output (Table A.30). As for exports, they continued to be entirely dominated by agricultural products, with coffee still coming close to 60% of total exports (Table A.31). Overall, the economy had significantly reduced its 'dependence' on foreign trade, halving the trade-GDP ratio to around 7%. To use, a cliché, by the mid-1950s Brazil had apparently completed the 'easy' stage of import substitution.

The first phase of Brazil's industrialization is quite controversial, notably the pre-1930 period. Taking the risk of oversimplification, the debate can be said to have revolved around three main divisive issues, that is: the importance of the linkages between the manufacturing and export-coffee sector, the impact of external shocks and the role of the government.[188] This controversy was prompted by Furtado's (1963) 'adverse shock theory' that, *inter alia*, argued that Brazil's industrialization had been triggered off by a series of external shocks (the First World War, the Great Depression and the Second World War), which, via trade disruption and relative price changes, had shifted the source of economic growth away from the coffee-export sector, towards manufacturing investment and the internal market. The Great Depression is seen as the great catalyst of this change, and is used to mark Brazil's passage from an agricultural to an industrial economy.

This theory was later criticized from at least three points of view. First, there was the criticism led by Dean (1971) which maintained that, given the linkages between the export and manufacturing sector, and taking up the latter's dependence of imported capital goods, industrialization would have progressed, not in the periods of crisis, but during the periods of export boom. Second, there was the so-called 'late capitalism' critique, which suggested, *inter alia*, that both the manufacturing-export sector linkages and the external shocks were crucial to explain the origins of industrialization. The former for similar reasons to those given by Dean, and the latter, for contributing to de-link manufacturing investment from the export sector's income (Mello 1982). Finally, there was the criticism that claimed that the behaviour of the export sector was 'neither favourable nor unfavourable to industrialization', and that the role of the government in promoting industrialization had been overlooked, notably the impact of tariffs and other incentives (Versiani 1979).

The issue of linkages and external shocks seem to have been largely settled by the evidence made available by Suzigan (1984, chap. 2), which showed that manufacturing investment was positively correlated with export earnings until the Great Depression, while presenting no direct relationship afterwards. However, the point about the role of the government, which is the main concern of this chapter, did not benefit from such conclusive evidence. Before turning to this issue, though, it is worth noting that the controversy over the government's role refers specifically to pre-1930 period. None of the interpretations available seems to deny that after the Great Depression and until the mid-1950s, government policies have somehow favoured industry, even if unintentionally. It makes sense then to look at these two periods separately.

Before the Great Depression

The dominant view in the literature is that the government's role in the first steps of Brazil's industrialization was minimal. No doubt, this perception seems to square with the liberal rhetoric of the first republican governments and their agrarian political base.[189] The fly in the ointment, though, is the existence of evidence suggesting, first, that tariffs were anything but low, and second, that the state has granted incentives and subsidies, notably, to the heavy industry.

Table 18   Brazil's actual tariff rates,* 1893–55 (%)

1823–32	1833–82	1893–1902	1903–12	1913–22	1923–32	1933–42	1943–50	1951–55
10.0	27.2	24.0	28.0	36.0	37.0	23.0	7.0	5.6

* Tariff revenue divided by total imports. Arithmetic average.

Source: Silva, G.A. (1983) 'A Reforma Aduaneira no Brasil', is *Estudos Aduaneiros* no. 11, ESAF, Brasilia, as quoted by Machado (1990).

Table 18, for instance, shows a significant, if not monotonic, increase in the actual tariff rates since the independence, to levels that cannot be dismissed outright as not affecting resource allocation. In addition, evidence on light industry sectors such as textiles, footwear and beverages, indicates that they were heavily protected, with actual tariffs reaching three-digits in certain periods.[190] As to the other incentives, they seem to have included, e.g., tariff exemptions for capital good imports, a 'law of similar'(1890) which prohibited tariff exemptions for goods produced domestically, and loans and profit-guarantees for heavy industries such as steel, cement and caustic soda. The latter appear to have grown in importance after the First World War, prompted by a security-conscious government.[191]

However, this evidence is played down on the grounds that it does not prove that the government was systematically pursuing industrialization, nor that the measures taken were effective. Much ammunition is spent on tariffs whose main purpose is thought to have been fiscal, and whose impact is believed to have been limited given that they were specific, and tended to be offset by international prices and exchange rate variations.[192] In Suzigan (1984:88), for instance, this argument is underpinned by evidence showing that the real landed price of imports (i.e. including actual tariffs and exchange rate variations) has actually fallen until 1930, except for the First World War period. As to the other incentives, the claim is that they were not used in a systematic fashion, and had more of a *de jure* than a *de facto* existence.[193]

Strong as these arguments may be, it seems difficult to deny that changes in the relative prices received a valuable, if modest, assistance from government incentives, particularly as far as tariffs and light industry go. That protection seems to have declined during the period does not tell us much about its absolute level. Moreover, if one takes into account that the light industry's productivity was apparently well below the international frontier, protection appears to have been all the more necessary.[194] The long arm of coincidence would have to be stretched too far to explain why the first spurts of manufacturing investment occurred only after quasi-free-trade 'agreements' with Portugal and England had expired.[11] This does not mean to say, however, that the state was interventionist or developmental. In fact, the limited service that it rendered industry by raising tariffs and giving incentives, appears to have been more than offset by its inaction regarding market failures in the financial markets, infrastructure, education and science and technology (S & T).

During all the period, the financial sector remained basically geared to cater for the coffee-export sector's financial needs, and even though the state owned the largest commercial bank – Banco do Brasil – there was virtually no source of long-term credit for manufacturing.[196] The government played an important 'functional' role in expanding the infrastructure, yet, as these investments were mainly targeted to serve the coffee-export sector (concentrated in the south-east), they neither provided industry with access to a unified national market, nor with an adequate energy supply. As to education, despite being free and compulsory, the share of total population enrolled in school in 1930 (6.3 %) was well below the already dismal Latin America's average (8%) (Albert 1983:38). Finally, government action in the area of S&T was limited to the creation of a few specialized institutions in the engineering and biomedical fields (the first university was established as late as 1920), with virtually no links with industry.[197]

After the Great Depression

In the post-1930 period, the government's hand became more visible, although most of the policies that favoured industrialization can be said to have had other targets in mind, i.e., balance-of-payment (BP) adjustment, and growth. Most accounts give trade and exchange rate policies the pride of place. In fact, the government handling of these policies took the classical contours of an import-substitution (IS) strategy. Its response to the Great Depression is seen to have been groundbreaking. Instead of pursuing the classical BP-adjustment policies of exchange rate devaluation and fiscal-cum-monetary contraction, the government opted for a different package that included the former but not the latter.[198] Given the size of the gap in the external accounts, this policy mix had to be complemented by foreign exchange and import controls.

The success of this policy in sustaining income levels, adjusting the BP and boosting manufacturing investment, seems to have left a permanent mark in Brazilian policymakers. From then on, except for a few short periods, import and foreign exchange controls would be a key element of government policies whatever the ideological colours of the incumbents.

During 1930-55, import and exchange rate controls took different forms and were combined with different exchange-rate policies, gradually becoming more favourable to industry. Customs tariffs were left playing second fiddle (they remained specific until 1957, see table 18). From 1930 until the outbreak of the Second World War, except for the brief 1934-37 liberal period, imports were controlled by a licensing system, used concurrently with a rising real exchange rate. Until 1934, foreign debt payments and government imports were given priority in the allocation of foreign exchange. This, however, changed after 1937, when producer goods gained precedence.

An improvement in the BP during the war led to a short-lived liberalization, but import controls were re-introduced in 1947. This time under a fixed and increasingly over-valued exchange rate, and with a tacit policy of not allowing competitive imports in.[199] In 1953, a complex multiple-exchange-rate system was adopted, with product-specific rates for exports, and a five-category auction system for imports. Imports of producer goods, however, continued to be favoured.[200]

These policies are seen to have helped industry in two main ways. First, by virtually eliminating import competition to the light industry, and by increasing protection for the fledgling heavy industry. This would have allowed these industries not only to survive and learn, but also to grow ahead of income through IS. Second, by subsidizing imports of capital goods and raw material, notably after 1947, with a highly overvalued exchange rate.[201]

The changes in Brazil's import structure (Table A.33), the behaviour of the manufacturing-import ratio (Chart 2 and Table A.32), and an annual growth rate of 8.4% for manufacturing output (1930-55), leave little doubt about the strength and accuracy of these arguments. However, the costs involved were no less visible. One could mention, for instance, the much-heralded rent-seeking and static costs of protection that came along with import controls. Yet, these costs can be said to have been attenuated, first, by the fact that the manufacturing structure remained dominated by light industries, very much in line with Brazil's factor endowment (Table A.29). Second, because the 1953 auction system reduced significantly the opportunity for rent-seeking. And third, because the welfare gains associated with rapid growth have probably made up for the consumer loss. More damaging losses were inflicted on two other interrelated issues, i.e., the industry's efficiency and the external balance.

Economic theory has already shown that the replacement of tariffs by NTBs leads to non-competitive behaviour, aggravating the infant industry problems of X-inefficiency and endless-learning periods.[202] The experience of countries like Korea (see Chapter 2), however, also suggests that these problems can be largely avoided, and monopolistic behaviour even turned into a positive factor, if protection is made conditional on export performance, forcing firms into the international market. In Brazil, during 1930-55, external competition was totally removed but nothing was put in place to push firms down the learning curve. Firms had, then, incentives to expand to fill the gaps left by imports, but little incentive to increase efficiency given the technologically poor domestic competition.

With the wrong set of incentives, it does not come as a surprise that manufacturing exports never really took off. Table A.32 shows that the manufacturing-export ratio decreased sharply over 1907-49 to a mere 2.3%, and in 1955 this figure must have been even lower, given that during 1950-55 manufacturing output outperfomed manufactured exports by a large margin.[203] This lack of incentives to export also led to a BP increasingly dependent on coffee exports (Table A.31), which, thanks to the price-inelasticity of its international demand, tended to be less affected by the exchange-rate policy.[204] Yet, this has not prevented regular foreign exchange crises from happening, or the external debt to grow, notably in the first half of the 1950s.[205]

These inefficiencies provoked by the trade policy were aggravated by the government's belated and, largely, unsatisfactory response to the industry's growing requirements for infrastructure, financing and human capital. It was not until the beginning of the 1950s, that effective steps were taken to tackle some of these market failures. Until then, ad hoc and isolated measures tended to predominate and the proliferation of regulations and institutions seem to have served more the government's political and bureaucratic needs (notably to administrate the trade policy) than industrial development.[206] An exception to this rule was the state's direct intervention in the production of intermediate goods in the early 1940s. Although this move had little to do with an industrialization strategy – it was prompted mainly by military reasons related to the Second World War – and was carried out only when the state had run out of private options, it would later prove to be economically sound. This intervention not only smoothed the transition towards a more integrated industrial structure, but also contributed to develop a major source of comparative advantage.[207]

But going back to the industry's needs, the state's actions in the area of infrastructure were hampered by a government torn between the virtues of public and private investment, and ending up with the worst of both worlds. Key sectors such as electric power and telecommunications were dominated by private firms (mainly foreign companies), but were regulated by state and municipal governments that constantly imposed unrealistic rates. The result was low and uncoordinated investments. On the other hand, services that had passed to public hands (e.g. railways), suffered from the lack of long-term planning and the state's inadequate financial and fiscal base. It was only in the early fifties that a clear option for public sector investments emerged, with key state enterprises (SEs) being created, particularly in the energy sector (oil and electric power).[208] This move was backed up by the establishment of a development bank (National Development Bank – BNDE – 1952), to be funded by fiscal and external resources, with the specific aim to finance improvements in the infrastructure.[209] Major investments, however, would only begin in 1956.

On the financial side there was little progress, if any. Government intervention, to a certain extent, was more of a hindrance than a help. For instance, the development of the financial sector was considerably delayed by the ill-conceived 'usury law' (1933) which limited the maximum annual rate of interest to 12%. This, coupled with inflation averaging 13% annually over 1940-55, led the financial sector to shrink exactly when the economy's increasing degree of industrialization and commercialization was demanding the opposite.[210] As a result, industry ended up without both long-term financing and short-term funds for working capital. Without proper credit, and with a negligible stock market, firms had to increasingly rely on internal finance, whose limits were pushed by constant, increasingly elusive, attempts to raise markups. In this endeavour, firms were 'helped' not only by the trade policy but also by government's use of monetary expansion to finance the Treasury deficit.

This disastrous intervention contrasted sharply with more positive, if timid, moves to provide industry with long-term loans. The first endeavour in this direction came in 1937, through Banco do Brasil, aiming at extending medium and long-term credit for the purchase of machinery and equipment. However, most of the loans ended up going for agriculture (Malan *et al.* 1980). A second attempt came only in 1952, with the already mentioned establishment of the BNDE. Industry, however, had to wait until the mid-1950s to benefit from a significant share of its loans, and even then the lion's share went for the government-owned heavy industries (Table A.38).

Finally, S&T and education continued not to figure among the government's priorities, even though important, if uncoordinated, steps were taken in this direction. In the case of the S&T infrastructure, the pre-1930 trend of establishing isolated institutions in military-strategic areas continued,[211] but two new institutions – the National Research Council (CNPQ) and the Campaign for the Improvement of the Higher Education Staff (CAPES) – were set up in 1951, with the more functional aim to finance investments in human capital. As to education, the establishment of National Service for Industrial Apprenticeship (SENAI) was an important and successful initiative in the area of vocational training.[212] Overall, though, no substantial improvement appears to have occurred. As of 1950, 50% of the population was still illiterate, and only 40% of the literate population had completed the first five grades of elementary education (Table A.35).

In all, it can be said that government intervention played an important, if incoherent and largely unintentional, part in this first stage of Brazil's industrialization. In the pre-1930 period, fiscal considerations seem to largely explain the tariff protection given to manufacturing, which, nonetheless, appears to have been instrumental in allowing Brazil's long-suppressed comparative advantages in the light industry to develop. Little else was done, though, to tackle other market failures.

After the Great Depression, government intervention clearly increased but, again, BP and growth considerations seem to have been the main motivation. As in the previous period, protection proved to be a powerful boost to manufacturing investment. Yet, the use of NTBs and of an overvalued exchange rate virtually eliminated the healthy pressure and guidance provided by international prices and competition (through either exports or imports). These policy mistakes were compounded by the government's timid and sometimes ill-advised action in key areas such as infrastructure, finance, S&T and education. As a result, local industry not only lacked incentives to go down the learning curve, but it also had to face social-overhead and financial costs above the international average.

3.2 HEAVY INDUSTRY 'AT ALL COSTS': THE 1956-64 PERIOD

As shown, more than half a century of 'unintentional' and inward looking industrialization had good results in terms of growth and manufacturing investment, but gave rise to an industry of dubious quality, suffering from distorted incentives, and burdened by serious bottle-necks in infrastructure, financing and human capital. However, it was not until the mid-1950s – with the so-called 'Targets Plan' ('T' plan, 1956-61) – that industrialization became part of the government's agenda.

Inspired by ECLA's (Economic Commission for Latin America) structuralism, the 'T' Plan, despite its rather pompous title, was not more than a collection of five-year targets for output and investment in infrastructure, heavy industry, food and education. As suggested by the make-up of the targets, the intention was to deal not only with functional market failures, but also to carry on with IS in the intermediate, capital and durable-consumer goods sectors. In the end, functional interventions were limited, in practice, to infrastructure (transport and energy), with the food and education receiving a perfunctory 6.6 % of the proposed investment (no mention was made of finance or S&T). The bulk of the investment went into IS.[213]

The decision to launch the plan was not accompanied by significant institutional changes. Even though a National Development Council, with the initial purpose of acting as a central planning agency, was set up in 1956, it was soon fragmented into several sectoral agencies, the so-called 'executive groups'. The programme was left then with little central coordination, except for the measures taken by the BNDE and SUMOC (sort of central bank), imposed by the financial and macroeconomic constraints.[214]

This institutional weakness was compounded by an inhospitable macroeconomic environment, particularly inappropriate to a plan whose expending programs would amount to about 5 % of GDP in the following five years.[215] On the external front, an erratic export performance compounded by a rising debt-service and falling terms of trade, suggested little room for the increase in imports implicit in the plan's investments. In the domestic front, inflation was above two digits reflecting not only the already high GDP rate of growth (8% in 1955), but also, as suggested earlier, the lack of proper funding for the state and private investments. In order to circumvent these macroeconomic and institutional constraints, the government went again for an eclectic policy mix, still dominated by trade and exchange rate policies, but this time, other important ingredients were added, i.e., incentives to foreign capital and a greater role for the state in infrastructure, intermediary goods industry and in the financial sector.

Table 19   Brazil's effective tariff rates, 1958–67 (%)

Sectors	1958[a]	1963[a]	1966[a]	1967[a]	1966[b]	1967[b]
Total industry	30	75	44	14	83	36
Agriculture	–47	–15	–13	–14	n.a.	n.a.
Manufacturing	106	184	108	48	118	66
Capital goods	53	113	69	52	100*	60*
Intermediate goods	65	131	68	39	110	67
Consumer durables	242	360	230	66	151	75
Consumer non-durables					173	101

* Machinery only.

Source: (a) Fishlow (1975:58) 'Foreign Trade Regimes and Economic Development: Brazil' Mimeo. as quoted in Carvalho and Haddad (1981:42). Non-specified method based on legal tariff. Sectoral figures are averages weighted by the 1959 value-added adjusted for tariffs. (b) Bergsman and Malan (1971:122) 1970 output as weights. Corden method based on legal tariff plus non-tariff barriers.

Government Policies

Beginning with trade and exchange rate policies, there was little change in the overall orientation. These policies continued to serve the dual purpose of avoiding a balance of payment crisis and promoting IS, and therefore, competitive imports continued to be kept out, while the non-competitive remained subsidized by exports. The aim to deepen the industrial structure, though, meant that the non-competitive group had to be streamlined even further to increase protection for the heavy industry. There was also a refinement of the instruments used. In 1957, seeking to make protection more selective and the exchange rate policy more flexible, the government revived custom tariffs and reformed the exchange rate-auction system. *Ad valorem* tariffs were introduced, ranging from 0 to 150%, and auction categories were reduced from five to two low (non-competitive producer goods) and high premium (consumer goods) groups. The average effective PPP exchange rate for imports, though, continued to be substantially higher than that of exports (Table A.36).[216] Moreover, the 'law of similar' was eventually put officially into effect.[217]

The net effect of these changes was a rise in protection, now consisting not only of the high premiums of the exchange rate auctions but also of generally prohibitive tariff rates.[218] Table 19 shows that all manufacturing sectors had very high effective tariff rates, with the structure of protection reflecting 'essentiality' rather than comparative advantages.

The now traditional policy of trade and exchange rate restrictions, though, was not enough to keep the plan afloat. Given the import intensity, and the capital and technological requirements of the heavy industry targets, a new element had to be brought in: foreign capital. To this end, the government reformed the already liberal legislation inherited from previous administrations, dropping the remaining restrictions and creating lavish incentives.[219] In addition to the deregulation of remittances (profits, interest and dividends), sectors of 'special interest' could benefit from a preferential, notably, overvalued exchange rate (with registration of the principal at the 'free' market rate). This process was crowned by Instruction 113 (1955), which authorized foreign investors to import equipment without exchange rate cover.[220] On the requirement side, investments had to be in the targeted sectors (virtually all manufacturing sectors) and a programme for domestic procurement of inputs had to be agreed, to name but the more important.

This legislation combined, on the one hand, with the potential loss of Brazil's fast growing and highly protected market, and on the other hand, with the virtually non-existent local capital market, had an immediate effect upon the inflows of foreign capital. Table A.37 shows that annual FDI surged in 1956, and suppliers' credits rapidly became the major source of autonomous capital, accounting for more than two thirds of the gross inflows over the 1954-61 period.[221]

The third prong of the government's strategy involved, as noted earlier, an increase in the state's presence in the infrastructure, intermediate goods and financial sectors. The public sector's average share of the gross fixed capital formation rose substantially (Table A.34), led by SEs' investments in the steel industry and infrastructure.[222] Likewise, the public sector's share of total loans went up from 26 (1951-55) to 36% (1956-63), whereas as a lender, its share rose from 48 to 57% over the same period.[223]

Leaving for the moment the financial aspects aside, these events rather than reveal the government's socialist tendencies, reflect mainly the plan's division of labour between the private and public sectors, with the latter taking on the targets where market imperfections (particularly the lack of a capital market) virtually ruled out a private solution. This explanation seems to be accurate even for the intermediate goods sector, where the case of the steel industry, which received the most of the public sector's investment, is quite revealing. Although both the size of Brazil's market and the characteristics of the industry's production function (mature technology, inputs which were abundant in Brazil, and the medium-skill requirements) were pointing to static and dynamic comparative advantages, not even US Steel accepted a government invitation to set up an integrated steel mill.[224]

On the financial side, the expanded state presence, both as borrower and lender, can be only partially justified by its greater role in infrastructure and heavy industry, and did little to remedy capital market failures. Much of this expansion reflected the inadequacy of the public sector's financing schemes. Despite the ambition of its targets, the Plan was short of specifics on how investments would be financed, and arrangements were virtually limited to various earmarked fiscal funds, placed under BNDE control. Even though this move, combined with the possibility of issuing foreign-loan guarantees, significantly increased BNDE resources, it proved to be thoroughly inadequate to the public and private sector's financial needs. Table A.38 shows that BNDE loans in the 1956-64 period were limited in average to 2.2% of the gross fixed capital formation.

In the case of the public sector, the lack of adequate financing was compounded by the SEs' unrealistic pricing policy, part of an ill-advised attempt by the government to control the rising inflation. As an increase in the national debt was not a viable option (the 'usury law' prevented the government from issuing securities with positive returns), the gap in the public sector's finances was almost entirely financed by monetary expansion under the guise of Banco do Brasil 'loans' to the Treasury.[225]

As to the private sector, whereas foreign firms had access to foreign loans at preferential exchange rates, local firms (LPFs) continued to have problems in arranging long-term financing, due to their diminished creditworthiness in the international markets. BNDE loans and guarantees, a possible answer to this problem, had a reduced impact since, as indicated, they were meagre and mostly directed towards the public sector (Table A.38). LPFs continued, then, to resort to auto finance via higher mark-ups, an option favoured by the lax monetary policy, but that became increasingly inefficient as inflation accelerated towards 30% in the late 1950s. Moreover, the supply of short-term funds was further restricted by the combination of high inflation with negative interest rates. The extent of this problem can be gauged by the fact that, in real terms, outstanding domestic loans to the private sector remained stagnant over 1956-61, despite a two-fold increase of GDP.[226]

Table 20   Targets Plan. Selected targets and performance (1956–61)

	Planned	Achieved
Electric power (10³ kW)	5 000	5 205
Oil production (10³ barrels per day)	100	95.4
Railways (km)	1 624	1 093
Roads (km)	12 000	13 169
Steel ingots (production, 10³ tons per year)	2 300	1 843
Cement (production, 10³ tons per year)	5 000	4 678
Passenger cars (10³ units and localization index)	58 (95%)	52 (89%)
Shipbuilding (capacity 10³DWT per year)	160	158

Source: Data from Lessa (1982) except for steel production (achieved) which is from Baer (1969).

Assessing the Results

At first sight, the Plan's overall results point to a remarkable success. As Table 20 shows, most of the targets, either in infrastructure or manufacturing, were met within a reasonable margin of error. In addition, GDP grew at an annual average rate of 9.4 % (1955-61), whereas the same figure for manufacturing output was 12% (Table A.48). IS and industrial diversification were successfully carried further down the road, notably in the heavy industry, whose import-ratio reached 9% in 1964 (Table A.32), and whose share of manufacturing output, rose from 35 to 48% over 1955-65 (Table A.29).[227] Yet, impressive as these results might be, one of the Plan's main objectives – the decision to a speedy move into the heavy industry – can be seriously questioned if the options involved, and the results achieved, are examined more carefully.

One can begin by arguing that in the mid-1950s there was hardly a sound case for a hasty and massive move into heavy industry. Looking first from a static point of view, Brazil was far from any Lewisian turning point as demonstrated by the falling unit labour costs (Table A.39). Factor prices, therefore, were suggesting that resource allocation would be improved not by widespread targeting of heavy industry, but by giving light industry the right incentives and financial means to 'grow' and sell in the international market (whose access in the mid-1950s was no longer restricted). Instead, as we have seen, not only exports continued to be discriminated against, but the light industry was almost completely left out of BNDE long-term loans (Table A.38). As a result, both manufacturing employment growth and its elasticity were halved (Table A.40) at a time when almost half of the economically active population was under-employed.[228]

From a dynamic and, say, 'strategic' perspective, it is true that a move towards the heavy industry was justified, first, by the possibility of exploiting dynamic economies of scale, particularly in technologically mature sectors, and second because of the human capital spillovers, higher productivity and above-the-average-cost profits, usually associated with this industry. However, it seems that in order to take full advantage of these benefits, any attempt in this direction would have to allow for the limitations of the existing resource endowment, and for the market failures and imperfections that affect competition in this industry. This, not only to prevent benefits being offset by excessive resource misallocation, in the static sense, but also to give LPFs realistic chances to grow and compete.

Yet, as we have seen, the government overlooked all these considerations. Despite Brazil's poor capital and human capital resources, several heavy industry sectors were targeted at once. Notwithstanding, the 'lumpiness', long-term maturation, and economies of scale that mark investment in this industry, very little was done to centralize capital in the hands of schumpeterian entrepreneurs, either through the stock market or banking credit, and an excessive number of producers was allowed in. Despite the obvious limitations of the domestic market, backward integration, through domestic content incentives, was excessively pursued. And finally, notwithstanding the industry's high technological and skill requirements, improvements in the S&T infrastructure and education remained out of the government agenda.[229] It was as if all these constraints and preconditions could have been quickly overcome by a large and unregulated inflow of FDI, thought to be in itself a guarantee of efficiency. True enough, the targets were met and manufacturing growth was high, yet the costs seem to have been too high.

Even though, as suggested earlier, the analysis of FDI costs and benefits tends to be controversial, the case for TNC affiliates protection is at best weak. Just to recapitulate the main arguments, whereas there is no doubt that these firms also face a learning curve, and generate pecuniary and non-pecuniary externalities, their unrestricted access to capital and technology in the international market does not make them legitimate candidates for protection. The more so if one takes into account, first, that their access to parent company technology tends to exclude the 'know why' from their contribution to domestic technological capabilities; second, that their protection is hardly compatible with that of those who really need to 'grow', i.e., the LPFs;

Table 21   1966 share of government (SE), foreign (FF) and local private
firms (LPF) in assets of the top 300 firms

Sectors	FF	LPF	SEs
Non-metal minerals	33	67	0
Metal products	22	42	36
Machinery	79	21	0
Electrical and commercial	61	39	0
Transport	82	18	0
Lumber	30	69	0
Rubber	92	3	5
Chemicals	69	25	7
Pharmaceuticals	100	0	0
Plastics	49	52	0
Textiles	47	54	0
Food	43	32	0
Miscellaneous	43	57	0
Total	51	41	8

Source: Newfarmer, R. and Miller, W. (1975)

and third, that foreign ownership invalidates the welfare gains related
to the 'profit-shifting' argument.

Therefore, even though heavy reliance on 'protected', inward-looking, and unregulated FDI allowed the government to ignore the resource and technological constraints, and the LPFs' human capital and
financial needs, it ended up compromising much of the dynamic benefits involved in a move into the heavy industry. In fact, by taking
this 'short cut', the government created a situation where, on the one
hand, LPFs were thoroughly exposed to the imperfect competition of
the affiliates, and, despite the highly protected internal market, had to
either leave the market, or to settle for marginal or subcontractor positions. And, on the other, the combination of high domestic prices and
lax investment licensing, produced the so-called 'crowd in' effect. An
inefficient industrial structure was then built – oversized *vis-à-vis* the
domestic market but with most of the plants below the MES – heavily
dependent on permanent protection, even though most of the heavy
industry sectors were either led or totally dominated by the most efficient
producers of the world (Table 21).[230]

Finally, a more selective approach to the heavy industry, coupled
with neutral trade incentives and supported by pro-market intervention
in the financial market (to overcome market failures not to aggravate
them), would have made the serious macroeconomic imbalances of the

first half of the 1960s less likely. During this period, inflation approached three digits, and the widening current account deficit had to be financed by increasingly costly short-term loans.[231] This alternative approach would also have acted in the direction of avoiding the deep recession that followed the implementation of the Plan. The rush into the heavy industry produced an industrial capacity well beyond what the internal market could absorb, which, in turn, made a slow-down in growth inevitable. Greater export orientation would have allowed growth to go on irrespective of the limits of the internal market, which could have become bigger had the resources been used more efficiently.[232]

3.3   THE PRAGMATIC 'MIRACLE'. THE 1964-73 PERIOD

The last section has shown that the government's first conscious attempt to promote industrialization led to a considerable, and long overdue, improvement in the country's infrastructure, and was very effective in taking IS to most heavy industry sectors. Yet, keen on removing the 'foreign exchange gap', the government pursued IS without due regard for the resource endowments, and the financial and technological requirements. Exports continued to be unduly discriminated against, and foreign capital was invited in to fill the micro and macroeconomic gaps, often at the expense of the LPFs. The side effects of this strategy did not take long to show their 'ugly face'. The lack of proper financing and the trade bias, led to high inflation and a BP crisis, which coupled with the polarization of the political situation, resulted eventually in a military coup, in 1964. A new team of neoclassical policy makers, then, took over.

Apparently utterly opposed to the interventionist ideas that inspired its predecessors, the new team set out to implement comprehensive institutional and policy reforms that would spark off a new period of rapid industrial and economic growth. Even though the reforms aimed at restoring 'the supremacy of the price mechanism', in practice, as we shall see, theoretical principles quickly gave way to a puzzling pragmatism, which did not fundamentally alter either the government's role or the previous pattern of industrialization. The reforms were largely designed to deal with two major issues – the inadequacy of the public and private sector financing, and the incentive-bias against exports and foreign capital – thought to have been the underlying causes of the chronic inflationary and BP problems. Moreover, at a less prominent level, there were also changes in the industrial and S&T 'policies'.

Reforming Public and Private Sector Financing

Looking first at the public sector, the main measures were: a fiscal reform to modernize taxes and protect fiscal revenue from inflation; more realistic SEs' prices; and compulsory saving funds to finance investments in infrastructure and housing. In addition, a central bank was finally created,[233] and the treasury allowed to issue bonds with monetary correction. As Sochaczewski (1980:360) pointed out, this last measure allowed the government to circumvent the 'usury law', whose 12% ceiling was then reinterpreted as referring to the real and not the nominal rate. As a result, the state improved its control over the monetary policy, and significantly increased its resources, which became more in line with its new responsibilities in the infrastructure and intermediary goods industry, whose legitimacy was not questioned by the newcomers. On the contrary, SEs expanded their investments in these areas, doubling their share of the gross fixed capital formation over 1965–73 (Table A.34).

As to the private sector, new non-banking financial institutions and assets were created, and old ones reformed. The principal innovation was the introduction of assets with monetary correction, which, as with public bonds, would allow interest rates to be positive.[234] These new assets were to be part of a specialized financial market, with commercial banks and credit societies supplying, respectively, short-term and consumer credit; and the stock and debenture markets, supported by fiscal incentives, the long awaited long-term funds. In this task, they would have the support of the newly created investment banks, authorized to undertake underwriting operations, and to supply medium-term working-capital. Foreign loans were also to be another important source of medium, long-term capital, and new legislation was enacted to expedite these operations (see below). The immediate impact of these measures was a substantial increase in financial savings that rose from 16 to 26% of GDP (1965–73), sustained by a two-fold increase in the financial-asset-to-GDP ratio and a stock-market boom.[235]

Reforming the Trade Regime and Foreign Capital Policy

Beginning with the trade regime, the government gradually moved towards a unified exchange rate via devaluation (Table A.36), and removal of most of the NTBs.[236] In addition, a crawling-peg system was adopted, aiming at curbing speculation and reducing the real exchange fluctuations. These measures were accompanied by the implementation of export incentives, and by a selective import liberalization. On the export side, manufactured exports were exempted from indirect and income taxes, granted product-specific fiscal subsidies, a system of drawback was implemented, and heavily subsidized export credits were made available.[237] Exports responded quickly, particularly manufactured exports, which grew at an average annual rate of 29% over the period, with an almost five-fold increase in their share of total exports (Table A.31).

On the import side, apart from the already mentioned tariff exemptions for export production and the removal of most NTBs, tariffs were reduced with the manufacturing average falling from 99 to 66% over 1966–73.[238] In addition, tariff exemptions were extended to capital goods imports of 'priority' sectors, irrespective of the market targeted, and an 'import processing zone' was created in the Amazon region, which allowed the assembling of products (mainly electric and electronic consumer goods) for the domestic market with inputs close to the international prices. However, legal and effective protection remained rather high and its inter-industrial structure unchanged (Tables 19 and A.40). The changes in import composition and the modest increase in import ratios (Tables A.33 and A.32) suggest that non-competitive, producer-goods imports, given the tariff and tax exemptions, were largely the sole beneficiaries of the liberalization.[239]

With respect to foreign investment, the government was quick to alter Law 4131 (1962), one of the last acts of the civilian government, which, *inter alia*, restricted profit remittances to 10% of the capital, and for the first time tried to screen and limit technology imports. Most of these restrictions were, then, dropped (Law 4390), but a supplementary income tax was levied on remittances that exceeded 12% of the registered capital.[240] As before, the manufacturing sector continued to be totally open to FDI. As to foreign loans, even though they still required Central Bank authorization, there were no restrictions on the borrower's nationality or sector of activity. In fact, the access to foreign loans was further facilitated by two new pieces of legislation: instruction 289 and resolution 63. The former allowed short-term loans to be registered and serviced, and the latter, granted local banks permission to raise funds abroad to be reloaned to local firms with a shorter maturity. These measures, in conjunction with economic recovery, triggered off a new spurt of FDI (Table A.37), and a rapid growth of the external debt (11% annually over 1965–73).

Changes in the Industrial and S&T 'Policies'

Despite the policy-makers' neoclassical credentials, the uncoordinated group of institutions that were the tools of the industrial and S&T 'policies' during the 'T' plan and earlier, were not wound up but reformed; and as regards S&T, there was even an attempt to come up with a strategy worthy of the term. On the industrial side, the government set up, in 1964, the Industrial Development Council (CDI), made up of representatives of the main economic agencies, which were to incorporate the executive groups (see last section), and to co-ordinate and establish criteria for the concession of fiscal and credit incentives to the manufacturing sector. These initial ambitions, though, never materialized. CDI incentives were distributed at random, without any clear criteria, but to increase investments.[241] Moreover, there were at least a dozen regional and sector-specific government institutions, conceding similar incentives, with the CDI having little or no control over them.

As to S&T, it finally became, in 1968, an explicit policy aim. The government eventually came to the conclusion that IS was not enough to assure *'self-sustained development'* and that it had to be complemented by the development of local technological capabilities.[242] A National System of Scientific and Technological Development (SNDCT) was then set up, which would co-ordinate the existing S&T institutions, formulate S&T development plans, and would be funded by the National Fund for Scientific and Technological Development (FNDCT). Particular emphasis was given to the need to develop more appropriate technologies to Brazil's resource endowment. This move was soon followed by a new emphasis on higher education, and by the reintroduction of the screening of technology imports (1971), whose responsibility fell to a new agency, INPI (National Institute of Industrial Property Rights).The alleged motivation of this last measure was to reduce the cost of technology imports and to facilitate its absorption. Its impact, though, would only be felt in earnest in the next period, in so far as it did not affect the contracts in force.[243]

Behind the 'Miracle'

As noted before, these measures sparked off a new period of exceptional growth. During 1965–73, GDP grew at an average annual rate of 10%, whereas manufacturing output reached 11% (Table A.48). The latter was spearheaded by the heavy industry, notably by the durable consumer goods sector. Other indicators point to better resource allocation, with a substantial increase in labour absorption in manufacturing (Table A.40), and a remarkable decline in incremental capital output ratios (ICORs), which reached its lowest level in the post-war industrialization (Table A.42). There was also a considerable reduction in inflation that fell from around 90 to 16% over 1964–70, reflecting not only the reforms examined above, but also a rather heterodox stabilization programme (1964–67), which combined a 'stop-and-go' monetary policy with outright intervention in the labour market.[244] Finally, the BP also improved – helped by the export take-off and the substantial inflow of foreign capital – showing an overall surplus in the whole period, except for 1967.

These impressive results prompted largely two sorts of reading. First, that they reflected industry reaching its maturity and, therefore, vindicated the previous IS strategy, and second, that they were no more than the product of an outward-looking trade regime.[245] Even though this involves the difficult, if not impossible, exercise of answering counter-factual questions, these apparently contradictory interpretations can be reconciled. For instance, it seems hard to accept that the 'miracle', particularly the export take-off, would have been possible without the industrial capacity and technological capabilities built during the IS period. It is equally difficult to accept that, given the market failures that burdened the Brazilian industry, these capacity and capabilities could have been built without government intervention. On the other hand, without the incentive changes and the financial and fiscal reforms, the achievements of the IS period would have been, in all likelihood, lost amid serious resource misallocation and macroeconomic imbalances.

Yet, even when cobbled together, these views can be misleading for two interrelated reasons. First, because despite being instrumental for export and economic growth, IS policies left a legacy that made a move towards a more open economy costlier and economic growth unsustainable. And second, because, it gives the wrong impression the reforms have successfully tackled the key shortcomings of Brazil's industrialization 'strategy', i.e., its excessive inward-orientation, lack of selectivity, inadequate finance, and lack of investment in education and S&T.

In order to clarify these points, we can begin by looking at the changes in the trade regime and its results. Whereas there is no doubt that the reforms reduced the bias against exports, they fell well short of turning Brazil into an outward-oriented economy. Growth accounting estimates show that exports played a minor role in the 'miracle', accounting for not more than 6% of manufacturing growth (Baumann 1985). As a number of authors have already pointed out, the 'miracle' was largely an 'internal matter', the upshot of the explosive combination of the industry's excess capacity, a consumer credit boom, and the public sector's investment in infrastructure and housing.[246]

While there is nothing wrong in principle with a domestic-market-led boom, the fact that manufactured exports remained marginal suggests that much of the old regime, and its drawbacks, were still in place. The government, as we have seen, continued to give incentives and highly protect virtually all manufacturing sectors (except for non-competitive capital goods). Inward, 'protected' FDI continued to be encouraged, and to expand its presence increasingly at the expense of the local firms. In 1971, TNCs accounted for more than 50% of heavy industry sales, and for 45% of those of the whole manufacturing sector (Table A.43). Morley and Smith (1971) estimated that in 1965 this last figure was 33.5%. Moreover, whereas during 1956–60, 33% of US-based TNCs were set up via take-overs of local firms, this percentage rose to 52% over 1966–70, and to 61% over 1971–72 (Newfarmer 1979).

With protection still high, the exchange rate remained overvalued. In other words, notwithstanding its liberal inclinations, the government instead of going for an across-the-board liberalization, leaving the exchange rate to bear the burden of the adjustment, the option was to maintain protection high enough not to upset the prevailing (inefficient) industrial structure, and to use subsidies to reduce the bias against exports.

While an apparently similar strategy was successfully pursued by other NICs such as Korea (see chapter 2), in Brazil, even though it succeeded in expanding manufactured exports, it turned out to be rather costly, and did not make exports more than a poor alternative to internal sales. Table 22 shows that during the miracle, export subsidies reached more than 50% of the value of manufactured exports, well above the figures for Korea. Yet exports remained accounting for less than 7% of manufacturing output (Table A.32).

The explanation for this poor and costly response seems to go beyond the often touted 'continental economy' argument. For instance, Germany and Canada, whose GDPs in 1970 were respectively 4.5 and 2.0 times bigger than Brazil's, had export-to-GNP ratios more than twice higher (18.5% in Germany and 20.4% in Canada, against 7.1% in Brazil)

Table 22   Korea's and Brazil's export subsidies and export related imports as a percentage of manufactured exports (FOB), 1969–85

| Year | Korea (%) | | | Brazil (%) | | |
| | Subsidies[1] | | Imports[3] | Subsidies[2] | | Imports[3] |
	Net	Gross	% of exp.	Net	Gross	% of exp.
1969	6.4	27.8	66.3	10.8	42.7	2.34
1970	6.7	28.3	56.2	21.0	52.7	6.51
1971	6.6	29.6	63.6	22.3	53.1	8.05
1972	3.2	26.8	54.8	25.8	58.8	8.55
1973	2.2	23.7	53.1	24.1	58.3	11.69
1974	2.1	21.2	49.3	19.9	55.2	10.50
1975	2.7	16.7	48.6	25.3	56.0	16.28
1976	2.5	16.9	43.3	29.0	65.8	14.07
1977	1.9	19.2	n.a.	33.5	72.5	9.37
1978	2.3	19.5	n.a.	31.6	68.1	10.04
1979	2.3	20.2	n.a.	30.3	67.5	n.a.
1980	3.3	21.3	n.a.	7.4	45.1	n.a.
1981	2.2	n.a.	n.a.	29.8	71.8	n.a.
1982	0.4	n.a.	25.9	34.6	76.7	n.a.
1983	0.0	n.a.	n.a.	20.6	58.5	n.a.
1984	n.a.	n.a.	n.a.	13.9	53.0	n.a.
1985	n.a.	n.a.	n.a.	10.0	49.2	n.a.

[1] Korea data for total exports. Yet manufactured exports averaged 94% during the period. Net subsidies include direct cash subsidies, export dollar premium, direct tax reduction and interest rate subsidy. Gross subsidies include net subsidy plus indirect tax exemptions and tariff exemptions. [2] Net subsidies comprise direct tax reduction, tax credits and interest rate subsidy. Gross subsidies include net subsidies plus indirect tax and tariff exemptions. [3] Export-related imports consist of parts and raw material used in export production which were exempted from import and indirect taxes.

Source: Original data from Kim, S.K. (1991:33), Hong (1979:68) and KFTA (1989) for Korea; and from Baumann (1990) and Musalem (1983:746) for Brazil.

(OECD 1989). Hence, the crux of the matter seems to lie elsewhere, that is:

(a) Brazil relied solely on export subsidies, whereas Korea made protection and incentives to industrialization conditional on export performance;

(b) Whereas in Korea, IS was selective, plants were built at international scale, and exporters were given full access to inputs at international prices; in Brazil, IS lacked selectivity, plants were

Table 23   Direction of manufactured exports, 1965–79

	Light[1]		Heavy[2]	
	DC	LDC	DC	LDC
1965	81.7	18.3	12.5	87.5
1970	81.4	18.6	30.3	69.8
1975	63.5	36.5	31.1	68.9
1979	89.8	10.2	37.2	62.8

[1] Includes food, textile and footwear. [2] Includes transport equipment, machinery and other equipment.
Source: Data from World Bank (1983a:194)

built below the MES, and given the limitation of its 'drawback' scheme,[247] exporters had to shoulder the burden of an excessively backward-integrated industrial structure. This point is illustrated by Table 22, which shows that the imported component of manufactured exports was minimal; and

(c) Unlike Korea, Brazil relied heavily on 'protected' FDI, a strategy that made export diversification easier, but that restricted mainly to intra-firm trade the access to the important developed country markets, in view of parent-subsidiary arrangements. Fajnzylber (1971) showed that in 1967, only 34% of the MNC's exports were to DC. Table 23, in turn, reveals that most of the heavy industry exports during the period were to LDCs, whereas Table A.44 shows that most of these exports were done by TNCs. BNDE (1988a), quoting ECLA/UN data, put the share of intra-firm exports from American affiliates at 70% in 1977.

This last characteristic of Brazil's strategy also raises doubts about the economic justification behind heavy subsidization of TNCs' exports. In contrast to the LPFs' case, the dynamic benefits to be gained there were unlikely to offset the costs involved, the more so because their protection was far from justifiable.

In short, in spite of the reforms, the trade regime continued to reflect neither static nor possible dynamic comparative advantages, but rather an urge to save foreign exchange. As the regime did not become more selective and outward-oriented, the export drive had to bear the burden of an excessively protected, integrated and fragmented industrial structure, imposing heavy costs to the Treasury. Moreover, as export success never really became a necessary condition for survival, it did not exert the necessary pressure to force firms down the

Industrialization, Trade and Market Failures

ı *Table* 24   International comparison of the manufacturing share of employment and GDP

	Brazil			USA			Japan			Canada		
	(a) % emp.	(b) % GDP	(b)–(a)	% emp.	% GDP	(b)–(a)	% emp.	% GDP	(b)–(a)	% emp.	% GDP	(b)–(a)
1960	12.9	28.3	15.4	26.4	28.3	1.9	21.3	34.6	13.3	24.6	n.a.	n.a.
1974	14.5*	28.9	14.4	24.2	23.4	–0.8	27.2	33.6	6.4	23.0	19.7	–3.3
1980	20.0	34.0	14.0	22.1	21.8	–0.3	24.7	29.2	4.5	21.5	17.9	–3.6
1987	15.3†	30.0	14.7	19.3	18.6	–0.7	29	24.1	–4.9	23.4	18.6	–4.8

* 1970 † 1988

Source: IBGE (1990) and ANESTBR for Brazil and OECD (1989)

learning curve, and to force the industrial structure to find more efficient and sustainable configurations.[248]

For not increasing the economy's outward-orientation, Brazil also missed the opportunity to have a more sustainable economic growth, combined with better resource allocation. As suggested earlier, the 'miracle' was very much built on the indebtedness of a tiny middle-class,[249] which could not keep on accumulating durable goods at a 22% annual rate forever; and for all the improvements in labour absorption, Brazil's manufacturing sector continued to employ, *vis-à-vis* its share of GDP, far less labour than its capital-intensive DCs' counterparts (Table 24).[250]

Apart from the trade regime, there are two other points worth making concerning the financial reforms, and investments in S&T and education. As to the former, while they were successful in improving the state's finances, and in providing funds for current activities, they failed to eradicate inflationary financing and to provide industry with a proper source of long-term funds. Inflation never went below 16%, and indexation was a mixed blessing. True, it allowed interest rates to be positive, and reduced the worst inflationary effects upon the government's income and the creditors' and savers' assets. Yet, those on fixed incomes continued to suffer, and as indexation swiftly spread throughout the economy (exchange rate, wages), changes in relative prices became increasingly difficult, since they were quickly fed into monetary correction and passed on to other prices. More to the point, in so far as indexation made the past inflation the floor to future price rises, inflation got increasingly resistant to any sort of therapy.

With respect to long-term financing, the stock-market boom soon proved to be ephemeral and the debenture market never really took off. Whereas risk-aversion and informational imperfections seem to have played a part, government policy was less than helpful. The combination of high inflation and short-term indexed assets, made long-term investment in non-indexed assets even riskier.[251]

Hence, BNDE and foreign loans continued to be the only sources of long-term funds. To be fair, the access to these sources was increased, first by expanding and redirecting BNDE loans to the private sector, and second, by the already mentioned new legislation to foreign loans. Yet, they remained well short of the industry's needs, particularly of those of LPFs. BNDE's manufacturing loans over the period were equivalent to only 19% of manufacturing investment (Table A.38), and the bulk of foreign loans went to state and foreign firms (Table A.45). In the face of it, LPFs, whose association with banks was forbidden by law, continued to rely heavily on internal and inflationary financing for their capacity expansion. No doubt, a conduct that curtailed their chances of growth and diversification. For instance, local firm share of the top 25 and 500 firms' sales in 1974 was zero and a mere 39%, respectively (*Exame*, various issues).

As for education, investments in basic skills continued to be inadequate. As of 1970, the illiteracy rate was still high, and less than half of the literate population over 20 had elementary education (Table A.35). Apart from the implications for industry's efficiency, the continuation of scarcity conditions in the market for skilled workers seems to have contributed – together with the economy's product mix and the high-inflation-cum-indexation policies – to the worsening of the income distribution experienced during the 1960s.[252]

Finally, in spite of SNDCT investments, R&D expenditures remained limited even by LDC standards (Table A.46), and the fact that investments came only after the heavy industry was set-up, and since the latter was done mainly through 'protected' FDI, posed the problem of who would demand the top quality human capital, technologies and infrastructure that the SNDCT was proposing to deliver. This would hardly come from either the TNCs or LPFs. The former because of their advantageous access to the parent company's technology.[253] And the latter because they were either located in the light industry, where technology is easily acquired off-the-shelf, or were sustaining marginal positions in the heavy industry, with TNC competition leaving no option but to license technology. In addition, the inward-orientation of the incentive regime added to the attractiveness of technology imports, since the usual export restrictions were not in practice binding.

3.4 HEAVY INDUSTRY REVISITED: THE 1974-79 PERIOD

For all its shortcomings, primarily for its narrow base of growth, the pragmatic 'miracle' could not last for long, but it took the oil shock in 1973 to convince the government the adjustments were necessary. Clearly something had to be done. In 1974, the current account deficit hit an unprecedented 6.5% of GDP and inflation was above 30%. The response came with the 'Second National Development Plan' – II NDP (1974-79). By then the liberal rhetoric had been forgotten, and the 'old' structural analysis was back in business. The inflationary and BP difficulties were put down to Brazil's 'unbalanced growth model', whose insufficient investments in the basic inputs and capital goods industry, would have created inflationary bottle-necks and an undue dependency on imports. The therapy prescribed, then, was massive IS investments in these areas, which would concurrently promote structural adjustment and growth.[254]

Even though it all looks very much like the previous IS strategy, there were new elements in the II NDP that suggested a more favourable treatment for exports and a more consistent approach to market-failures. In fact, the government seemed to have come to realizing that there is more to infant industry promotion than import protection and FDI. For instance, the plan emphasized the need to carry out IS in conjunction with the promotion of exports and local private conglomerates, capable of competing against TNCs in the scale, technology-intensive heavy industry. There were also references to the importance of promoting sustainable market structures, technological capabilities, and of changing the role of the TNCs. The latter were now supposed to increase exports, carry out R&D, and form joint ventures instead of taking over local firms. SEs, in turn, were seen continuing their investments in infrastructure and in key basic input industries such as steel, fertilizers, basic petrochemicals and mining.[255] Before discussing the results of this 'neo-IS' strategy, though, let us look at its policy mix.

Trade and Exchange Rate Policies

The adjustments in the trade regime sought, in the short term, to avoid a BP crisis, and in the long term, to carry out IS and to promote exports, in this order of importance. Right from the start, a real exchange rate devaluation was ruled out on the grounds, first, that it would be ineffective given the widespread indexation, and second, that it would impose heavy losses on externally indebted firms, and discourage further borrowing abroad.[256] Hence, the bulk of the changes was in the trade policy. On the import side, the government reintroduced a whole range of NTBs and raised tariffs (Table A.41), virtually banning consumer good imports, and imposing tough restrictions on those of intermediate and capital goods.[257] The latter were particularly affected by a curb on tariff and tax exemptions, a stricter interpretation of the 'law of similar' (notably for SEs), and by the imposition of tougher localization indices and 'participation agreements' on projects benefiting from CDI incentives. In addition, the fiscal incentives available for manufactured exports were extended to domestic sales of locally made capital goods.[258]

As to exports, the government increased subsidies (Table 22) mainly by expanding the credit available, and by keeping interest rates at around 8%, despite the 41% average annual inflation during the period. In addition, the 'drawback' was made more attractive by giving its users access to fiscal subsidies, and the CDI began to 'suggest' long-term export agreements (so-called BEFIEX), particularly to foreign firms, as a pre-condition to exempt capital goods imports from tariffs and NTBs.[259] This increase in incentives more than offset the appreciation of the official exchange rate, keeping the PPP-export rate well above the 1973 level (Table A.36).

Financial Policies

The financial side of the II NDP did not involve any significant institutional change, and the traditional combination of 'policy' loans, foreign capital incentives and a permissive attitude towards inflation continued to hold sway. There were, though, some adjustments. BNDE resources were beefed up by compulsory saving funds, allowing a significant increase in manufacturing loans. Table A.38 shows that the bank's approved manufacturing loans rose to 43% of manufacturing investment during the period,[260] with heavy industry and LPFs being the major beneficiaries. The subsidy implicit in these loans was also increased, notably during 1975-76 when the interest rate charged became sharply negative.[261] In addition, new BNDE programmes were set up, seeking to offer competitive finance for the purchase of locally made capital goods; and to capitalize and 'equity strengthen' the LPFs, particularly in the capital goods and basic input sectors.[262]

As for foreign capital, there was a certain swing towards portfolio investments (Table A.37), with some restrictions being imposed on FDI (see below). Yet, both forms of investment kept on growing rapidly.

The average annual inflow of FDI during the period (US$ 1.1 billion) was well above that of the 'miracle' (US$ 0.2 billion), whereas the external debt trebled to US$ 50 billion in 1979. This exceptional increase in foreign borrowing resulted largely from the government's strategy of using the cheap Eurocurrency funds available, to finance the plan's investments and the BP. This strategy involved the concession of foreign borrowing incentives, the liberalization of domestic interest rates in 1976, and, as noted earlier, a passive exchange rate policy.[263] Unlike BNDE credits, though, there was no attempt to control the allocation of these loans, which were supposed to be guided by relative prices. This, despite the distortions provoked by the trade policy, and high-inflation-cum-indexation.

Finally, the government continued to look at inflation as a necessary evil, a price worth paying for growth and structural adjustment. To be sure, there were attempts to pursue a tight monetary policy but, as the finance minister of the day put it, '[they were] *soon abandoned because wage-indexation was considered to be encouraging the wage-price spiral. Eventually the government chose monetary accommodation, which kept the annual inflation rates in the range of 30-40 a year until 1978*' (Simonsen 1988:293). This 'stabilization' of the inflation rate was, to a large extent, achieved at the cost, first, of a substantial increase in the government's internal debt, issued to finance policy loans and to offset the monetary expansion provoked by the massive foreign capital inflow. And second, of compromising the SEs' financial position with an unrealistic pricing policy.[264]

Industrial and S&T Policies

Part of what can be understood as the II NDP industrial policy was already discussed above, and involved greater protection and an increased amount of subsidized credit to the capital goods and basic input industries, in general, and for LPFs, in particular. These measures were supposed to be part of a broader strategy, which, as suggested earlier, aimed not only at carrying out IS but also at fostering large LPFs, sustainable market structures, and technological capabilities. The pursuance of the first two objectives was left to the discretion of the government's loosely co-ordinated 'army' of federal, sectoral and regional 'incentive' agencies – which still had the CDI formally on top— and to BNDE and SEs (through procurement).[265]

These institutions, though, had different interpretations of what would be a LPF or a sustainable market structure, and had different instruments and capacities to pursue the government guidelines. As a result, quite a few policy regimes emerged during the period, even in technologically related segments of the capital goods and basic input industries. In some sectors, strict investment licensing was enforced together with different sorts of FDI restrictions, ranging from the imposition of joint ventures (e.g. petrochemicals and telecommunications equipment) to a complete ban on foreign firms (e.g. micro and minicomputers). In others – the great majority – restrictions continued to be limited to localization requirements, and the objectives of promoting LPFs and efficient market structures, were left to BNDE credit and CDI incentives, despite the obvious limitations of these institutions.[266]

As to technological capabilities, investments in S&T were significantly increased, particularly regarding graduate education and research.[267] This was combined with initiatives aiming at financing R&D activities at the private firm level, and at imposing stricter controls on technology imports. The former was done through the concession of subsidized credit by BNDE and SNDCT institutions, and the latter, through new guidelines issued by the INPI, which made new contracts conditional upon absorption of technology by the recipient firms.[268] In addition, the SEs were used to foster the LPFs' technological capabilities by favouring the purchase of locally developed capital goods, and by offering technological support through, either their research institutes, or via NAIs (centre for co-operation with industry).[269]

The Results

The results of this neo-IS strategy are controversial. Enthusiasts claim with reason quite a few successes. They argue, first, that economic growth was kept at a relatively high rate (6.4%)[270] and exports, notably manufactured exports, continued to grow fast (6 and 16%, respectively), substantially increasing their share of world exports (Table A.47). Second, that export growth was accompanied by diversification towards the heavy industry (Table A.29), reflecting the success of IS investments during the period. Industries that were targeted by the government such as steel, paper pulp, aircraft and some sectors of capital goods became major exporters. Third, that IS contributed not only to export diversification, but also to reduce dependency on imported capital goods and basic inputs (Table 25), assisting therefore in the structural adjustment whose first signs came out in the early 1980s.[271]

Yet, critics draw attention to the costly macroeconomic 'side-effects',

Table 25   Selected results of II NDP investments

	(a) *Capital goods*		(b) *Rolled steel*		(c) *Aluminium*		(d) *Paper pulp*		(e) *Oil*
	Imp ratio[1]	*Exp. ratio*[2]	*Imp ratio*	*Exp. ratio*	*Imp ratio*	*Exp. ratio*	*Imp ratio*	*Exp. ratio*	*Imp ratio*
1974	29.0	7.0	39.1	2.2	50.4	1.6	16.6	11.8	79.7
1978	20.0	8.0	5.7	5.4	26.3	2.0	4.4	14.8	84.7
1983	23.0	19.0	1.0	39.1	2.3	40.0	0.8*	27.7*	68.7
1987	25.0	20.0	0.5	50.7	n.a.	n.a.	n.a.	n.a.	52.0

[1] Imports divided by domestic supply. [2] Exports divided by total production.* 1982.

Source: BNDE (1988b) for (a), Batista (1992) for (c) and (d), and IBGE (1990) and ANESTBR, various issues.

whose most obvious manifestations were a huge external debt, whose service was taking up 62% of export revenue even before the interest and second oil shocks, and a record inflation (38% in 1978) fuelled by indexation and by the deterioration of public sector finances. The latter, provoked by the combined effect of the mounting indexed domestic debt, credit subsidies, fiscal incentives and the SEs' external debt.[272] In addition, IS contribution to BP adjustment is viewed with scepticism, particularly when measured by import coefficients, since these indicators would also reflect the slowdown in growth and investment during the 1980s.[273]

Even though the task of disentangling macroeconomic from industrial strategy failures is fraught with difficulties, it seems that the problem with the neo-IS strategy went well beyond unsound macroeconomic policies. In fact, a case can be made out that these macroeconomic imbalances were just part of a series of adverse results, overlooked by the enthusiasts, which were rooted in the government's failure to go beyond a mere patch-up of the old IS strategy.

To begin with, despite the government's attempts to increase the selectivity of the incentive regime by better targeting BNDE credits and CDI incentives, the clamp-down on imports and the lack of control over the allocation of foreign loans, ensured that resources remained dispersed across virtually all manufacturing activities, regardless of the existence of static or dynamic comparative advantages. This was made particularly worse by the increased obsession with localization indices, which kept mocking Adam Smith's insight[274] that the division of labour is limited by the extent of the market. As a result, exports became an even more subsidized and costlier business (Table 22).[275] Despite responding to greater subsidies, they remained at 9% of the manufacturing output, and under 7% of GDP (Tables A.32 and A.27). Apart from efficiency implications, this result – given the low level of imports – left the bulk of the BP adjustment to foreign loans, which in turn led to the debt build-up.

On the issue of targeting the basic input and capital goods industries, whereas the potential static and strategic benefits were unquestionable (as the export success of some of these industries was to prove), a number of considerations regarding the choice and implementation of the targets seemed to have been overlooked. Looking first at the target chosen, there were still clear gains to be made from better resource allocation by increasing investments in the light industry. Brazil's under-employment in mid-1970s was unabated and unit labour costs were still falling (Table A.39).[276] This opportunity, though, was largely missed since, amid an incentive bias against exports, BNDE credits and fiscal incentives were concentrated in the heavy industry. As expected, light industry's export performance was disappointing,[277] and labour absorption in the manufacturing sector slumped (Table A.40).

Moreover, the technological and strategic externalities involved in the production of capital goods should have been set against: a) the benefits of intra-industry trade and access to state-of-the-art embodied technology, and b) the disadvantages of spreading scarce resources too thinly. Yet, although the ratio of capital goods to GDI in 1975 was lower than that of the US (Frischtak and Dahlman 1990), the government went on to substitute as much of capital goods imports as possible.

As for the implementation, despite the measures taken to promote LPFs and sustainable market structures, the results were mixed, and on the whole unsatisfactory. In the basic input sector, strict investment licensing, FDI restrictions, and greater outward-orientation, seemed to have guaranteed plants close to the MES and an efficient number of producers, but SEs remained as the dominant player. In the capital goods sector, the fact that the TNCs were already firmly installed, combined, as noted earlier, with an inconsistent industrial policy, led, more often than not, to the entry of LPFs in already 'crowded' and inward-oriented industrial structures. Apart from aggravating the latter's inefficiency, this process precluded LPFs from benefiting from economies of scale and specialization, doing no wonders for their learning process or for the prospects of a limited period of protection.

The custom-built segment, where the entry of LPFs was more successful, is a case in point. BNDE (1988b) speaks of inward-oriented

Table 26   International comparison of the number of producers of
selected capital goods, 1980

	Brazil	Germany	US	Japan
Water turbines	4	2	1	3
Hydrogenerators	4	2	3	4
Rolling mills	7	3	3	3
Blast furnaces	4	3	1	4
Large mechanical presses	5	2	2	n.a.

Source: Lago *et al.*, 'A Indústria Brasileira de Bens de Capital', *Estudos Especiais*, 1. BRE/FGV as quoted in Vilella (1984).

and excessively diversified LPFs, struggling with the large number of producers and the limited and cyclical internal market. It also points out that vertical-integration was unduly pursued. Table 26 shows that despite Brazil's limited internal market, the number of custom-built capital goods producers in 1980 was clearly higher than in developed countries.

In view of this environment of inconsistent industrial policy, inward-orientation, and fragmented and often FDI dominated industrial structures, the objectives of fostering LPFs' technology capabilities and large private conglomerates turned out to be elusive. In the former's case, whereas the S&T infrastructure was significantly improved, its links with manufacturing remained weak. Facing the imperfect competition of the affiliates, precluded from taking advantages of scale economies by the crowded market, and looking inwards, the majority of the firms did not go beyond the routine and adaptive technological tasks, to use Lall's (1992a) taxonomy. The evidence available suggests, *inter alia*, that only 0.7% of the industrial firms conducted formal R&D during 1974-79, the great majority (63%) SEs. In addition, it shows that the private sector's outlays on technology (R&D and royalties in 1978 and 1982) were under 0.2% of net sales.[278] The comparison with Korea, shown in Table 27, gives the full measure of the government's failure to promote domestic technological effort.

In this context, it could be no surprise that the bulk of the successful technological developments over the period came from SEs in the steel, arms and aircraft industries. Growing up protected from FDI and enjoying more sustainable industrial structures, these firms had more favourable conditions to invest in domestic technological capabilities.[279]

As for the formation of large, internationally competitive, private conglomerates, the limited evidence available suggest modest advances. For instance, as of 1980, the LPFs' share of the top 100 non-financial

Table 27   Brazil and Korea R&D expenditures-to-sales ratio

Sectors	Brazil (1982)	Korea (1983)
Metallurgy	0.2	0.4
Machinery	0.3	2.0
Electrical equipment	0.4	3.0
Transport	0.4	1.5
Lumber	0.0	0.6
Rubber	0.0	1.0
Chemicals	0.0	0.5
Plastics	0.0	1.7
Textiles	0.0	0.7
Food	0.0	0.7
Manufacturing	0.1	0.8

Source: For Brazil, Braga *et al.* (1988:198) and for Korea, Minister of Science and Technology cited in World Bank (1987a, vol. 2:25)

groups' sales was only 30.7%, with TNCs and SEs taking 31 and 38% respectively (Willmore 1987:169). At the firm level, as of 1980, LPFs had still only 6% of the top 25 firms' sales, 20% of the top 100, and their share of the top 500 fell from 39 to 35% over 1974-80 (Exame, various issues). Again, a comparison with Korea shows that even by NICs' standards, Brazil's private conglomerates by the end of the 1980s were still small. As of 1989, the sales of Brazil's largest private group (US$ 3.8 billion) were lower than that of Korea's twelfth *jaebol* (US$ 4.2 billion) (Table 28).

Apart from the factors already indicated, the small scale achieved by Brazil's private groups seems to have also a bearing on the precariousness of government intervention in the financial sector. Table 29 indicates that, despite the increase in BNDE credits, the LPFs' financing pattern did not change significantly during the period. Retained earnings continued to be the main source of long-term financing, a characteristic that put them side by side with American firms, even though they did not have anything like their size, or their access to intra-firm capital markets. This contrasts sharply with the position of the Korean firms, which relied heavily on external sources to finance their growth and investments.

It seems clear, then, that government intervention led to a financial system that was neither credit- nor capital market-based, to use Zysman's (1983) categorizing. Since BNDE, at its peak, did not control more than 8% of private sector loans (Table A.38), and the private commercial and investment banks remained largely out of the manufacturing

Table 28   A tentative comparison of Brazil's and Korea's leading and locally-owned private conglomerates, 1989/90.
US$ billions

Groups	1990 sales*	Groups	1989 sales**
1. Andrade Gutierrez	3.76	1. Samsung	34.33
2. Votorantin	2.15	2. Hyundai	32.49
3. Camargo Correa	2.08	3. Lucky-Goldstar	23.13
4. Ipiranga	1.94	4. Daewoo	18.06
5. Pão de Açucar	1.93	5. Sunkyong	9.40
6. Copersucar	1.77	6. Ssangyong	7.46
7. Gerdau	1.31	7. Hyosung	5.22
8. Villares	0.86	8. Hanjin	4.78
9. Alpargatas	0.85	9. Korea Explosives	4.63
10. Vidigal	0.83	10. Kia	4.42
11. Steinbruch	0.78	11. Lotte	4.19
12. Brahma	0.36	12. Doosan	3.73
13. Dedini	0.21	13. Dongah	3.16
14. Matarazzo	0.19	14. Donghu	2.79
15. Mangels	0.19	15. Kolon	2.24

* Originally in Cruzeiros. It was converted to US dollars according to the year's average exchange rate.
** Originally in Won. It was converted to US dollars according to the year's average exchange rate.

Source: 'Quem é Quem, Visão 1991', for Brazil and FEER, March 1990, for Korea.

sector (even though legal restrictions were removed), LPFs never had the amount of credit available to their Koreans, Japanese and German counterparts.[280] This is illustrated by Table 30, which shows data on the debt-equity ratio of these countries. On the other hand, high inflation-cum-indexation, continued to preclude the development of a capital market, and encourage inflationary financing.

In sum, for all its success in deepening the industrial structure, diversifying exports, strengthening the LPFs' position and improving the S&T infrastructure, the II NDP did not go far enough to change substantially the pattern of Brazil's industrialization. The incentive regime continued to be largely non-selective, biased towards the internal market, and exports a heavily subsidized and lesser business. Under total protection, largely market-oriented credit allocation, lax investment and FDI licensing, 'crowded' and inefficient industrial structures continue to survive and proliferated as IS moved upstream. On the financial side, the key issue of long-term financing for LPFs was only precari-

Table 29 Brazil, US, and Korea source of funds by the corporate sector, 1978–84 (%)

	Autofinance	External	Total	External		
Brazil				loans	shares	other
1978	58.8	41.2	100	51.1	35.9	13.0
1980	62.5	37.5	100	69.6	24.1	6.3
1982	65.7	34.3	100	58.8	29.0	12.1
1984	76.8	23.2	100	54.7	24.8	20.6
Korea						
1977–81	23.3	76.7	100	53.7	24.8	21.5
1982	27.0	73.0	100	55.4	31.8	12.8
1984	33.3	66.7	100	60.5	32.1	7.4
US						
1979	78.7	21.3	100	84.5	15.4	—
1982	78.7	21.3	100	71.8	28.1	—
1984	83.5	16.5	100	124.8	−24.8	—

Note: Data for Brazil was based in a sample of the 90 largest locally owned firms.

Source: For Brazil, D.G. Rodrigues (1986).
For Korea Amsden and Euh (1990:66), and for the US, Ross *et al.* (1988:378)

Table 30 Debt-equity ratios for Brazil, Korea, Japan, USA and Germany, 1964–83*

Year	Brazil	Korea	Japan	US	Germany
1954	92.3	n.a.	n.a.	n.a.	n.a.
1964	112.7	100.5	n.a.	n.a.	n.a.
1973	92.6	272.7	449.0	92.0	185.0
1976	137.5	364.6	488.0	86.0	212.0
1978	120.0	366.8	421.0	93.2	222.7
1980	142.0	487.9	377.8	101.5	215.3
1982	115.0	385.8	298.6	106.1	247.8
1983	114.0	360.3	277.0	103.5	241.7

* For Brazil debt-equity ratios are for the non-financial sector while for the rest of the countries they are for the manufacturing sector. Ratios are liabilities divided by net-worth.

Source: For Korea, BOK, Financial Statement Analysis, various years. For Brazil, Goldsmith (1986) for 1954–76 and Almeida (1988) for the rest of the period. Other countries, Bank of Japan (1990).

ously solved. In this sort of environment, LPF growth was bound to be hampered and macroeconomic imbalances, inevitable, regardless of any 'macroeconomic failure'.

3.5   THE DISMAL DECADE. THE 1980S

When the interest and second oil shocks struck at the turn of the decade, Brazil could not be in a more vulnerable position. As noted earlier, a huge external debt had been accumulated, inflation was high and reinforced by widespread indexation, and oil made up more than one third of imports (Table A.33). In such a scenario, the three-fold increase in oil prices and the two-fold increase in international interest rates over 1978-82, could only play havoc. In fact, the current account deficit reached 5.8% of GDP in 1982, and the debt-service ratio 98%. Inflation, in turn, broke the three digit barrier in 1980. Unlike previous BP crises, this time there were no substantial imports to substitute, and the option of 'borrowing its way out the crisis' received its *coup de grâce* with Mexico's default in 1982. With little room to manoeuvre and resorting to misguided stabilization policies, the government would pass the rest of the decade struggling with these macroeconomic imbalances, creating an environment of low, unstable growth and near hyperinflation, hardly appropriate to industrial development.

Facing chaos in the short-term management of the economy, and apparently influenced by a simplistic structuralist notion that the II NDP had 'completed' industrialization, the government would also forsake any attempt to formulate a long-term industrial strategy. In practice, this meant that the previous pattern of intervention lingered on, and given the depth of the BP crisis and the sharp deterioration of the public sector finances, its shortcomings were further aggravated by extra cuts in imports, S&T expenditures, and curbs on long-term financing.

This troubled decade can be roughly divided in two periods, marked by different policy responses to the growing macroeconomic difficulties. That is, the 1980-84 period, when an orthodox BP-adjustment policy was adopted, and the 1985-89 period, when the threat of hyperinflation led to a series of heterodox stabilization plans. Let us look at their implications for industry.

Under Orthodox Adjustment

Living up to the country's tradition, the government's first response to the crisis was to pursue a strategy designed to adjust and stabilize the economy without hurting growth. At its core was an attempt to shift relative prices in favour of public sector and tradable goods. This was done by adjusting public sector prices and devaluing the currency in 30% (December 1979), while imposing strict price controls (including interest rates), and a pre-fixed monetary and exchange rate correction for 1980 well below the expected rate of inflation. In this process, fiscal subsidies to exports, advanced deposits on imports and CDI tariff exemptions were eliminated. By the end of 1980, though, expansionary policies had allowed the relative price changes to be reversed by a two-fold increase in inflation, while the BP situation continued to deteriorate.[281]

The government, then, finally caved in, adopting an orthodox programme in 1981. At first, given the 1979 experience, a real exchange devaluation was avoided (crawling-peg was reintroduced) and efforts were concentrated on restricting demand and escalating export subsidies and import controls. On the demand side, fiscal policy was tightened, wages partially de-indexed, quantitative credit controls imposed and interest rate ceilings removed. On trade policy, fiscal subsidies to exports were reinstated and export credits expanded.[282] Moreover, new NTBs were introduced including import surcharges, mandatory import programs for major importers, and an expanded list of prohibited imports.[283] The interruption of voluntary capital inflows provoked by Mexico's default, led eventually to a new maxi devaluation in early 1983, this time already under IMF supervision.[284]

These measures eventually adjusted the BP, with the current account showing a small surplus in 1984. Even though, as noted earlier, II NDP investments seem to carry considerable weight in explaining these results, the 34% growth in exports and the 39% fall in imports accumulated over 1980-84, cannot be dissociated from the all-time high reached by export subsidies and import controls, and from the brutal recession that hit the country. The GDP fell by 0.7% per year over the period, with output falling sharply in 1981 (–4.2%) and 1983 (–3.6%). The aggregate investment ratio fell continuously from 21 to 16% (Table A.48).

Industry was severely hurt in this process. The slump in domestic demand combined with restrictions on BNDE loans[285] and *real* interest rates averaging 25% per year, led output to fall on average by 3%

Table 31   Brazil's effective and legal tariff rates, 1975–89 (%)

Sectors	Legal				Effective (Corden)		
	1975	*1980*	*1984*	*1989*	*1980*	*1985*	*1988*
Total manufacturing	86.4	99.4	90.0	43.1	46.4	42.9	32.6
Capital	62.9	83.3	69.4	58.6	71.9	14.5	19.0
Intermediate	77.3	76.5	76.9	33	42	45.9	42.2
Consumer	125.4	132.5	131.5	62.7	35.7	38.7	13.6
Durable	163.9	n.a.	173.6	58.5	n.a.	−15.5	−10.5
Non-durable	117.4	n.a.	122.7	46.6	n.a.	50.1	18.9

Notes: (a) All sectoral data are averages weighted by the 1975 output at international prices, except for 1980 that is weighted by the 1979 value-added. (c) Effective rates were derived from direct price comparisons, and used 1970 (1980) and 1975 (other years) technical coefficients.

Source: Tyler (1983:553) for 1980, Braga *et al.* (1988) for 1975, 1984, 1985 and Kume (1988) for 1988 and 1989

yearly over the period. Likewise, manufacturing investment fell 36% in 1981, and was around the 1976 level in 1984. Among the manufacturing sectors, capital goods, a key II NDP target, was worst hit. Output in 1984 was 22% below the 1975 level, and its share of the manufacturing structure fell below the 1970 mark (Table A.30).

The depth and length of the recession helped to put into perspective the much-heralded manufactured export performance over the period. True enough, Brazil managed to increase its share of world exports in most sectors (Table A.47). Yet, despite the highest ever subsidies (Table 22) and the collapse of domestic demand, the shift to exports was less than impressive, with its contribution to recovery coming only in 1984. Even then, exports made up less than 10% of the manufacturing output (Table A.32). The external constraint argument does not seem to hold against the fact that countries like Korea, increased manufactured exports at an annual rate of 12% against Brazil's 4% (1980-84). More to the point, in the crucial machine and transport equipment sector, its share of world exports fell to 0.6%, whereas Korea's nearly trebled to 1.9% (UN ITSY, HIT).

All those years of 'protected' FDI, non-selective and inward-oriented incentive regime seem to have produced an industry that was not prepared to take on the international market. An increase in the already comprehensive NTBs could only aggravate this situation. Estimates of effective protection rates, for what they are worth[286], put the average protection for manufacturing at the end of the period as high

Table 32   Labour productivity in manufacturing.*

1949–64	4.5
1965–73	4.5
1974–79	3.1
1980–84	−1.3
1985–88	0.0

* Compound rate of growth of value added per production worker, 1986 prices.
Source: IBGE (1990).

as 43%, with an inter-industry structure that bore no logic (Table 31). Apart from competitiveness considerations, the prospect of having another period of unchallenged inward-oriented growth after the recession, might have certainly precluded a stronger commitment to exports.

Needless to say that this scenario of falling output and investments, coupled with a limited shift towards the external market, did not help much the long-term competitiveness of the industry. The static and dynamic diseconomies of scale associated with a prolonged recession added to the old problems of fragmented industrial structures and suboptimal plants, causing productivity to plunge (Table 32). Moreover, investments in R&D fell from its modest levels (Table A.46), with the public sector cutting back drastically its investments in the modest S&T infrastructure.[287] Technology imports also fell by 35% over 1979-84 (BACEN).

To complete the picture, the orthodox adjustment failed to stabilize the economy and ended up aggravating the problem. Inflation more than doubled to 213% in 1984, reflecting again the widespread indexation and the increasing deterioration of the public sector finances.[288] Apart from turning cost accounting into a nightmare, this rampant inflation, coupled with short-term indexed assets offering stratospheric interest rates, made the prospect of developing a proper source of long-term financing even gloomier. Not surprisingly, LPFs moved even further into internal financing (Table 29).

Paradoxically, it was amid this inhospitable environment that the government, or at least part of it, took the most important industry related initiative of the 1980s. That is, to consolidate the so-called 'market-reserve' for mini- and micro-computers, set up in 1977, and to expand it to much of the professional electronics industry.[289] Among the several policy regimes originated in the late 1970s, this initiative stands out for its almost unique attempt to apply correctly the infant industry principle. That is, to protect LPFs (instead of affiliates) in an industry where the importance of strategic benefits and positive externalities are widely recognized.[290]

Unfortunately, the basic IS, inward-oriented notion remained dominant. The government did not act as if it was keen on promoting an internationally competitive industry. For instance, despite market imperfections such as R&D and production related economies of scale, there were about 37 different firms producing PC-clones in 1985 (Schimtz and Hewitt 1992). Despite the limited human capital base,[291] and the benefits of intra-industry specialization, vertical and horizontal diversification was unduly encouraged. Finally, despite the capital market failures, BNDE loans came only late in the day, a problem somewhat mitigated by the unprecedented decision of some commercial banks (heavy user of computer systems) to enter the industry.

The results achieved so far seems to reflect these shortcomings. On the one hand, despite the macroeconomic chaos, the local computer industry grew at about 23% annually during the 1980s (Evans and Tigre 1989), and 'the skilled technical and engineering component of the labour force has grown substantially' (Hewitt 1992:196). But on the other, after more than a decade of protection, exports remained negligible and prices are said to be twice that of US, despite the obvious differences in quality.[292]

Under Heterodox Stabilization

If the implications of the orthodox adjustment for industry were disastrous, and the flaws of government intervention aggravated (except perhaps for the isolated case of the computer industry), things were not much better under the heterodoxy. The BP adjustment gave the newly installed civilian government (March 1985) more room to manoeuvre, and after a short-lived austerity, fiscal and monetary policies became clearly expansionary. As a result, the recovery initiated in 1984 continued in 1985 with GDP growing 7.9%. Yet, the combination of fast growth, a higher fiscal deficit and a food supply shock in a very closed and indexed economy, put the monthly inflation by year-end at 15%, or at an annualized rate of 435%.

With hyperinflation knocking at its door, and believing that indexation was to blame, the government launched the Cruzado Plan in February 1986 – a heterodox attempt to stabilize the economy that had at its core a price-wage freeze and the abolition of monetary correction.[293] Despite its success in reducing inflation to a monthly average of 0.5%

in the first six months, expansionary fiscal, monetary and wage policies led to a consumer boom that, in turn, raised inflation to above pre-plan levels in early 1987. To add to the gloom, the frozen exchange rate coupled with the domestic boom produced a 2% of GDP current account deficit, which, given the low level of reserves, led the government to an interest moratorium in February 1987.

After the failure of the Cruzado Plan, another two stabilization plans were implemented (mid 1987 and early 1989) pursuing variants of the price-freeze-cum-de-indexation formula, but combined with more restrictive fiscal and monetary policies. Even though they managed to slow down the economy – GDP growth fell from 7.6% in 1986 to an annual average of 2% over 1987-89 – and adjust the BP, they both went down the Cruzado path. Initial successes were followed by unprecedented rates of inflation and re-indexation. By December 1989, inflation had reached a mind-boggling monthly rate of 49%. Underlying these failures was an increasingly intractable fiscal deficit approaching 7% of GDP in 1989.[294]

Reflecting this highly unstable macroeconomic environment, the performance of the manufacturing sector was erratic and on the whole poor. After growing on average 11.3% in 1985 and 1986, output fell annually by 0.3% until 1989 (Table A.48). Manufacturing investment in 1986 was still well below 1980 levels, and fell even further in 1987, following the decline of the aggregate investment ratio.[295] The latter, after recovering to 18.7% in 1986, fell continuously to 16.7% in 1989. Labour productivity, in turn, stagnated around the dismal 1980-84 levels (Table 32), and the whole decade produced the worst ICOR of the post-war period (Table A.42).[296]

As one would expect, manufactured exports were also affected. Apart from the disruption of relative prices, low investment and low productivity, competitiveness also suffered from a higher incentive bias against exports. The steep appreciation of the PPP-exchange rate prompted by the price freezes (Table A.36), coincided with a gradual and substantial reduction of export subsidies (Table 22),[297] which was not properly balanced by a meaningful import liberalization.[298] These events reinforced the position of the export market as a poor and occasional alternative to domestic crises, discouraging long-term commitments. This is clearly indicated by an export performance that mirrored the 'boom and bust' developments of the internal market, with exports growing on average 18.7% in the years of negative or no growth (1987–88), and stagnating or declining when growth resumed (-0.2 over 1985–86 and -16% in 1989).

Not surprisingly, Brazil's share of world manufactured exports over 1984-87 fell or stagnated in most segments, including the light industry despite falling unit labour costs.[299] This decline could have been worse had it not been for the long-term export agreements under the BEFIEX scheme, which forced firms to export whatever the costs, and that continued to receive, until 1989, the fiscal subsidy eliminated for the regular exports in 1985. BEFIEX's share of manufactured exports rose from 17 to 40% over 1979-86 and reached 50% in 1989.[300]

Amid the disruption and stagnation provoked by the failure of successive stabilization plans, there were two attempts to reform the policy regime that are worth noting. The first came in the beginning of the period, when worries about the industry's competitiveness led to a new emphasis on developing the local S&T infrastructure.[301] The Ministry for Science and Technology (MCT) was then created in 1985, giving the subject an unprecedented ministerial status, with investments increasing sharply in 1986.[302] Yet, this revival was short-lived, and expending cuts initiated in 1987 brought investments back to the depressed 1984 levels, with the MCT being abolished in 1989. The cuts in S&T expenditures, coupled with falling LPF investments, not only worked against increases in the latter's technological capabilities, but also widened the gap between the productive sector and the S&T infrastructure. To add to the problem, human capital indicators showed little progress over the 1980s (Table A.35), with Brazil still ranking poorly among NICs.[303]

The second attempt came only in 1988, with the so-called 'New Industrial Policy.' Seeking to increase productivity, technological capabilities and reduce government intervention, this initiative comprised: (a) a limited import liberalization involving a partial removal of NTBs[304] and a tariff reform that reduced the average manufacturing tariff from 90 to 43% (Table 31); (b) the re-introduction of fiscal incentives to capital good imports, coupled with new incentives to R&D activities and BEFIEX exports, to be administered by a revamped CDI; and (c) legislation allowing the establishment of export processing zones (EPZ).[305] These measures, though, had little impact. First, legal tariffs remained high and the system of import licensing remained in place, including NTBs such as the 'law of similar'. And second, the dire financial conditions of the public sector left little room for fiscal benefits, a fact that largely prevented their implementation, including the anachronistic EPZs. Serious changes in the incentive regime would have to wait until the following decade.

In sum, the impact of external shocks magnified by previous misguided intervention in the product (trade bias) and financial markets (indexation), largely reduced government action over the 1980s to a series of unsuccessful adjustment and stabilization attempts. Facing a highly unstable environment, industry fell into a vicious circle of falling output, investments and productivity, which coupled with a higher trade bias, produced declining market shares abroad. This decline in competitiveness, however, cannot be dissociated from the industry's structural weaknesses fostered by decades of an ill-conceived approach to market failures. That is, its fragmented and excessively integrated structure, its sub-optimal plants, its weak local private sector, the lack of long-term financing, the limited and isolated S&T infrastructure, and the poor human capital endowment.

3.6 SUMMING UP

The mixed results presented by Brazil's industrialization seem to closely reflect the dubious quality of government intervention throughout the various stages of its development. It seems clear that instead of being moulded and disciplined by international prices, and by the nature of the relevant market failures, government action was largely guided by the pressures to keep the economy growing at all costs, and by the need to remove what was seen to be the most binding of the constraints, i.e., the foreign exchange gap. This, coupled with a solid export pessimism – deeply rooted on the backwardness caused by centuries of 'export-oriented' colonial history – set the stage for an industrialization strategy that blindly followed the country's import composition.

This strategy, as shown, cannot be considered a complete failure. Far from it. *Import controls combined with fiscal and credit incentives were very effective in turning an agrarian country into a highly sophisticated industrialized economy.* Yet the indiscriminate use of protection amid an inconsistent and often misguided approach to market failures, led not only to a damaging waste of resources, but also produced serious structural weaknesses that seriously compromised the industry's efficiency and competitiveness, while exposing the economy to violent macroeconomic imbalances.

Decades of a non-selective, inward-oriented incentive regime coupled with 'protected' FDI, lax investment licensing and largely market-oriented credit allocation, took industrial diversification and vertical integration beyond what would be economically sound. It also produced unsustainable market structures, held together only by high and permanent protection. Facing inward-oriented incentives, squeezed by the TNCs' imperfect competition, lacking a proper source of long-term financing, having a poor human capital base to build on, and handicapped by a limited S&T infrastructure, LPFs did well to survive and grow. Yet, this growth, as we have seen, was largely modest both in terms of size and technological capability. The macroeconomic chaos of the 1980s only added to these problems.

Since the beginning of the 1990s, the government has been taking important steps towards a serious overhaul of the incentive regime. A program of import liberalization was adopted, including the removal of the relevant NTBs and a four year advanced schedule for tariff reductions, which reduced the average nominal tariff to 17 in 1993, with a maximum of 35 for infant industries.[306] However macroeconomic stability continues to be elusive, with yet another heterodox stabilization plan failing to control inflation. Moreover, the reforms have been taking place amid a liberal, anti-government rhetoric that threatens to throw away the baby with the bath-water.

The source of most of Brazil's problems, as suggested, is not government intervention *per se* but the quality of this intervention. Deficiencies such as a weak local private sector, lack of long-term financing, low domestic technological effort, poor human capital base and limited S&T infrastructure, are not going to be solved by market forces alone. They all arise from market failures in the product (static and dynamic economies of scale) and factor markets (informational imperfections and externalities), and they all call for government action. Not of the type that Brazil had in the past, but one focused on the nature of these market failures, and disciplined by the need to increase industry's competitiveness in a more open and outward-oriented economy.

4 Summary and Conclusions

As noted in the introduction, this book aimed at challenging the neo-classical explanation of industrial success, by looking into the role of government intervention in two prominent NICs: Brazil and Korea. According to the neoclassical view, the differences in industrial performance among LDCs, would have been related to two different policy regimes, with divergent trade orientations and distinct degrees of government intervention. That is, the EP, outward-looking regime, deemed intrinsically liberal and adopted by the best performers, notably the East Asian NICs; and the IS, inward-looking strategy, viewed, by contrast, as intrinsically interventionist, adopted by the majority of LDCs, notably the Latin America NICs and India. In order to test this hypothesis, the cases of Korea, representing the EP strategy, and Brazil, representing the IS regime, were then chosen, and the role of government intervention analysed.

The study of these two cases has suggested, first, that trade orientation really matters. More open, outward-oriented economies such as Korea tend to perform better because of allocational (more efficient use of the resource endowment), technological (economies of scale and specialization, access to the technological frontier), behavioural (competitive pressure) and macroeconomic (external balance) benefits.

Second, that even though trade orientation matters, its relationship with government intervention is hardly the one stated by the neoclassical view. Both the outward-oriented Korean and inward-oriented Brazilian governments were heavily interventionist.

Finally, that rather than being inimical to outward-orientation or simply ineffective, government intervention can be a powerful complement. On the one hand, outward-orientation and good fundamentals alone cannot remedy the crippling market failures that affect industrialization in LDCs. These imperfections – externalities, dynamic and static economies, and informational failures – require, as Korea's case has shown, decisive government action. On the other hand, governments need the guidance and discipline of an open economy, to confine interventions to the relevant market failures, and to reduce the risk of government failures. As revealed by the case of Brazil, inward-oriented regimes tend to lead to wholesale government intervention, with far from satisfactory diagnosing and correction of imperfections.

It is, then, the interaction between these two elements – outward-orientation and selective intervention – and not the dichotomy of open-liberal and closed-interventionist regimes, that emerges from the analysis as the main factor behind industrial success in general, and the performance differential between Brazil and Korea, in particular. To reinforce this point, let us now recapitulate the main traits of government intervention in the industrialization of these two countries.

4.1 KOREA

In the case of Korea, the origin of its industrialization can be traced back to the first decades of this century when under Japanese occupation a sizeable and diversified industrial structure was built. Although impressive, the shortcomings of this 'colonial industrialization' became clear after WWII, when the Japanese withdrawal left Korea with limited industrial skills, with a poorly integrated industrial structure and without its main market. The North–South split followed by civil war made things worse, with Korea losing most of heavy industry and power supply to the North, and having what was left of its industrial base, destroyed. The government response was to adopt an IS 'strategy', which succeeded in rebuilding the light industry and in improving the human capital stock, but that failed to deliver growth and reduce dependency on aid. This, however, appears to have been not so much the result of a 'disastrous' industry and trade bias, but the inexorable outcome of a situation that combined the difficulties of learning and reconstruction, with a government more interested in its political survival, than in remedying market failures.

The 1960s saw the military taking over and responding to the failures of the 1950s with what became known as an outward-oriented policy regime. Building on the industrial reconstruction of the IS period, this strategy was remarkably successful in promoting industrial, export and economic growth. Neoclassicals were quick to attribute this success to the allegedly neutral, hands-off and outward-looking traits of the new regime. Yet, even though the regime was undoubtedly outward-oriented, and the economy was opened up, it was not market, industry or firm neutral, nor protection for the domestic market was low. Behind this paradox was concerted government action to overcome market failures in the product and factor markets, which allowed Korea to fully exploit the advantages of an open economy, without the drawbacks of a free-trade regime.

In the product markets, the main actions were threefold:

(a) A selective trade regime was set up, which granted exporters free access to producer goods at world prices, while offering – under strict export performance conditions – light industry and selected heavy industries an exclusive domestic market, where to reap static and dynamic economies;

(b) A conglomeration policy that led to the optimization of dynamic and static economies at firm level, and that allowed an early entry to the export market via cross-subsidization and price discrimination; and

(c) FDI restrictions that limited the benefits of protection to those who really needed it, allowing local firms to be protected from the imperfect competition of TNCs; and ensuring a prompt private sector's response to local incentives.

In the factor markets, the government intervened in the financial sector to make sure that manufacturing investment – particularly in those sectors where the dynamic benefits, externalities and barriers to entry were high – and exports, would not be discouraged by the lack of proper financing or by interest rates above the social opportunity cost. Moreover, its control over loan allocation was one of the main instruments of the conglomeration policy. The government also intervened to promote the acquisition of technological capability, investing or giving incentives to the S&T infrastructure, education and R&D, all activities where externalities prevent an optimal market solution.

In the 1970s, concerned mainly with factor price changes and with an eye in the industrial restructuring of the developed countries, the government promoted a shift in the industrial structure towards the HCIs. Contrary to what Neoclassicals claim, this 'push' did not involved major alterations in the policy regime. It remained outward-oriented – the very reason of the 'push' was to maintain high export growth in the face of changing comparative advantages – and there was no significant change in the pattern of government intervention. There were though some adjustments. Given the scale of HCI market imperfections, adjustments were made in the policies towards the product and factor markets to help local firms to overcome high entry barriers. That is, HCIs were granted, *inter alia*, higher, but still selective, import and FDI protection; greater access to preferential credit; and, to meet their technological requirements, government investment in human capital and S&T was stepped up.

Even though policy mistakes happened, the 'HCI push' results had little to do with the apocalyptic picture that its critics like to paint. Industrial, export and economic growth remained high, thanks to the exceptional performance of the HCIs, which, despite their infancy, began to export very early in the day, boosted by government incentives and the *jaebols'* ability to cross-subsidise and price-discriminate their products. By targeting the HCIs, the government precluded a steep rise in labour costs that would have fatally compromised the competitiveness of the light industry. The more so, because, given the market imperfections in the HCIs, the private sector would have been, at best, slow to respond to the factor price changes. The overall result would have been a poor industrial and export performance, not only in the 1970s but throughout the 1980s.

Finally, in the 1980s, the government moved to liberalize the policy regime, amid a misleading and politically motivated criticism of state intervention in the previous decade. If anything, by overcoming market failures in the product and factor markets, state intervention had created the conditions by which liberalization could be particularly beneficial. This and the gap between the government's rhetoric and its actions, have to be taken into account when one examines the remarkable industrial and export performance of the Korean economy during the 1980s. It seems quite clear that the government, notwithstanding its rhetoric, continue to intervene selectively to ensure that 'irreparable' market failures did not prevent Korea from fully exploiting its static and dynamic comparative advantages.

4.2   BRAZIL

In the case of Brazil, the colonial heritage was more of a hindrance than a help to industrialization. Nearly three centuries of an 'outward-oriented' agrarian regime, combined with prohibitions to manufacturing activity and exclusive trade agreements with Portugal, did very little to developed the required capabilities to industrial development. This situation hardly changed with independence in 1822. The rulers of the independent state continued to believe in Brazil's 'agrarian vocation', and embraced unconditionally the free-trade strategy. Hence, the first spurts of manufacturing investment came only at the end of the nineteenth century, driven by the cyclic expansion of the coffee export sector. Despite being mainly market-led, these first steps of the industrialization also benefited from changes in the government policy. These changes, however, did not go beyond a limited increase in tariff protection (mainly for fiscal reasons), and industry had to make do without proper infrastructure, financing, and human capital.

After the Great Depression, the foreign exchange gap and full-employment considerations drove the government towards an IS strategy, which gradually took the contour of a full-fledged IS regime. Industrialization progressed at fast pace, mostly in the light sector. Yet, under the cover of total protection and without incentives to export, quantitative prevailed over qualitative expansion, limiting the build-up of technological capabilities. More to the point, industry continued to be handicapped by timid and ill-conceived intervention in key areas such as infrastructure, finance, S&T and education.

In the mid-1950s, the government finally took up industrialization as an explicit policy objective, promoting a massive move into the heavy industry. As in previous periods, growth was exceptional and the industrial structure was effectively diversified and deepened. Yet, unlike Korea's HCI 'push', Brazil's 'T' plan did not take into account the advantages and limitations of resource endowment, nor the market imperfections affecting competition in industry. Despite falling labour costs and a poor human capital stock, light industry was neglected and several HCI sectors were targeted at the same time. Market failure considerations gave way to a 'magic' solution – 'protected' FDI – which for all externalities it might have generated, ended up damaging LPF growth, and produced an inward-looking, crowded, and inefficient industrial structure. By mid-1960s, the side-effects of this strategy were clear: serious resource misallocation, evidenced by a large labour under-employment; negligible manufactured exports; shortage of both long- and short-term financing; a poor S&T infrastructure; and very limited progress had been made in building up human capital.

In 1964, an outward-oriented, liberal regime was announced. Vowing to get relative prices right, the government implemented policy and institutional reforms aiming at eliminating the trade bias and at providing proper financing for the state and private sectors. These reforms, building on the 'T' Plan IS achievements, sparked off a new period of rapid growth, this time accompanied by the take-off of manufactured exports. Yet, despite the rhetoric and the impressive results, the pattern of the industrialization was not fundamentally changed.

The policy regime continued to largely ignore comparative advantages and firm ownership, offering indiscriminate protection. As a result, improvements in resource allocation were limited, LPF growth continued to be hampered, and the export take-off was only achieved through heavy subsidization. On the financial side, the reforms were successful in providing funds for current activities, but ended up institutionalizing inflationary financing and failed to provide industry with long-term funds. Moreover, the belated attempts to beef up the S&T infrastructure, run against an industrial structure whose fragmentation, inward-orientation and heavy TNC presence, discouraged investments in domestic technological effort.

In 1974, forced by macroeconomic imbalances triggered by the oil shock, the government abandoned its liberal rhetoric, and launched a revamped IS programme in the heavy industry. This time, the strategy was supposed to include neutral trade incentives and a more consistent approach to market failures. Export subsidies were then raised, and local private conglomerates, domestic technological effort and sustainable market structures were singled out for promotion. Despite having considerable success in substituting imports and diversifying exports, it fell well short of correcting key structural weaknesses of Brazil's industrialization.

The incentive regime continued to be largely non-selective, biased towards the internal market, and exports a heavily subsidized and lesser business. Under heavy protection, largely market-led credit allocation and lax investment licensing, the new wave of IS continued to produce 'crowded' and inefficient industrial structures. On the financial side, the key issue of long-term financing remained unsolved. In this environment, investments in technological effort continued to be thin, and LPFs remained weak *vis-à-vis* affiliates and SEs. To add to the gloom, the failure to significantly expand the export-to-GDP ratio and to provide sound financing for both public and private sectors, led to growing macroeconomic imbalances, whose main symptoms were a huge external debt and an ever increasing inflation.

Finally, in the 1980s, the macroeconomic chaos provoked by the interest and second oil shock, combined with a misguided notion that the IS program of the 1970s had 'completed' industrialization, led the government to forsake any attempt to formulate a long-term industrial strategy. In practice, this meant that the previous pattern of intervention lingered on, and given the depth of the BP crisis and the sharp deterioration of the public sector finances, its shortcomings were further aggravated by extra cuts in imports, S&T expenditures, and curbs on long-term financing. Moreover, a succession of failed stabilization plans produced a very unstable macroeconomic environment, which led the industry into a vicious circle of falling output, investments and productivity.

The 1990s has been witnessing renewed government attempts liberalize the policy regime, particularly concerning trade policy. The similarities with Korea of the 1980s are tempting but deceptive. Korea's liberalization was preceded by two decades of a policy regime that combined the right incentives (outward-orientation) with decisive government action to remedy key market failures in the product and factor markets. Moreover, the liberalization was carried out amid a stable macroeconomic environment, and did not destroy the state's capacity to tackle irreparable market imperfections. In Brazil, the antecedents were quite distinct.

As we have seen, more than half a century of inward-looking policies combined with a wholesale, often misguided government intervention has produced a weak local private sector, an overcrowded and inefficient industrial structure, a financial sector that does not properly finance long-term investment, a poorly qualified work force, and a modest S&T infrastructure. Moreover, macroeconomic stability remains elusive, with hyperinflation just next door. So, if in Korea's case liberalization was a logical step, in Brazil, given the scenario described, it is hardly so. Particularly, if by liberalization the government means the minimalist state, limited just to functional interventions. The sort of weaknesses just mentioned above, *require a new pattern of government intervention and not its elimination*. This pattern demands, without doubt, a more open economy, which provides the private sector with the right incentives and the government with the necessary discipline and guidance. It does not require, however, a free-trade, hands-off regime, whose remedy is bound to be worse than the disease.

4.3 CONCLUDING REMARKS

In short, if both Brazil's and Korea's experiences with industrialization confirm the advantages of outward-orientation, they, by no means, constitute an indictment of government intervention. The success achieved by Korea, and some of the positive aspects of Brazil's experience suggest exactly the contrary. Yet, these experiences, particularly that of Brazil, do not give governments a blank cheque either. *Government intervention can be a powerful instrument of industrialization as long as it is used within the discipline of an outward-oriented economy, and with selective and clear objectives of remedying specific market failures.* Within these constraints, and assuming that the capacity to intervene is there, the cost or non-intervention is bound to be higher than any potential government failure.

Notes

*This book was prepared with financial support from the National Research Council (CNPQ), Brazil, and the Central Research Fund of the University of London, both gratefully acknowledged.

1. For recent reviews of the evolution of development thinking see Krugman (1993), Shapiro and Taylor (1990), Colclough (1991), Weiss (1988) and Chenery *et al.* (1986).
2. See, e.g. Balassa (1981a), Chenery *et al.* (1986) and World Bank (1987b:82). The latter, unlike the others, classifies Brazil as moderately outward-oriented. Yet this definition ('overall incentive structure is biased toward production for domestic rather than export markets') does not differ in any significant way from the usual IS definition.
3. The neoclassical view or 'reaction', as others prefer to call it, was pioneered by the work of Little *et al.* (1970), which compared trade and industrialization policies in seven countries: Argentina, Brazil, Mexico, India, Pakistan, the Philippines, and Taiwan. This was followed by works such as Balassa (1975, 1981a, 1989), Little (1982), Krueger (1981, 1984, 1985, 1990a, 1990c) and World Bank (1991) upon which most of this review is based.
4. The potential adverse impact that such exchange rate would have on importables is seen to be neutralized by quantitative restrictions (QRs).
5. The distinction between functional and selective (sector-specific) government intervention is made in World Bank (1987a:101, vol.1)
6. 'The appropriate role for government in a market friendly strategy is to ensure adequate investments in people, provide a competitive climate for enterprise, keep the economy open to international trade and maintain a stable macroeconomy.' (World Bank 1993:10)
7. For a review of the arguments and counter-arguments about the significance of Hong Kong case see Wade (1988, footnote 11) and Krueger (1985:196). There seems to be no doubt, however, that for historic reasons (the *entrepôt* role and the communist revolution in China) market failures in Hong Kong were less pervasive.
8. See Varian (1984, chap.7) for a formal treament.
9. See e.g. Corden (1974).
10. Corden (1974:270) gives the example of two industries A and B that produce complementary products: 'If capital is invested to produce or to expand A with no production or expansion of B, the return on capital would be only 2%. But if B were expanded at the same time the return on capital in A would leap to 10%. Similarly, expansion of B alone would mean a very low return, but expansion in combination with A would yield a 10% return to investment in B.'
11. In an alternative formulation, Stiglitz (1989:198) postulates the learning function as $\ln ct - \ln c_{t+1} = a + b \ln Q_t$. This means that in order

to catch up with incumbents, latecomers have to have a higher *b* coefficient. Stiglitz calls this coefficient 'learning to learn'. One can also add that different industries have different '*b*'s reflecting the degree of technological complexity.

12. Lall (1992b) gives a full account of the technological capabilities necessary for a successful entry in the manufacturing sector, both at firm and country level.

13. See Scherer and Ross (1990) for details. According to the 'two-thirds rule' the output of the processing unit tends within certain limits to be roughly proportional to the volume of the unit, while the investment costs required to construct the unit is more closely proportional to the area of the unit.

14. The incompatibility of economies of scale with marginal cost pricing arises from the fact that under these circumstances firms are operating in the areas of the production function where average exceeds marginal cost, and accordingly, marginal pricing would imply selling products below the average cost. See Helpman and Krugman (1985, chap. 2).

15. Dynamic comparative advantages are understood as being those not directly linked to factor prices differences, but to the dynamic effects of learning. In a sense, they can be called Ricardian advantages because they are related to the existence of different cost functions. See Posner (1961).

16. For a recent review see Helpman (1990).

17. The Mill-Bastable test requires that infant industries not only dispense with protection after a limited period of time, but also that the cumulative discounted cost of protection (production and consumer loss) is lower than the cumulative discounted value of the benefits of protection (difference between the domestic and import costs after the period of maturation). See Corden (1974).

18. Price discrimination involves two pre-conditions. First, that the industry is imperfectly competitive and secondly that the markets are segmented (Krugman and Obstfeld, 1988:146). The existence of increasing returns or differentiated products satisfy the former pre-condition and protection, the latter. Firms, then, will maximise profits when they equal marginal revenue in the two markets. Since $MR = P_i(1 - 1/e_i)$, where MR is marginal revenue, p price and e the price elasticity, the market with the most elastic demand (usually the more competitive export market) have the lowest price. Rodrik (1988a) models a firm which operated in a protected domestic market and has a cost function presenting increasing returns. The model shows that if export prices are higher than the marginal cost, the firm will find it profitable to export. As Rodrik (*op cit.* p.171) explained 'protection allows the firm to make some excess profits at home which can be used to cover its fixed costs; exports then become attractive even if the world price is below the firm's average cost.'

19. See, for instance, Johnson (1965a), Westphal (1982) and Graham (1991).

20. This phenomenon was modelled by Horstmann and Markunsen (1986), who showed that the case for an import tariff/export subsidy based in increasing returns, largely collapses when there is free entry and no

price discrimination. See also Rodrik (1988a, 1988b) for the effects of trade liberalization on a 'crowded' industrial structure.

21. The chart below illustrates a situation where a firm with increasing returns is faced with a segmented market due to protection. D is the demand curve in the domestic market and ($p*$O) the perfectly elastic demand in the export market. In order to maximise profits, the firm equals marginal revenue (MR) in the two markets, producing Oq_1 for the home market at price p, and producing q_1q_2 for exports at $p*$. If, however, there is excessive entry, firms might not be able to reach the level of production Oq_1 for the home market and therefore, the equalization of the marginal revenue in the two markets (i.e. price discrimination) would not be possible. Marginal cost would be higher than the export price.

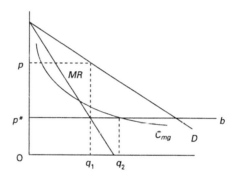

22. As of 1980, the ratio of M_3 to GNP in Korea, Taiwan and Brazil were 0.33, 0.75 and 0.17 respectively (McKinnon 1991:14)

23. The last World Bank Report (1993), adept of the so-called market friendly view, corrects this deficiency.

24. The preparation of this part involved a month trip to Korea (April 1991), hosted by the local Ministry of Trade and Industry. Apart from the collection of data and government documents, the field research also included interviews with government officials and academics.

25. See, for instance, Frank *et al.* (1975), Krueger (1979, 1985), Hong (1979), Mason *et al.* (1980), Westphal and Kim (1982), Balassa (1985, 1991), World Bank (1984a, 1987a).

26. The figures related to the pre-1950 period, unless stated otherwise, were taken from Jones and Sakong (1980, chap 2).

27. All growth rates of this study, unless stated otherwise, were computed in constant prices using the least-squares method, with the regression equation taking the form $\log X_t = a + bt + e_t$, which is the equivalent to the logarithmic transformation of the compound growth rate equation $X_t = X_0(1 + r)^t$ where X is the relevant variable, r is the rate of growth, and t is time (World Bank 1991:273).

28. The country division resulted from the political polarization that followed the Second World War. With the Soviet Union supporting the

left and the US the right, the conflict came to a head in 1947, with the country being divided along the 38th parallel.

29. In 1950, North Korea invaded its southern counterpart provoking the US intervention. The war ended with an armistice in 1953, without a clear winner. For a detailed analysis of the political and economic situation in the 1950s, see Cole and Lyman (1971).

30. As of 1954, 74% of the imports were financed by aid (Krueger 1979:67).

31. During the 1950s, apart from the official rate, importers had to deal with at least three exchange rates according to the foreign exchange source, i.e., exports, government held foreign exchange or foreign aid. As of 1957, the weighted average tariff rate was around 35.4% (Table A.10), with the tariff structure ranging from zero (producer goods) to more than 100% (consumer goods). During 1949-53, imports were controlled by a quota system, replaced in 1953 by a more flexible scheme, based on a positive list of imports. Imports were divided into two categories: automatic approved and restricted. See Jones and Sakong (1980) and Frank *et al.* (1975).

32. The major export incentives introduced up to 1959 were: export-import link scheme whereby exporters were allowed to import popular items normally banned, commodity tax exemption, export financing, export insurance, trade licensing based on export performance, export bonus with preferential exchange rates, payment of direct export subsidies, discount on railroad freight rates, tariff exemption on imports of inputs. See Table A.11.

33. As Suh (1975) pointed out, the full extent of IS in the light industry does not show in the import coefficients (Table A.3) given that the imported component of domestic supply was already very low in 1953, reflecting the foreign exchange shortage. In conjunction with stringent import controls, though, IS reduced the consumer goods share of total imports from 70 to 25% over 1953-60 (Krueger 1979).

34. EPBa. The LDCs' average (GDP) was $150 in 1960 (Little *et al.* 1970:33)

35. As of 1959, 73% of imports were still financed by aid (Krueger 1979:67). See Table A.8 for BP data.

36. Both rates were calculated in current dollars. Total exports from EPBa and manufactured exports from Suh (1975:84 ff.).

37. See, e.g., Krueger (1979).

38. See Frank *et al.* (1975: 36 ff.)

39. The textile industry that spearheaded the 1960s export drive is a case in point. Output grew at 13.4% p.a. over 1954-59, and a considerable industrial capacity was built, which by early 1960s was roughly only half used (Michell 1988 and Amsden 1989).

40. Following Lall (1992a:12) non-economic interventions are 'those not directed at remedying market failures but at bypassing the markets and replacing them with administrative rules that do not seek to promote competitive markets.'

41. See Jones and Sakong (1980, chap. 8)

42. See Amsden (1989, chap. 2) and Cole and Lyman (1971) for details.

43. Korea's market for manufactures in 1960 was $1 billion while India's and Brazil's were $23 billion and $14 billion, respectively (Kuznets

1977:155). The current account deficit in 1960 amounted to 9.3% of GNP (EPBa).

44. There is something of a disagreement over the exact dates of the transitional period. Suh (1975) and Balassa (1985) treat 1960-63 as the transitional period, whereas for Frank *et al.* (1975) it would be 1961-66 and for Krueger (1979), 1960-65.

45. Items not listed in these categories were also subject to restrictions.

46. For a detailed account of the trade and exchange rate reforms of the 1960s see Frank *et al.* (1975, chap. 4), Luedde-Neurath (1986, chap. 2) and Hong (1979, chaps. 3 and 5).

47. Modelled on Japan External Trade Organization (Jetro), Kotra was founded to assist exporters in their relations with foreign buyers. It maintains trade centres abroad to provide information about products and services that Korean exporters and importers buy or sell. It also explores potential markets for Korean exports and provides training for salesmen (Rhee *et al.* 1984:52).

48. See Table A.11. Table A.9 shows that net export subsidies (excluding tariff and indirect tax exemptions and export premium) more than double over 1960-64.

49. At first, the exchange rate was allowed to float. However, after six months, the government introduced a unitary fixed exchange rate system with *ad hoc* adjustments to make up for the domestic inflation. See (Kim, S. K. 1991:57).

50. They included wastage allowance (1965) and end-user-and-related-product schemes (1966). The former, artificially increased the input-coefficients for certain inputs and commodities allowing the excess to be used for domestic production or to be sold with considerable profit in the internal market. The latter, linked the imports of certain popular consumer items and inputs to the export performance of producers of related products (in the case of consumer goods) and end users (in the case of inputs).

51. As of 1965, the main types of export credit available were: short-term export credits via unlimited rediscounts by Bank of Korea; long-term loans for investment on export production; credits for importers of raw materials and equipment for export industries. For details see Frank *et al.* (1975:49) and Hong (1979:57). Table A.21 shows that exports more than trebled their share of total domestic credit over the 1963-72 period.

52. According to this system, exporters could issue letters of credit to local suppliers, who in turn could use them to benefit from all export incentives available.

53. Table A.12 despite not including all subsidies, shows that they clearly increased after 1965. The performance of the export zones Masan (1970) and Iri (1972), despite all the incentives involved, was disappointing. As of 1980, they accounted for only 2.3% of total exports (BNDE 1988a:46). See USITC (1985) for a description of the incentives.

54. The low level of nominal and effective protection would be further confirmed by a comparison with other LDCs. For instance, as of 1969, Argentina's nominal and effective protection for manufacturing was 70 and 112%, respectively, whereas the effective subsidy was 110% (Balassa 1982:36).

no

55. Balassa (1975: 376), e.g., suggests that in an outward-looking regime, the uniform level of protection should be no more than 10–15%, with protection for a very limited number of infant industries at a maximum of 30%.
56. After fruitless endeavours by its predecessors, the practice of formal economic planning was eventually implemented by the military. Despite not being normative, the guidelines of these plans were taken very seriously by the private sector given the government's control over the economy. See Jones and Sakong (1980 chap. 3) and Hong (1979 chap. 3). During the second Five Year Plan, the government introduced a series of promotion laws for heavy industries (machinery, shipbuilding, iron and steel, electronic, and petrochemicals) whereby specific tax-cum-subsidies were assigned to each industry. For sectoral case studies see, e.g., Amsden (1989) for shipbuilding and steel; Jones and Sakong (1980) for machinery; and Enos and Park (1988) for petrochemicals and machinery.
57. The steel industry is a case in point. See Amsden (1989, chap. 12). In 1972, state enterprises accounted for 9% of GDP (a figure similar to India's) with 35% of them in the manufacturing sector (Jones and Sakong, 1980:150)
58. Kuznets (1977) cites data for 1968 from the *Korea Times*, which states that the profit margin on exports was only 2.1% while on domestic sales it averaged 9.5%. There is no reference, however, to how these figures were calculated. For reference on non-profitable exports see also Jones and Sakong (1980, chap. 4), Amsden (1989, chap. 3) and Rhee *et al.* (1984, chap. 3).
59. The use of protection (free trade) technical coefficients in a free trade (protection) context tends to over or underestimate ERPs depending on the elasticity of substitution between primary factors and inputs (the so-called *index number* problem). See Ramaswami and Srinivasan (1971).
60. Westphal and Kim (1982:221). Tariffs were considered prohibitive when imports accounted for less than 10% of domestic supply.
61. The use of AA imports to measure the scope of NTBs tends to underestimate government control because even these imports were affected by instruments such as special laws ('welfare' and security checks), import-source diversification system and government procurement. See Kim, S.K. (1987) and Luedde-Neurath (1986).
62. The government controlled the production of coal, iron, steel, fertilizer and oil refining. See Nam (1985: 203). The existence of constant monitoring of the private sector's prices is mentioned, e.g., by Jung (1989:13) and Amsden (1989:17).
63. In 1972, the share of consumer goods (not including food and beverage) in total imports of the US, West Germany, Brazil and Korea were 15.9, 14.2, 4.2 and 2.9%, respectively (UN, various years).
64. See Table A.8. This view is supported even by Frank *et al.* (1975:54) who state that: 'The most that can be said is that liberalization probably laid the groundwork for continued rapid growth of exports over the following decade and that without those efforts, such phenomenally rapid export growth could not have continued'.

65. The non-pecuniary incentives derived mainly from the government's deliberate politicization of export activity. Major exporters were celebrated as national heroes and given special awards in the so-called *Export Day* (30 November). See Rhee *et al.* (1984:16).
66. As stated in the introduction, price discrimination involves two preconditions. First that industry is imperfectly competitive and secondly that markets are segmented. There seems to be no doubt that the Korean government created these pre-conditions by protecting the domestic market and by stimulating conglomeration through industry licensing and credit rationing.
67. The cotton textile industry is a case in point. Whereas in 1965 labour productivity was 65% below Japan's, by 1972 the gap had been reduced to 48% (Y.B. Kim 1980:280).
68. Cole and Cho (1986:26). Access-to-borrowing ratio is the amount of total bank and foreign loans divided by total assets.
69. For a comparison between Korea's *jaebol* and Japanese *zaibatsu* see Hattori (1989). For a comprehensive analysis of the *jaebols* see, *inter alia*, Jones and Sakong (1980), Jones (1987) and Amsden (1989).
70. Jung (1989:12) was equally brief, but more explicit stating that 'the Korean government is heavily involved in the determination of the firms that can enter certain sectors of the economy. In many industries, private firms have to get approval from the government to start a new business.'
71. For instance, specialists on finance, feasibility studies, training and recruitment, technology contracts, civil construction, equipment procurement and export marketing, to name but a few. For a detailed discussion on how the *Jaebols* took advantage of these economies of scope see Amsden (1989:125 ff.).
72. See, for instance, Frank *et al.* (1975) and Koo (1982, 1985).
73. Full or partial exemption from income tax was granted on income accruing from the provision of technical services, and FDIs enjoyed a full exemption from individual or corporation income tax for the first three years, a 50% reduction in tax for the next five years, a full exemption from customs duties on imported capital goods and no capital gains tax (Frank *et al.* 1975:104).
74. The policy on technology licensing will be examined in the section concerning intervention in the factor markets.
75. Westphal *et al.* (1985) and Westphal *et al.* (1979:372).
76. Koo (1985:200)
77. For recent surveys of the literature, see Weiss (1988) and Helleiner (1989).
78. In 1963, the stock market value as a percentage of GNP was a meagre 2% (Cole and Park, 1983:98).
79. The banks were nationalized on the grounds that they were 'illegally hoarded property' (Cole and Park 1983:57). The financial system consisted of a central bank (Bank of Korea); deposit money banks (DMB) including commercial and specialized banks (among the latter, development banks like the Korea Development Bank, set up in 1954 to supply long-term industrial credit), non-banking financial institutions (NBFI)

and securities markets. The only institutions that remained in private hands were the local banks, created in 1967, and some of the NBFIs whose shares of total deposits and loans until 1980 were too marginal to have had any importance. See *ibid.* for details.

80. At first, all guarantees were issued by the Korean Development Bank and by the Bank of Korea, and had to be formally approved by the National Assembly. From 1966, though, commercial banks began to issue repayment guarantees (according to government approval) without the need for approval by the National Assembly. See Hong (1979:143). Foreign firms were not allowed to officially borrow money abroad (Park 1985:290).

81. These figures tend to overestimate government control insofar as they include local and foreign banks, and NBFIs that were privately owned. Their share of total loans during the period, though, seems to have been insignificant. Local banks had an average of 3.6% of the bank deposits during 1967-72, while the same figure for the foreign banks was 0.6%. As to NBFI, the volume of indirect securities issued in late 1960s was no more than 15% of M_2 (Cole and Park 1983:68 ff.).

82. Gurley, J., Shaw, E. and Patrick, H. (1964) 'Financial Structure of Korea'. Study commissioned by the US Aid Program on the occasion of the 1965 monetary reform, as quoted by Cole and Park (1983:201).

83. The financial-asset-to-GNP ratio fell from 1.0% to 0.8% during 1962-64. After 1965 it began to grow fast reaching 2.1% in 1972. (Cole and Park 1983:26).

84. For instance, the 1962 credit guidelines required financial institutions to give special preference on loans to export and IS activities, together with business that produced daily basic necessities and contributed significantly to growth or employment. 'Nonessential' consumption goods, luxury goods, entertainment and restaurant services were virtually ruled out as borrowers (Hong, 1979:112).

85. See Hong (1979:163), Cole and Park (1983:173) and Hong and Park (1986:167).

86. Hong (1979:204) estimated that the interest subsidy was around 40% of gross fixed capital formation during 1962-66, and about 75% during 1967-71.

87. Long-term loans assumed the form of continuos roll-over of short-term loans. See Cole and Park (1983: chap. 5) and Amsden and Euh (1990:16)

88. See Hong (1979:116).

89. The share of the latter in total export loans over 1970-72 was on average 43% (Hong and Park, 1986:165). Long-term export loans were far from being automatic and had to be approved not only by the banks but also by the 'competent minister' (Hong 1979:124).

90. Yearly average of 54% of total manufacturing credit over 1966-72 (BOKa).

91. Harbison, *et al.* (1970) *Quantitative Analyses of Modernization and Development.* Princeton University. Princeton. As quoted in Amsden (1989:217)

92. Quantity apparently prevailed over quality. See, e.g., McGinn *et al.* (1980:36 ff.) who speak of larger class sizes, of the failure of vocational education to compete against the academic side, and of the lack of

emphasis on science and technology. See also Amsden (1989, chap 9).

93. As Luedde-Neurath (1986:57) pointed out, Korea had some nasty experiences with technology licensing in the early 1960s, notably with cosmetics and pharmaceuticals. 'The contracts were aimed essentially at obtaining the foreign trademark for use in the domestic market, and more importantly involved little more than simple repackaging of semi-finished products by the Korean partner'.

94. See Lee *et al.* (1991) for details.

95. See below. The number of scientists and engineers increased fourfold over 1960-70 (Kim, L. 1989:3).

96. See, e.g., World Bank (1987a, 1993:309), Balassa (1985) and Jung-ho (1990).

97. The third five year plan set two specific targets to the HCI: to increase the HCI share of GNP from 35.2 to 51% over 1971-81, and to increase the HCI share of exports from 19% to 60% over the same period. Steel, chemicals, non-ferrous metals, machinery, automobile, shipbuilding and the electrical-electronic industry were listed as key industries. (Kim, J.H., 1990a:4)

98. See Jung-ho (1990), Kim, J.H. (1990) and World Bank (1987a:38, vol. 1).

99. The import content of exports (imports for exports divided by exports) rose from 5.8 to 48.2% over 1964-73 (Jung-ho 1990:23). Chenery *et al.* (1986:217), using a more refined measure based on input-output data, estimated that the direct and indirect import content of Korean exports increased from 15.8% to 25.5% during 1963-73.

100. In 1973, for instance, Korea introduced 'voluntary' export restraints on textile exports to the US and in 1974, restrictions were extended worldwide with the signing of the Multi-Fiber Agreement. See Jung-ho (1990:20).

101. The chairman of the Planning Council of the HCI Promotion Committee, in an interview with Jung-ho (1990:19), stated that defence needs and economic considerations were given weights of 20 and 80%, respectively.

102. The analysis of the mid-1970s adjustments in trade policy was based mainly on Hong (1979), Westphal (1979) and Yoo (1990).

103. For instance, in 1973, the 50% reduction of corporation and income tax on export earnings was abolished, and interest rates on short-term export credit raised by two percentage points (Table A.13) These credits were also limited to 85% of the export value (it was approximately 95%).

104. Exporters, though, were allowed to pay the tariff in instalments. The exemption criteria were as follows: essentiality for the manufacturing process, *age* of the technology and availability in the domestic market. Although capital goods financed by foreign capital continued to be exempt from import duties, the government established minimum domestic content requirements for large plant facilities and for those built with foreign loans.

105. The decision to fix the exchange rate resulted apparently from an attempt to control inflation and subsidize capital goods imports for the HCIs. The first oil shock in 1973 led to a period of high inflation.

During 1974–75, the WPI grew in average 34.5% p.a., well above the 1965–73 average (8.8%) [BOK (a)].

106. The promotion of trade companies (TC) was aimed at reducing Korean exporters' dependency upon Japanese TCs, lowering transaction costs and facilitating access to international credit. Incentives included immediate access to short-term loans without letters of credit, relaxed controls on inventories of imported inputs and increased allowances of foreign exchange to conduct overseas marketing (Westphal 1979:268). The TCs ended up being no more then a new label for the *jaebols* and in the early 1980s their incentives were abolished (FEER, June 1983). The TCs increased their share of exports from 12 to 50% over 1975-83. In 1990, however this share was reduced to roughly 40% (Rhee *et al.* 1984:148 and FEER 1990, 1 March).

107. During 1973–79 there were three major tariff reforms: 1973, 1977 and 1979. In the first reform, the special tariff (introduced in 1964 to eliminate windfall profits produced by NTBs) was abolished, but more significant reductions in the simple and weighted average rates had to wait for 1977 and 1979 reforms, particularly the latter. However their impact would only be felt in the 1980s, after the HCI *push* was over. See Kim, S. K. (1991:48).

108. In this respect, the case of the Hankook Machine Industrial Co., analysed by Enos and Park (1988, chap. 3), is quite illustrative. This company was taken over by a *jaebol* in 1976, and the new management asked the government to impose a ban against the imports of medium-sized diesel engines, one of the company's most important products. The government agreed with the demand but asked in exchange the right to control the price of the product. By 1978 the whole domestic market for the product was being supplied by Daewoo.

109. See Hong (1979:83), World Bank (1987a:42, vol. 1) and Enos and Park (1988:36).

110. As with Westphal and Kim's (1982), Nam and Young's estimates also used direct price comparisons. Moreover, as Nam acknowledged, the estimates for 1978 are even more problematic because of the pervasive price controls imposed in 1977. The divergences between Young and Nam's results, reinforce our doubts about the accuracy of the instrument.

111. As pointed out before, these figures underestimate the *jaebol* bias since smaller subsidiaries were included among the SMF.

112. This rapid expansion seems to be caused by the diversion of Japanese investment from Taiwan to Korea, following Japan's normalization of diplomatic relations with mainland China (Kim, Il-Hwan 1987:4).

113. See Koo (1985:178). Moreover, restrictions on capital repatriation were also introduced, limiting its withdrawal to two years after the initial investment, and restricting the annual repatriation to less than 20% of total investment (Bark 1989:16)

114. These figures, though, appear to have been strongly affected by the 1972–73 surge. For the sake of international comparison, during 1977–79, the stock of FDI as a percentage of GNP was 4.7% for Argentina, 6.4% for Brazil, 5.6% for Mexico and 3.2% for Korea (Westphal *et al.* 1985:191).

115. The stabilization was prompted by Korea's rapid increase in foreign borrowing during 1968-69, reflecting the gap between the foreign and domestic interest rates (Table A.13). See Cole and Park (1983) and Amsden (1987).
116. See Cole and Park (1983:158).
117. The NFI was set up to finance both fixed and working capital mostly of HCIs. During 1974–79, roughly 60% of the NFI loans were to HCIs constituting 3 to 4.5% of total domestic credit (World Bank 1987a:111, vol. 2).
118. Together with Taiwan, Singapore and Hong-Kong. See Table A.1 and Lall (1991).
119. MOST (1988) and Lee *et al.* (1991). The specialized institutes included shipbuilding, marine resources, electronics, telecommunications, machinery and metals, chemicals and standards. The incentives of the Technology Development Promotion Law included tax exemption for R&D funds and special depreciation for R&D equipment.
120. For the sake of comparison, the R&D share of sales in Brazil in 1978 was less than 0.2% (Braga and Matesco 1986) while in 1981 Korea it was 0.7%.
121. Technology licensing outlays over 1967–71 were $ 16.3 million. It then shot up to $96.5 million over 1972–76, and during 1977–80 reached $ 344.2 million (Kim and Lee 1990:94). Yet, Korea's royalty payments remained well below other NICs such as Mexico and Brazil. During 1977–79, Korea's payments for disembodied technology were only 0.17% of GNP, while Brazil's and Mexico's were 0.33% and 0.23%, respectively (Westphal *et al.* 1985:191).
122. See Enos and Park (1988:36).
123. See World Bank (1987a:45, vol. 1)
124. See, e.g. Amsden (1989), Michell (1988) and Westphal (1990). Kim, J.H. (1990a:13) draws attention to the fact that most of the HCI investment was carried out in a short span of time (1977–78), placing unnecessary strain on the economy. On a sectoral level, the heavy machinery industry is one of the most cited government's HCI 'mistakes', leading to overcapacity and uncompetitive prices. See World Bank (1987a:46), Enos and Park (1988) and FEER (1981:44, June 5).
125. For details of the macroeconomic performance see Amsden (1987).
126. In 1979, Brazil' HCI import ratio was 8.4% against 23.8% in 1980 Korea (Tables A.4 and A.32).
127. The measures were wage per worker and value-added per worker.
128. Westphal (1979:271). Moreover, Won-Am Park states that even though the won, on a PPP basis, was overvalued against the US dollar throughout the whole 1963–79 period, the degree of overvaluation was higher during 1963-72 than afterwards ('Exchange Rates, Wages, and Productivity in Korea', *The Korean Economic Review*, vol. 2, 1987, p. 19 quoted in Mihn 1988:31).
129. They were 41.0 and 40.8%, respectively (World Bank 1987a:116, vol. II). Moreover, as Hong (1979:71) argued, the fact that the HCI investments were carried out by the same entrepreneurs who had been engaged in light manufacturing, casts doubt over the 'starvation' argument.

130. The profitability of the light industry (the ratio of profits minus financial expenses over capital stock) fell from 9.9% to 3.8% over 1973-79. (World Bank, 1987a: 120, vol. II).
131. World Bank (1991) and Chang (1989:144). The light industry was the most affected by import restrictions. The textile and clothing, e.g., had their share of restricted exports increased from the already high 48% in 1976 to 51% in 1981.
132. Overall, Korea's share of world manufacturing exports rose from 0.8 to 1.45% over 1975–80 (UN ITSY, HIT). Fujita and James (1989), using the source-of-growth methodology, showed that during 1973-80, the export expansion effect in the growth of the HCI's output was second only to domestic demand expansion effect.
133. For a formal and stylized model of import protection as export-promotion see Krugman (1984a).
134. See Brander (1986).
135. This seems to have been particularly the case of steel and shipbuilding. See Amsden (1989: chaps. 11 and 12). Jung-ho (1990:28), quoting a document from the HCI Promotion Committee, stated that 'plants were to be of "international scale" to reap the economies of scale that were important in the heavy and chemical industries. It was considered desirable to import the cutting edge technologies rather than the "appropriate" technology from abroad.'
136. This is illustrated by a comparison with the US shown below (USA=100):

Manufacturing	1970	1972	1976	1977	1978	1979	1980	1982	1984
Capital utilization	83.2	78.6	90.4	94.7	99.0	91.6	87.0	98.7	100.0

Source: Table A.24 and OECD (1989).

137. Rate of return is defined as operating profit plus non-operating income minus financial expenses, over total assets. BOK (b) and EPB (b).
138. Bai (1982:131) shows that the labour supply elasticity declined significantly in the mid-seventies while the job opening-applicant ratio surged. The labour share of value-added also started to grow rapidly after 1975 rising from 23% to 32% in 1979 (EPB (b)).
139. Despite the wage hike, Korea's wage rate in the early 1980s was still just a fraction of those of the developed countries and therefore still a significant edge in the technologically mature capital-intensive industries. For instance, the 1980 hourly compensation rate in the steel industry was only 9.2% of that of the US (UNIDO 1988). Dornbusch and Park (1987) use a Ricardian model with a continuum of goods to develop this point.
140. EPB (a).
141. See Table A2. For details of the macroeconomic crisis see Amsden (1987), Jung-ho (1990) and Kim, S. K. (1991).
142. Quoted by Balassa (1991:51).
143. The first attempt to liberalize trade happened in 1978, as part of an anti-inflationary policy. Even though it led to a noticeable reduction on

NTBs and tariffs, the Korean economy began the 1980s, still highly protected from imports. In 1982, nearly 74% of manufactured imports were under NTBs, and 74% of the AA items were raw materials (Table A.14). The simple average tariff, 24.7% (Table A.10), was still well above the 6% OECD average. Moreover, ERP estimates show a substantial increase over 1978–82 (Table 6). See Kim, S. K. (1991).

144. The stabilization policies involved, first, a 17% devaluation associated with a wage squeeze. Second, interest rates were raised, access to domestic and foreign credit restricted and the budget deficit virtually eliminated. These measures led to a rapid drop in inflation (WPI) which fell to 0.2% in 1983. In addition, boosted by the devaluation and by a strong import demand in the US, exports resumed high growth while imports faltered, improving the current account condition (Table A.8). See Amsden (1987).

145. Moreover, the programme projected a reduction in the dispersion of the tariff rates, bringing, in 1988, the overall range of 0–150% down to compressed sub-ranges of 5–10% for raw material, 20% for intermediate products and capital goods, and 20–30% for consumer goods. IMF (1984:300).

146. World Bank (1987a:71, vol. I) and Rhee (1987). The new technology industries comprise machine parts, general machinery, electrical machinery and electronic materials.

147. According to Kim's (1991) estimates shown in Table A.12, net export subsidies were eliminated in 1983. However, this tends to be misleading since the interest rate subsidy was calculated using the commercial banks' general loan rate, which, notwithstanding the liberalization, was still controlled by the government.

148. Young (1987, 1989) and (USITC 1985). As of April 1989, the major tax free reserves were for overseas market development, price fluctuations and export goods inventory. As for long-term credits, they are provided by the Korea Eximbank for post-shipment financing or imports of producer goods, usually at an interest rate below that of the international market. Finally, exporters also continued to benefit from institutions like KOTRA and Korea Traders association.

149. According to this system, the exchange rate is set each day based in the middle rate prevailing in the interbank market in the previous day within 'certain' limits. The liberal nature of this new scheme seems to be disputable. As the *Financial Times* (1990:11) put it, 'giving the overwhelming power of the Bank of Korea in the tiny foreign exchange market – average turnover US$ 200 million – claims that they can no longer influence the exchange rate are being treated with scepticism at home and abroad.'

150. To qualify for the AA system, the project had to have a foreign equity share of less than 50%, amount up to US$ 3 million, and not require tax exemptions.

151. See Il-Hwan Kim (1987:8) for incentive details. In March 1991, a Notification System was implemented and FDI incentives were substantially reduced. This new system is supposed to automatically approve projects in the liberalised sectors, where foreign ownership is less than 50%. In

these cases, the foreign investors 'will be able to start operations by simply notifying the contents of their investment to the authorities concerned.' (MOF 1991:7) On portfolio investment, the government began in 1981 to open the market to foreign investors through domestic investment trusts. Direct dealing by foreigners, though, was postponed to the first half of the 1990s. Exchange controls only began to be relaxed as late as 1987, but were tightened in 1989 when the current account surplus, which arose in 1986, began to wither away. See Amsden and Euh (1990) and BOK (1985:8).

152. See FEER (1985, 12 December and 1988, 29 September) and World Bank (1987a, vol. I: 93).

153. The selected strategic industries were naphtha cracking, iron and steel, machinery, electronics shipbuilding and aviation industry. As of 1984, the functional incentives included accelerated depreciation, preferential fiscal treatment of reserves for various purposes and losses, and exemption or reduction of income taxes. The activities eligible included SMF investment, R&D and overseas investment or other overseas operations (Koo 1984:36).

154. Kim, J. H. (1989:35). The decisions to intervene in a specific sector were now to be made not only by government ministries but also by 21 new advisory councils under the Ministry of Trade and Industry (MTI) aegis, made up of entrepreneurs, academics and public researchers (World Bank 1987a, vol. I).

155. For details see, e.g. BOK (1985), Cole and Cho (1986) and Kang (1989).

156. In 1980, the stock market as a percentage of GNP was a meagre 7%. It started then to grow steadily reaching 14,3% in 1986, and jumping to 72.5% in 1989. In 1984, the same figure for Japan was 48.0% (Amsden and Euh, 1990, and World Bank, 1987a:111, vol. I).

157. The preferential tax treatment for R&D (i.e. tax credit or exemption, tariff exemption and preferential depreciation) was extended to foreign engineer's wages, corporation tax of research institutes, reserve funds for technology development, research facility investments, job training expenses, imports of R&D equipment, royalties from technology sales and venture business. The financial incentives included preferential loans from the KDB and Small and Medium Industry Bank, direct subsidies from special government funds, as well as loans and equity investments from venture capital companies set up by the government (Rhee 1987).

158. Other measures included the set up of 'science towns' (4 were planned until the year 2000) to take advantage of externalities associated with localization, and a "Long Range Plan of Science and Technology towards the 2000's", which, *inter alia*, envisage R&D expenditures at 3% of GNP. See MOST (1988).

159. Kim, L. (1989:5). Since June 1988, screened contracts have been those with a duration over 3 years and with royalties exceeding $100.000 or 2% of sales. Tax exemptions were limited to 'high tech' industries (MOST 1988:41).

160. Table A.8 and World Bank (1991:204). Korea's share of world manufactured exports rose from 1.4 to 2.5% over 1980–87 (UN ITSY, HIT).

161. The figure for textile and leather was heavily influenced by the lack of

raw material for the leather industry. For instance, in 1983, the import penetration ratios for textile, apparel and leather products were 19%, 4%, and 58%, respectively.

162. Information at a more disaggregated level is scarce, but the few existent studies also suggest that, at least until 1985, the adjustment cost was limited. See Young (1986:55) and Rhee (1987:65).

163. For the 1970–79 period, the average elasticity (arithmetical mean) was 1.26 and varied between 0.95 and 1.35, whereas for 1980–88 the average was 0.74 and the range 0.64–0.83. The regression equations for the two periods were,

(1) $M = -0.99 + 0.33$ GNP (2) $M = 7.86 + 0.25$ GNP
    (-0.84) (13.4) (5.10) (16.5)
    $R^2 = 0.96$ $R^2 = 0.98$

whereas M is imports and GNP is the gross national product both at 1985 US dollars.

164. Rhee's (1987) and Yoo's (1990) analyses follow along these lines.

165. These points are amazingly underpinned by later statements of the Korean government. For instance, in 1989, the deputy prime minister described the economic policy of the 1960s and 1970s as follow: 'The economic policy regime of those days has also given rise to a *mercantilist trade policy*. Exports were promoted, and imports restricted, to save scarce foreign exchange and to promote import substitution. Imports were large, not due to import liberalization, but rather because they were the necessary minimum; importing to encourage market competition or to increase consumer welfare have only recently become considerations.' EPB (1989b: 4). Italics are ours.

166. Import liberalization was accompanied by a build-up of 'contingency' safeguards. The government added a new 'adjustment' tariff (up to 100% of the legal tariff) to the already existent arsenal of 'emergency' tariffs, import quotas, import surveillance, special laws, anti-dumping and countervailing duties. See World Bank (1987a:71, vol. I) and Young (1987:52) for details.

167. In the case of computers, for instance, the government introduced in 1982 a presidential order placing all computer related imports under strict MTI and Electronics Industry Association supervision. This regulation effectively prohibited imports of mini, micro and personal computers, together with its peripherals and parts. The imports of 'mainframes' were permitted only if accompanied by technology transfer. Moreover, the regulation gave MOST the power to require governmental agencies to purchase Korean-made computers and peripherals where appropriate. The imports of computers were finally liberalised in 1988, but the government procurement scheme remained in place. The rest of the sectors mentioned were all granted with similar legislation. See, e.g. Chung (1986), Allgeier (1988) and Evans and Tigre (1989).

168. See MTI (1990b) and Young (1988, 1989) for details of the Korea–US trade relations. In addition to NTB removal, an administrative reform was carried out in 1987, that was supposed, *inter alia*, to make contin-

gency protection less restrictive. Both import surveillance and contingency measures were placed under the control of commissions sponsored by the MTI and the MOF, respectively. See IMF (1988:301) and Young (1987, 1989).

169. See Tables A.7 and A.8.

170. FEER (1990, 19 July), for instance reports two incidents occurred during 1990, involving US-made refrigerators and cars. It is worth noting that up to 1989, the reforms did little to establish a more competitive market in foreign trading, wholesale and retailing. Until that year, trade licenses were conditional on export performance and were restricted to foreign companies that had production facilities in Korea. In addition, only nine out of 66 retail and wholesale business categories were open to foreign investors. See EPB (1989a).

171. The major industries involved in the 1980-83 restructuring programme were: heavy power-generating equipment (reduction in the number of producers); motor vehicles (mergers and market segmentation); shipbuilding (market segmentation); fertilizers (mergers and capacity reduction); electronic exchange (reduction in the number of producers); smelting of copper (mergers); shipping (mergers and capacity reduction). See, e.g., World Bank (1987a, vol. I), Rhee (1987) and FEER (1981, 5 June).

172. The World Bank (1987a:106, vol. 1), e.g. stated that the IDL lacked, 'A mechanism for explicitly picking winners.'

173. The sectors selected were textile and fabrics, ferro-alloys, dying and fertiliser, as sunset industries; and automobiles, diesel engines, heavy electrical equipment and heavy construction equipment as the sunrise ones (Kim, J. H. 1989). In an interview with FEER (4 August 1988), Korea's finance minister stated that between 1986–87, the government bailed-out 78 bankrupt companies, with the government and commercial banks writing-off US$1.36 billion in debts, and rescheduling, for periods as long as 30 years, another US$8.4 billion.

174. A 1988 EPB survey revealed market entry regulations in 84 industries, price controls in 26, equipment regulations in 10 and quantity regulations in 15 (PCRER, 1988: 75).

175. Lee *et al.* (1986) and PCRER (1988). The data for exports present a similar trend, with the share of the five largest groups increasing from 24% to 27% during 1977–85, despite the two-digit export growth (FEER 29 September 1988).

176. FEER (1990, 1 March). This indicator cannot be taken as an absolute measure of economic concentration because of the double-counting problem. Further evidence of the increase in concentration is the 1988 presidential report that emphasized that, 'Conglomerates dominate entire markets not only for materials, manufacturing, and assembly but also for sales, trade, finance, and real estate by taking advantage of superior financing ability and information resources.' PCRER (1988:72).

177. For example, as of 1985, 100% foreign owned electronics manufacturers were obliged to export at least 50% of their production (USITC 1985), whereas up to January 1990, sectors like excavators, heavy electrical equipment, diesel engines, optical fibres and electronic switching systems were subject to local equity participation requirements (MTI 1990b).

Korean companies that were authorized to sell foreign goods or use licensed trade marks were also subject to export requirements. See USITC (1985). These and other restrictions were somewhat relaxed in the beginning of the 1990s, under the 'Super 301 Accords' with the US.

178. EPB (1989a:23). As if the regulations were not enough, foreign investors also had to face an unsympathetic bureaucracy very keen on tax audits on foreign companies. See *Financial Times* (1990, 16 May) and FEER (1989, 15 June).

179. In December 1988, the ceiling on most lending and deposit rates for instruments with maturities of more than two years were lifted. However, restrictions on short-term deposits remained (*Financial Times* 1990, 16 May).

180. The government direct and indirect control over loanable funds (ratio of deposits at commercial banks and development institutions to total deposits) was 71% in 1980, 70.2% in 1985 and 42% in 1989 (BOK (c)). Table A.21, in turn, shows that as of 1986, the share of policy loans was still 45%.

181. KDI (1991:24). As of 1986, the gap concerning the curb market rates was also sizeable, amounting to 14.3% in real terms (Table A.13).

182. BOK (1985:25), for instance, states that '. . .most of insurance companies, and large short-term credit companies are owned or controlled by the industrial groups'. Despite regulations that limited the maximum ownership of any single shareholder to 8% of the total capital, not even the commercial banks seem to have escaped from *jaebol* dominance. As of 1986, the top 10 *jaebols* held together between 22.4% to 56.5% of each commercial bank's capital. Individual holdings in certain cases were as high as 23.8%. See World Bank (1987a:92, vol. I)

183. In 1991, the government was again using its control over banks to force the *jaebols* to reduce the scope of their business and increase therefore the advantages of specialization. See *Korea Economic Journal* (1991, 29 April).

184. During 1982-88, the government invested $311 million in National R&D projects against $218 million for the private sector. As of September 1989, the MTI was about to set-up a new five-year technology development project that would include microelectronics, machine tools, robotics, aerospace, new materials, fine chemicals, laser and biotechnology (FEER 1989, 28 Sept.). In an interview to *Korea Trade & Business* (November 1989), the director of MTI Import Policy Division explained why the government was targeting technology-intensive industries. 'The comparative advantage of the industries among the Asian newly industrialised economies will be shifted from textile, shipbuilding and iron & steel, to knowledge-intensive industries such as automobile, machinery and electronics in the 1990s. On the other hand, advanced countries will keep the comparative advantage in areas such as biotechnology and aerospace.'

185. The preparation of this part involved a month trip to Brazil (September 1991) which included the collection of data, government documents and interviews with academics and government officials.

186. Wells (1987:96).

187. A 1907 industrial inquire gave the textile, food, beverage and apparel sectors the combined share of 62%. See IBGE (1990).
188. For a through review see Suzigan (1984: chap. 1). See also Barros and Versiani (1977).
189. The first republic was proclaimed in 1889, overthrowing the monarchy which had ruled since the independence from Portugal in 1822. One of the republicans aims was to 'free' the economy from the excessive regulations of the monarchical era. See, e.g., Topik (1980).
190. See Versiani (1979) on the textile-cotton industry, and Suzigan (1984: chapters 3 and 4) on the other industries. In 1916, the United States Federal Trade Commission found that Brazil had the highest tariff in the Western Hemisphere (Topik 1980:606). This seems to confirm M. J. Muller's 1913 report on custom tariffs (quoted in Villela and Suzigan 1977:284) which put Brazil actual tariffs in the footwear, beverage (beer) and textile (cotton cloth printed) industries in 155.4, 837.5 and 127%, respectively. The same figures for the Germany were 13.4, 18.7 and 20%, respectively.
191. See Topik (1980) and Villela and Suzigan (1977) for details.
192. During 1893-1932, customs revenues accounted in average for 52% of the government revenue (Machado 1990:79). Tariffs were fixed on an *ad-valorem* basis, but were levied not on the market price of the imports but on an 'official' price fixed by the government, denominated in the local currency. As these prices were not regularly adjusted to make up for inflation or changes in international import prices and exchange rate, the actual rates tended to fluctuate as if they were specific. In 1890, the government introduced a 'gold-quota' whereby 15% of the tariff was fixed in terms of gold. This was later increased to 25%, reducing but not eliminating the exchange-rate-related instability of the customs revenues. See Villela and Suzigan: (1977: appendix E).
193. The tariff exemptions for capital goods and the 'law of similar' are cases in point. The former is said to have lacked any clear criteria (being an easy prey to rent-seekers), and to be limited in scope for fiscal reasons (tariffs were the main source of government revenue). The latter is believed to have been strictly enforced only in the 1950s.
194. According to Clark, W. (1910) 'Cotton Goods in Latin America, Part II'. Department of Commerce Special Agents Ser. n°36. 1910, quoted in Fishlow (1972:18), labour productivity in the Brazilian textile-cotton industry was in 1910 between 50 to 30% below that of the US, and even somewhat below that of the American industry 50 years earlier.
195. The last trade agreement expired in 1844. According to this agreement, the tariff rates on English products could not exceed 15%. See Machado (1990) for details.
196. See Tavares (1973) and Villela and Suzigan (1977) for details. During 1914-1945, Banco do Brazil accounted for approximately 30 to 40% of total loans (Goldsmith 1986:171).
197. A notable exception was the Institute for Technological Research at the São Paulo Polytechnic School which according to Leff (1968:19) '*played an important role in promoting the early technical development of this [capital goods] and other São Paulo industries.*'

198. The expansionary policies took the form of a coffee-support programme
     aimed at sustaining international coffee prices, partially financed by fiscal
     deficits and related domestic credit expansion. The innovation, though,
     was not the coffee support programme, which had been in place since
     1906, but the way it was financed. Up to the Great Depression, this
     programme was financed by foreign loans. However, the shortage of
     foreign funds provoked by the crisis led the government to resort to
     export taxes and domestic credit expansion, a solution which was dubbed
     proto-Keynesian by some. For details of the coffee support programme
     and its effects see Furtado (1963) and Villela and Suzigan (1977).
199. During 1939-53, the official exchange rate remained virtually constant
     despite the fact that domestic prices had grown at an annual average
     rate of 18.6%, a rate more than double that of the US.
200. A minimum premium was set for each category of the auction, which
     varied in accordance to the goods perceived priority. Capital and inter-
     mediary goods had the lowest premium while consumer goods the highest.
     As for exports, a system of bonuses was used to obtain product-speci-
     fic exchange-rates. All financial transaction were carried out in a 'free'
     exchange rate market. See Bersgman (1970), and Malan *et al.* (1980).
201. See Furtado (1963) and Fishlow (1972).
202. See Bhagwati (1965) and Helpman and Krugman (1989: chap. 3).
203. During 1950–55, manufactured exports nominally decreased (Table A.31),
     while manufacturing output has increased 65% in real terms (IBGE 1990).
204. Some authors try to justify the exchange-rate policies of the period ar-
     guing that the importance of coffee as a source of foreign exchange,
     the price-inelasticity of its demand and the problems affecting interna-
     tional trade (e.g. inconvertibility of European currencies) would have
     made an exchange-rate devaluation ineffective as a means of increasing
     export earnings. The alternative of a coffee-export-tax-cum-devaluation,
     which would have made more economic sense, is ruled out because it
     would have been politically unacceptable (see e.g. Malan *et al.* 1980:
     chap. 3 and Malan and Bonelli 1990). Even though these points seem
     to be generally correct, their importance appears to have been exagger-
     ated. A fixed-exchange rate seemed to have been as unpopular with
     coffee-growers as perhaps an export tax would have been. Moreover,
     the fact that Brazil's export performance during 1950–60 (–0.2% of
     annual average growth) was well below that of the developing countries
     (2.4%) (UNCTAD 1990) suggests that there was room for export growth.
205. The external debt which had been stable around US$ 600 million in the
     second half of the 1940s, shot up to US$ 1445 billion in 1955 (IBGE
     1990).
206. See Malan *et al.* (1980, chap 5) for details. Public sector expenditures
     as a percentage of GNP increased from 12.5% in 1920 to 19.2% in
     1941 (Trebat 1983:15).
207. During 1941–45 the government built Latin America first fully inte-
     grated steel mill (Cia Siderúrgica Nacional), established the Vale do
     Rio Doce Co. to mine and export iron ore, set up a factory to produce
     barilla and caustic soda (Cia. Alcalis), and, in its only venture out of
     the intermediary good sector, started to assemble aeroplanes engines

and trucks (Fabrica Nacional de Motores). The share of this state enterprises investment in the total capital formation, though, was only 3% during 1947–55. See Table A.34.

208. In 1953, the government set up the public enterprise Petrobras which was given the monopoly for research, exploitation, refining and transport of oil. In 1954, the government sent a bill to the congress proposing a similar enterprise for the electric power sector (Eletrobras). This, company, however, would only be approved in 1962.

209. These measures were inspired by the reports of two joint Brazil–US technical commissions (1948, 1949), set up to look into Brazil's development problems. Both reports maintained that the poor infrastructure was a major bottleneck to be overcome. See Malan *et al.* (1980). Tendler (1968) gives an accurate account of the acute power supply problems facing the industry in the post-war period.

210. The M2/GDP ratio increased from 28.3% to 34% during 1930–45 but fell to 19.2% in 1955 responding to the acceleration of the inflation in the post-war period (Goldsmith 1986:245).

211. The most important specialised institutes set up during this period were an aerospace engineering training institute (ITA) in 1946, and an aerospace research centre (CTA) in 1954 which would later provide the human capital basis for the internationally successful Brazilian aircraft industry.

212. SENAI was established in 1942, financed by a pay-roll tax on industrial firms with 500 or more employees. See World Bank (1979).

213. The plan also envisaged the construction of the new capital, Brasilia. The total proposed investment had 43.4% going for energy, 29.6% for transport, 3.2% for food production and distribution, 3.4% for education and 20.4% for the heavy industry. As to the latter, the most important targeted sectors were steel, cement, automobile, shipbuilding, and machinery. See Lessa (1982:35).

214. The executive groups were made up of private sector and government representatives of the various agencies providing finance and incentives for the relevant sector. They had the task of overseeing the implementation of the sectoral programmes, and of suggesting fiscal and financial incentives. See Lessa (1982) for details.

215. Sochaczewski and Orenstein (1990:178).

216. Exports continued to have product-specific exchange rates up to 1959, when their proceeds were allowed to be sold on the free market.

217. On the 1950s trade policies see Bersgman (1970) and Doellinger *et al.* (1977).

218. One estimate put tariffs for the goods in the general category up to about 80% plus 15% of average premium, and for the ones in the special category, tariffs ranging up to 150% plus a premium of 100 to 200% (Bergsman 1970:33).

219. Until 1953 restrictions to foreign capital were limited to investments in infrastructure and in the financial sector, but even there they were not strictly enforced. There were attempts to control and limit remittances in 1946 and 1952 but only survived for a brief period. For details see Abreu (1990:101) and Guimarães *et al.* (1982: Appendix A).

220. As the exchange rates for imports were generally higher than the 'free' market rate, avoidance of the foreign exchange transaction was a substantial subsidy. In addition, when these imports were financed, the debt could be also serviced at a preferential exchange rate.

221. Malan and Bonelli (1990:37). Imports without foreign exchange cover rose from 8% of total imports in 1955 to 34% in 1958 (Doellinger *et al.* 1977:34ff). As Table A.37 shows, during the period of the plan, FDI amounted to roughly 30% of the manufacturing investment. In 1960, 90% of the FDI was invested in manufacturing of which 24% in the automobile sector, 10% in chemicals, 9% in food and 8% in machinery (Villela and Baer 1980:20).

222. During 1956–61, 65% of SEs' investments were in infrastructure (energy, transport and telecommunication) and 17% in the steel industry. The rest was scattered in other manufacturing sectors, mining, financing (Werneck 1969:99).

223. Boletim SUMOC various years.

224. See Baer (1969).

225. The Treasury deficit rose from 1.2% of GDP in 1955 to 5.1% in 1962 (Boletim SUMOC). During 1950–64, Brazil's financial system had a very peculiar structure, with the monetary authorities being composed of three institutions: (a) SUMOC, the normative and controlling institution, which performed usual tasks of a traditional central bank, except for the fact that the execution of its policies was carried out by the BB; (b) the BB, which acted simultaneously as SUMOC executive agent, as the treasury financial agent, and as major commercial bank; finally, (c) the Treasury, responsible for currency issues. As the BB used to make no distinction between its various operations, it had no limits to expand its loans, which had the same effect of a primary expansion of the money supply. See Sochaczewski (1980) for details.

226. Boletim SUMOC, various years. The financial sector continued to shrank with the financial-asset-to-GDP ratio falling from 45% in 1956 to 34% in 1964 (Goldsmith 1986:245). At the end of the 1950s, the increasingly restricted supply of finance by the institutionalized banking system led to the appearance of a curb market, which in 1963/64 reached about 5% of total bank credit. See Sochaczewski (1980, chap. 6) for details.

227. From an 'end-use' perspective, the capital goods sector almost doubled its share of the manufacturing output, while durable and intermediate goods also expanded their participation at the expense of non-durable consumer goods (Table A.30).

228. Wells (1987:96). One could also argue that low-labour absorption resulted from subsidies to capital via the exchange-rate mechanism, and from a minimum wage legislation implemented in 1943. Yet, as Clements (1988:31) put it, there is no conclusive econometric evidence regarding the magnitude of capital–labour elasticity of substitution, and most of the qualitative evidence seems support the view that the possibilities of factor-substitution are, and were, limited, particularly the heavy industry.

229. In fact, between 1956 and the end of the 1960s, the already poor S&T infrastructure fell into decline because of lack of government support.

See Bielschowsky (1978). As to education, progress continued to be sluggish (Table A.35), despite some success in the areas of technical and vocational training, mainly through the SENAI. Leff (1968:61), commenting on the capital goods industry in 1963 argued that 'the supply of engineers has not keep pace with the demands of the labour market principally because of insufficient expansion of the educational system.'

230. The automobile industry is a case in point. Despite the fact that investment was, to a certain extent regulated by the GEIA (Executive Group for the Automobile Industry) no less than 8 firms were assembling passenger cars (including pick-ups) in 1962 (see Bergsman 1970). According to Suzigan (1978:47) the industry's capacity utilization until 1967/68 was less than 50%. Leff (1968:29) also reports widespread excess capacity in the capital goods industry in the beginning of the 1960s.

231. As Malan and Bonelli (1990:38) pointed out, in 1960, Brazil was already the largest international debtor among LDCs (US$3.9 billion), with 70% of the debt scheduled to be paid in the following three years. As to inflation, GDP deflator reached 50% in 1962 and 90% in 1964.

232. The real GDP annual growth rate fell from 8.5% in 1961 to 0.6% in 1963. For details of the economic policy over the 1961–64 period see Abreu (1990).

233. See footnote 57. BB, though, retained its double role as the government's financial agent and major commercial bank, continuing to compromise the transparency of governments accounts.

234. For details, see Sochaczewski (1980) and World Bank (1984a). Although positive, interest rates continued to be controlled by the government until 1974.

235. World Bank (1984a:11). Real savings though increased only slightly, from 16% (1956–64) to 18% (1965–73) (IBGE 1990). The total stock market value, as percentage of GDP, increased from 3% in 1968 to 41% in 1971 (Goldsmith 1986:422).

236. A less restrictive version of the law of similar remained in place, with the nature of the prohibition changed from a total ban on import of goods produced domestically, to a veto on the concession of government incentives to these imports.

237. The indirect tax exemption involved the IPI (federal tax on industrial products), and the ICM (state turnover tax). Both are value-added taxes, and the former varies according to the type of product. The fiscal subsidies took the form of a tax credit equivalent to a percentage of the IPI and ICM exempted. These incentives were limited to manufactured and semi-manufactured goods. For details see, e.g., Doellinger *et al.* (1974) and Tyler (1976). Export credits were given mainly to pre-shipment activities, for a maximum of one year, and were supplied by the commercial banks that had access to unlimited rediscounts at the Central Bank. See Baumann and Braga (1985).

238. The 1967 tariff reform almost halved legal tariffs for most manufactured sectors. However, BP difficulties in 1968 led to a revision of this reform, which ended up moving tariff rates upward again, although to levels below to those of 1966 (Table A.41). Importers were also required

to make a pre-payment for goods with tariff above 50%. See Doellinger *et al.* (1977) for details.

239. Table A.33 shows that, in 1972, the share of consumer goods in total imports remained negligible, whereas that of capital goods increased 61%. Yet, even in this sector, the growth in imports seem to have been mainly non-competitive, since production grew 13% p.a. over the period, and the import ratio has never gone beyond 28%, a level below the 32% achieved at the end of the 'T' Plan. See Bergsman (1970) for the pre-1964 period and Bonelli and Façanha (1978) for post-1965 data. See also Coes (1991) for a detailed account of the 1967–73 trade reforms.

240. A restriction to intra-firm royalty payments remained, but not for 'technical assistance'. In addition the investment registration system made no allowance for inflation in the country of origin. See Guimarães *et al.* (1982) for details.

241. Until 1970, these incentives included: exemption from indirect and import taxes for capital goods imports, access to subsidized credit from state banks such as BNDE, and accelerated depreciation for income tax purposes to buyers of local capital goods. After 1970, the latter were granted exemption from indirect taxes and fiscal credit. See Suzigan (1978). During 1969–74, the projects which received CDI incentives averaged 82% of the total manufacturing investment (Central Bank Annual Reports).

242. 'Plano Estratégico de Desenvolvimento'. Presidência da República. 1968.

243. INPI imposed a ban on contracts that restricted the absorption and dissemination of the imported technology, or included export restrictions. Moreover, it put a ceiling on royalty rates that amounted to 5% of net sales, and limited to five years the concession of tax brakes for technology imports. See Guimarães *et al.* (1982).

244. On the stabilization policy see Resende (1990). Until the 1960s, government intervention in the labour market had been limited to labour union legislation (1931) and to the introduction of a minimum wage (1940). In 1965, the military government introduced a 'wage formula', bringing public and private sector nominal wages under its control. According to this formula, wages were to be adjusted once a year according to the government's expected inflation, plus a productivity-related bonus. As the former was consistently underestimated, the average real wage fell 9% between 1965–67. In 1968, this formula was changed with wages being indexed not to the expected but to the past inflation.

245. See, e.g., Tyler (1976) on the former, and Balassa (1979) on the latter.

246. See Serra (1982).

247. Drawback users, until 1975, would lose part of the fiscal subsidy, and both drawback incentives and export credits were conditional on localization indices above 70% (Pastore *et al.* 1979:75 and Guimarães 1989).

248. Sustainable in Baumol *et al.*'s (1982) sense. For instance, a 1973 study of the machinery sector by an Italian consultancy firm, revealed that productivity in most product lines was well below that of Italy, because, *inter alia*, plants were below the MES and lack specialization (Villela and Baer 1980).

249. According to Hoffman (1989:217) 42 percent of the population in 1970

was below the 'poverty line', defined as the prevailing minimum wage.

250. Despite being more labour-intensive than importables (see Carvalho and Haddad 1981), the export contribution to greater labour absorption was limited, given its small share of total sales.

251. The total stock market value, as percentage of GDP, fell from 22 to 7% over 1972-77 (Goldsmith 1986:422). The ratio of indexed to non-indexed assets increased from 5 to 43% over 1965–73 (World Bank, 1984a:9).

252. As Lago (1990:286) pointed out, skilled workers during the 'miracle' had wage rises well above those of the unskilled workers. As to income distribution, the share of the 20% highest income group increased from 55% in 1960 to 62% in 1970 (IBGE 1990).

253. In a study of foreign technology contracts over 1965–70, Biato *et al.* (1973) revealed that the TNCs' share in value terms was 73%, 52% of which consisting of parent-subsidiary deals.

254. In 1974, raw material, intermediate and capital goods accounted for 87% of total imports (Table A.33). The plan also envisage substantial investments in transport and communication.

255. II Plano Nacional de Desenvolvimento. Brasilia. For a thorough analysis, see Batista (1992).

256. Simonsen (1988:299). Simonsen was the finance minister in charge during the II NDP.

257. The NTB barriers included advanced deposits, outright ban on 'non-essential' products (e.g. cars, motorbikes), imposition of import ceilings on state enterprises which were also prohibited to buy imported consumer goods, and restrictions on certain types of import payments. See Dib (1985).

258. The share of imported equipment in the CDI approved projects fell from 67 to 19% over 1973–79. The 'participation agreements' were restricted to large scale industrial and infrastructure projects, and consisted of the withdrawal of import restrictions for capital goods imports in exchange for the purchase of a certain amount of these goods locally. Finally, the fiscal 'export' incentives to locally-purchased capital goods were restricted to equipment considered 'sophisticated' by the Ministry of Finance. See Suzigan (1980) and Tyler (1981).

259. These agreements, first used in 1972, allowed firms to import equipment and inputs, tax and NTB free (on top of the regular export incentives), in return for a commitment to reach export targets over a long-term period (usually 10 years). Imports of inputs were limited to one-third of the value exported. BEFIEX share of manufactured exports rose from 9% in 1974 to 17% in 1979. TNCs in the transport equipment sector accounted for 87% of these exports (1974–79) (Guimarães 1989:22).

260. The figure for loans effectively disbursed was a great deal more modest, averaging 28%.

261. During 1975–76, monetary correction on BNDE loans was limited to 20% annually despite the 37% average annual inflation. As of 1976, their nominal interest rates varied from 0 to 8% plus monetary correction (Revista do BNDES 1978).

262. Subsidized finance to the purchase of locally-made capital goods had been on offering since 1964 by the BNDE subsidiary FINAME. However,

it received a major boost in 1974, when a new programme targeting the made-to-order sector was set up. On the capitalization programmes, see Villela and Baer (1980).

263. Foreign borrowing incentives included reductions in the loans minimum maturity, fiscal concessions on interest rate payments, and the assumption by the Central Bank of a portion of the exchange rate risks. See Cruz (1984) and World Bank (1984a).

264. The federal debt increased from 5 to 9% of GDP over 1973–79 (ANESTBR). Credit subsidies favoured not only industry and exports, but also small firms and agriculture. During 1977–78, they were estimated at 5.5% of GDP, with agriculture accounting for 60% of the total (World Bank 1984a:38). Excluding oil and derivatives, SEs' prices in real terms fell 12% in average over 1974–79 (Dinsmoor 1990).

265. Public sector procurement was a particularly powerful instrument. Table A.34 shows that the state enterprises' share of gross fixed capital formation increased to 22% during the period.

266. None of these institutions could block investments, and BNDE credit was only relevant for LPFs. For a review of the industrial policy see Suzigan (1978) and Villela and Baer (1980).

267. Elementary education, though, continued to be neglected. The FNDCT's share of federal expenditures, which average 0.4% over 1970–73, increased to 0.9% over 1974-79 (World Bank 1983a, IBGE 1990). Graduate enrolments grew at annual average rate 18% over 1974–79 (Castro 1989).

268. This was supposed to be done by requiring full disclosure of technical knowledge by the licensers, and by requiring the licensees to present plans for the absorption of technology and for local personnel training. Import of technology, though keep, on growing fast. As a percentage of GDP it averaged 0.3% over the period against 0.2% during the 'miracle'. World Bank (1983a) and IBGE (1990).

269. In 1975, the government set up NAIs in the most important SEs, aiming at fostering technological links between them and the local capital goods industry. See Villela (1984).

270. See Table A.48.

271. See, e.g., IPEA (1979), Castro and de Souza (1985), and Batista (1992).

272. According to one estimate (*Conjuntura Econômica*, February 1982) the global federal deficit as a percentage of GDP was 8.1% in 1979. Subsidies as a percentage of tax revenue increased from 13 to 41% over 1974–79 (C. G. Langoni, 'Bases Institucionais da Economia Brasileira' BACEN as quoted in Dinsmoor (1990:129).

273. See, e.g., Balassa (1979), Fishlow (1986), and Tavares and Lessa (1985).

274. This insight was later developed by Stigler (1951).

275. To make things worse, a increasingly disproportionate amount of subsidies were directed to the TNCs, with no obvious dynamic benefits. In 1978, Braga (1981) estimated that TNCs accounted for 42% of the fiscal subsidies whereas their share of total exports was 37%. The results in terms of greater outward-orientation were not impressive. According to one estimate (Baumann 1985) affiliates increased marginally their export ratio from 15.4% in 1971 to 18.6% in 1978. Blomström (1987)

estimated in 8.7% the export ratio of the American affiliates in 1977, well below the LDCs' average.

276. As of 1980, under-employment was still at 35% of the economically active population (Wells 1987:96).

277. In fact, Brazil's share of world exports of textiles and basic industry increased significantly during the period (Table A.47). Yet, it remained unimpressive *vis-á-vis* other NICs. For instance, Korea's share of textile exports in 1980 was 5.5 times larger than Brazil's. As Lucke (1990:23) put it 'The very modest export performance [1960–85] of the textile and clothing industries in Brazil contrasted sharply with that of the Asian NICs . . . this confirm the conclusion that the sector is still very inward oriented.'

278. Data on R&D reviewed by Frischtak and Dahlman (1990). Data on formal R&D involved the universe of legally established firms. Data on R&D ownership is for 1983, for a sample of 1118 firms. As to technology outlays, the source was Braga and Matesco (1986), who using income tax data for approximately 5000 large firms, find out that LPFs, 81% of the sample, accounted in average for 92% of the R&D outlays in 1978/80/82, whereas TNCs, 19% of the sample, accounted for only 8%. With respect to royalties, the TNCs accounted for 45% of the payments.

279. On the steel, aircraft and arms industries see, e.g., Fischer *et al.* (1988), Baldwin (1988) and Gouvea Neto (1991), respectively.

280. LPFs' access to foreign loans were mainly for medium-term working capital (resolution 63) (Table A.45) which unlike the direct, long term loans, had high positive interest rates. For instance, even if 1979 is left aside, the average annual real interest rate for these loans during 1974–78 was 11.8% (including spread, commissions and taxes) (Cenarios, various issues).

281. The PPP exchange rate for exports in 1980 was below that of 1979 (Table A.36). See Belluzzo and Coutinho (1983) for details of the macroenomic policies during the period.

282. During the Tokyo Round, Brazil had agreed to phase out the fiscal subsidy to exports until 1983. Yet, as mentioned, it was abruptly eliminated in December 1979. When reinstated in 1981, it lost its product-specific character and a flat 15% rate of the export value was introduced. This rate was to be phased out until 1983. In 1982, however, Brazil negotiated with the US, which was threatening to impose countervailing duties, the extension of the subsidy until 1985 (CEPAL 1985b).

283. According to a conservative estimate, the percentage of imports affected by NTBs (in item terms) rose from 4 to 56% over 1975–84 (Guimarães 1989). Yet, Moreira and Araújo (1984) estimated that, as of 1983, 75% of total imports were affected by NTBs, while, if oil is excluded, only 12% of imports entered the country without being related to a specific government programme of fiscal incentives.

284. On the adjustment policies see Carneiro (1987).

285. See Table A.38. In 1979, BNDE had its priorities changed towards agriculture and infrastructure, and stopped receiving resources from the treasury. See Zoninsein (1984).

286. To add to the effective protection conceptual (e.g. fixed technical coefficients) and direct price comparisons (i.e. non-homogeneous goods) shortcomings, the estimates for Brazil are further compromised by the widespread price controls, high inflation, out-of-date technical coefficients (5 to 10 years) and by the use of export prices as international prices.

287. The FNDCT fell *74%* in real terms over 1975–84 (Becker and Egler 1992:93). See Castro (1989) on the effects of the cuts on the research establishment.

288. Despite the draconian cuts in government expending, which reduced the operational fiscal deficit from 6.8 to 3.1% of GDP over 1982-84, the PSBR rose from 16.6 to 27.5%, due to the impact of higher inflation on the indexed internal debt (BACEN). PSBR stands for public sector borrowing requirements. Unlike the operational deficit, it includes the monetary correction on the internal debt.

289. The market reserve began officially when CAPRE (Coordination of Electronic Processing Activities), ultimately responsible for issuing import licences for electronic processing equipment and components, put to tender, in mid-1977, the production of minicomputers and selected only LPFs. In 1979, CAPRE was replaced by SEI (Special Secretariat for Informatics) which gradually expanded its control over the professional electronics industry except for mainframe computers and telecommunication equipment. This process was crowned in 1984, by the introduction of the 'informatics law'. See, e.g., Piragibe (1985) for details.

290. See, e.g. Krugman (1984a).

291. Apart from the deficiencies of the educational system, there was a limited manufacturing tradition on electronics to build on, since production of mainframes and consumer electronics had been long dominated by TNCs or pseudo-joint ventures. As Erber (1985:301) pointed out, LPFs could not rely on human capital externalities created by the TNCs since the majority of the university trained personnel was used in administrative and marketing activities. Hewitt (1992) gives more up-to-date information on the continuing problem of skill shortage.

292. Schimtz and Hewitt (1992:28ff). According to these authors, the technological lag of the industry at the end of the decade was 'below two years'.

293. For details see, e.g., Modiano (1990) and Dinsmoor (1990).

294. Operational concept. The PSBR in 1988 was estimated in 48.5% of GDP (BACEN) . On these two plans see Dinsmoor, *op. cit.*

295. Manufacturing investment estimates are from *Sondagem Conjuntural* and IDB as quoted in Dinsmoor (1990:69). They are not available for the post 1987 period. FDI also plunged to record levels (Table A.37) reflecting uncertainty surrounding the government policies.

296. A survey of the views of the most important industrial producers in October 1987, revealed that only 53% of those interviewed considered its sector to be technologically update (*Sondagem Conjuntural*, FGV/PEC/CEI). Another survey in 1990 by the National Confederation of Industry revealed similar findings. See Frischtak and Dahlman (1990).

297. It began in early 1984, triggered by the deterioration of public finances

and pressures from trade partners. First, monetary correction (MC) was introduced on export loans. Then, the Central Bank's open-ended discounts to export credits were abolished and interest rates raised from 3% plus MC to market interest rate less 10%. In March 1985, the fiscal subsidies were finally dropped, and in 1989 the corporate tax exemption raised from 0 to 3% (Guimarães 1989 and IMF(a)).

298. The most 'daring' attempt to liberalize imports came only in mid 1988. See below.

299. The ratio of Brazil's unit labour cost to the East Asia NICs' average (Korea, Taiwan, Hong Kong and Singapore), measured in dollars per hour, fell from 1.4 in 1975 to 0.6 in 1986 (US Bureau of Labour Statistics as quoted in Araujo Jr. *et al.* 1990:17). With regard to the rest of the world (weighted average) Brazil's unit labour costs fell 25% over 1976–87, although it has presented heavy fluctuations over this period (BNDE 1992b).

300. Baumann (1990). The elimination of the CDI tariff exemptions for capital goods in 1979, also boosted BEFIEX exports since this benefit could be obtained under the scheme.

301. These worries were expressed in a series of industrial policy proposals commissioned by the new administration. None of this documents, though, were of much consequence, except for the S&T policies. See Suzigan (1986,1988).

302. The FNDCT, for instance, almost doubled over 1984–86 (Becker and Eagler 1992).

303. For instance, the tertiary education enrolment ratio for Brazil in 1988 was 11.1% against 36.8% in Korea, 40.8% in Argentina (UNESCO). See Frischtak and Dahlman (1990) for an assessment of the present conditions of Brazil educational system.

304. Import surcharges were removed, the list of prohibited imports shortened from 2400 to 1200 items and the minimum financing requirements for some imports lifted (IMFa).

305. For details see Matesco (1988) and IMF(a).

306. For an analysis of the reforms during the Collor government (1990-92) see Horta *et al.* (1991), Erber (1992) and IMF(b).

Appendix Tables

Table A.1   Korea's selected human capital indicators, 1940–88

	Illiteracy rate	≥14[1]	Primary WF[2]	Primary Enr. ratio[3]	≥14	Secondary WF	Secondary Enr. ratio	≥14	Tertiary WF	Tertiary Enr. ratio
1944	86.7	11.3	53.0*	n.a.	1.7	7.4*	n.a.	0.2	—*	n.a.
1953	78.0	n.a.	n.a.	59.6	n.a.	n.a.	16.7	n.a.	7.6	3.1
1960	27.9	36.0	53.0†	86.2	17.3	33.9†	26.6	2.5	6.1†	6.4
1970	10.6	39.9	67.4	102.8	31.7	26.4	41.3	5.5	7.3	9.3
1980	—	n.a.	49.1	101.0	n.a.	43.0	76.0	n.a.	7.8	15.8
1986	—	n.a.	41.2#	100.2	n.a.	48.6#	90.0	n.a.	10.2#	34.2
1990	—	n.a.	n.a.	108.0	n.a.	n.a.	87	n.a.	n.a.	39.2

Notes: (1) Education attainment of the population aged 14 and over. (2) Education attainment of the work force (WF). From 1970 onwards figures for primary education includes no schooling. (3) Enrolment as a percentage of the age group. *1946 † 1963 #1983.

Source: Kim, L. (1989) for 1953–1986 and UNESCO for 1990 data on enrolments and literacy. Data on education attainment for over 14, McGinn et al. (1980:111); and Amsden (1989:222) for the work force.

Table A.2   Shares of heavy and chemical (HCI) and of light industries in Korea's manufacturing output, value added and manufactured exports, 1953–89

Variable	Industry	1953	1960	1972	1976	1980	1988	1989
Manufacturing	HCI	20.7	25.2	32.0	44.4	51.9	59.6	60.9
output[1]	Light	79.2	74.8	68.0	55.6	48.1	40.4	39.1
Manufacturing	HCI	n.a.	n.a.	36.7	43.9	49.2	62.0	63.5
value added[2]	Light	n.a.	n.a.	63.3	56.1	50.8	38.0	36.5
Manufactured	HCI	19.9	7.2	24.2	33.1	45.6	55.5	n.a.
exports[3]	Light	80.0	92.8	75.8	66.9	54.4	44.5	n.a.

[1] At current prices. [2] At 1985 constant prices. [3] At current prices.
Note: HCI includes industrial chemicals, petroleum refineries, other non-metallic mineral products, basic metals, fabricated metal products, machinery, electrical electronic machinery and appliances, transportation equipment and precision equipment according to the Korean Standard Industry Classification.

Source: Economic Planning Board as quoted by Suh (1975:204) for 1953 and 1960, and EPB (a) and KFTA (1989) for 1972–89.

Table A.3   Korea's basic macro indicators, 1953–89 (%)

Periods	(a) GNP growth	(b) Mnf. output Growth	(c) GFCF/GDP deflator	(d) GNP
1953–59	4.6	14.7	n.a.	8.9†
1960–72	9.9	20.5	19.5	16.0*
1973–79	10.8	17.2	26.9	20.5
1980–84	8.4	12.0	30.8	8.2
1985–89	11.5	13.8	29.4	4.3
1980–89	10.0	13.1	29.4	5.2

Note: (a), (b) and (d) real least square averages. (c) arithmetic average.
† 1955–60. * 1961–72.
Source: EPB (a) and BOK.

Table A.4   Korea's export and import ratio by manufacturing sector, 1953–83 (%)

Import ratios[1]	1953	1960	1965	1972	1974	1980	1983
Total manufacturing	10.2	12.1	10.2	15.3	24.1	16.8	17.6
HCI	26.0	33.3	23.6	33.0	39.0	23.8	23.8
Light	6.0	5.0	3.7	7.1	12.7	8.1	8.4
Export ratios[2]							
Total manufacturing	1.1	0.8	5.3	17.9	26.5	17.5	21.1
HCI	1.0	0.6	3.5	14.0	22.3	19.0	22.0
Light	1.1	0.9	6.3	19.8	31.7	18.3	19.9

[1] Imports divided by the total domestic supply. [2] Exports divided by total output.

Notes: (a) heavy and chemical industry (HCI) includes nonmetallic minerals, metallurgy, machinery, electrical and communication equipment, transport equipment, chemicals, and pharmaceuticals. (b) Ratios are the weighted average (output) for the two-digit sectoral data (Korean Industrial Classification.

Source: Suh (1975:84ff) for the 1953–74 period, and Bank of Korea's Input-Output Tables for the rest of the period.

Table A.5   Korea's GDP structure, 1953–90

	Agriculture	Industry	Manufacturing	Services	Total
1953	42.3	8.96	7.9	48.7	100
1960	35.2	15.6	13.5	49.2	100
1965	37.6	19.9	14.4	42.5	100
1972	26.8	23.5	18.4	48.8	100
1980	14.9	31.0	22.2	54.1	100
1989	10.2	31.9	22.6	57.9	100

Note: current prices.

Source: Suh (1975:277) for 1953–60 and EPBa.

Table A.6   Korea's export structure by main categories and selected commodities groups, 1960–85 ($ million and % of total exp.)

Categories	1960	1965	1972	1980	1987
Total exports	31.8	175.0	1624.0	17488.6	47206.6
Primary &	27.5	68.4	265.3	1736.4	3433.1
semi-mnf.[1]	[86.5]	[39.0]	[16.3]	[10.0]	[7.2]
Manufactured	4.3	106.6	1358.7	15752.2	43773.5
products[2]	[13.5]	[60.9]	[83.6]	[90.0]	[92.7]

[1] Includes STIC divisions nº 0, 1, 2, 3, 4, 9, 68. [2] Includes STIC divisions n° 5 to 8 minus 68. *Note*: Numbers in square brackets are the shares in total exports.

Source: U.N. International Trade Statistical Yearbook. Various years.

Table A.7 Korea's purchase power parity exchange rates, 1956–88 (won/dollar)[1]

Year	Export[2]	Import[3]	Official rate
1956	248.0	138.3	n.a.
1958	286.3	163.0	n.a.
1960	311.7	232.3	166.6
1962	265.0	251.0	220.4
1964	273.3	259.0	229.1
1966	268.0	279.7	254.9
1968	252.7	258.3	236.8
1970	258.3	261.0	242.5
1972	294.0	299.0	282.9
1974	298.3	305.3	291.4
1976	269.3	279.7	263.3
1978	263.7	278.7	258.3
1980	257.0	265.3	250.3
1982	256.7	269.7	254.5
1984	257.0*	273.0*	280.0
1986	n.a.	n.a.	311.4
1988	n.a.	n.a.	305.7

[1] Three year moving average except for 1988. 1965 prices. Each exchange rate is multiplied by the ratio of the weighted average of the major trade partners' WPI (US and Japan) to the Korean WPI. The Japanese WPI was adjusted by the index of the exchange rate of the yen to the dollar. [2] Includes official exchange rate, export premia, direct subsidies and interest rate subsidies. [3] Includes official exchange rate, tariff and foreign exchange tax collections and export premia. * 1983 only.

Source: Data from Krueger (1979: 48 ff.) for 1955–58, Frank *et al.* (1975: 70) for 1958–62, Kim, S. K. (1991: 24) for 1962–83; and EPB (a), IMF (b) and OECD (1989) for 1984–88.

Table A.8 Korea basic foreign trade indicators, 1952–90

Year	Exp. Growth (%)[1]	Imp. Growth (%)[1]	Trade Balance[2] US$10⁶	Current Account GNP	Debt ratio[3] %	Year	Exp. Growth (%)[1]	Imp. Growth (%)[1]	Trade Balance[2] US$10⁶	Current Account GNP	Debt ratio %
1952	n.a.	n.a.	-187	n.a.	n.a.	1972	45.5	0.8	-898	-3.5	33.9
1953	n.a.	n.a.	-306	n.a.	n.a.	1973	75.2	48.4	-1015	-2.3	31.5
1954	n.a.	n.a.	-219	-6.2	n.a.	1974	16.5	36.1	-2391	-10.8	32.0
1955	-26.6	37.3	-323	-8.7	n.a.	1975	4.3	-2.8	-2193	-9.0	40.5
1956	33.1	8.5	-362	-11.7	n.a.	1976	45.2	15.3	-1059	-1.1	36.7
1957	-14.4	11.4	-420	-10.5	n.a.	1977	22.7	16.1	-764	0.0	33.7
1958	-23.8	-15.7	-362	-8.7	n.a.	1978	17.4	28.5	-2261	-2.1	29.7
1959	17.4	-19.7	-284	-7.5	n.a.	1979	5.5	20.9	-5283	-6.7	31.7
1960	64.8	13.0	-311	-9.3	n.a.	1980	1.7	-4.1	-4787	-8.8	44.7
1961	24.6	-7.9	-275	-8.6	n.a.	1981	11.2	7.3	-4878	-7.0	48.3
1962	33.9	33.3	-367	-2.4	n.a.	1982	0.8	-9.0	-2398	-3.7	52.6
1963	58.7	33.1	-474	-5.3	4.06	1983	10.5	6.7	-1747	-2.0	53.2
1964	36.5	-28.0	-285	-0.9	5.29	1984	16.9	14.3	-1387	-1.6	53.2
1965	46.7	14.3	-288	0.3	6.81	1985	4.1	2.2	-853	-1.0	50.9
1966	38.2	49.7	-466	-2.8	10.3	1986	18.0	4.4	3131	4.5	43.2
1967	28.0	39.1	-676	-4.5	13.6	1987	32.4	25.8	6414	7.6	27.6
1968	38.5	43.0	-1007	-8.4	20.0	1988	23.6	22.1	8886	8.2	17.9
1969	31.7	19.9	-1200	-8.3	24.0	1989	-2.2	12.9	913	2.4	14.5*
1970	29.5	5.1	-1148	-7.7	25.5	1990	n.a.	14	-1854	n.a.	n.a.
1971	24.0	17.0	-1326	8.9	30.0						

[1] $ 1980. [2] Customs clearance basis. [3] Debt service divided by exports. * Preliminary.

Source: Krueger (1979), UN, EPB a, EPB (1990) and KDI (1991).

Table A.9 Importable items in Korea, 1961–91

Year[1]	Positive list			Negative list					
	AA	Restr.	Prohib.	AA	Restr.	Prohib[3]	Total	AA/Total (%)	AA-S.L /Total[4]
1961	1015	17	305				—	—	
1962	1377	121	433				—	—	
1963	109	924	414				—	—	
1964	496	n.a.	631				—	—	
1965	1495	124	620				—	—	
1966	2307	127	2446				—	—	
1967/ July 24[2]	2950	132	362	(156)	(1114)	(42)	1312	(11.9)	(11.9)
July 25	—	—	—	792	402	118	1312	60.4	52.4
1969	—	—	—	723	530	74	1312	55.1	47.1
1971	—	—	—	721	518	73	1312	55.0	47.0
1973	—	—	—	683	556	73	1312	52.1	44.7
1975	—	—	—	649	602	66	1312	49.5	41.6
1977	—	—	—	691	560	61	1312	52.7	40.8
1979	—	—	—	683	327	—	1097	67.6	56.2
1981	—	—	—	5579	1886	—	7465	74.7	60.7
1983	—	—	—	6355	1560	—	7915	80.4	66.6
1985	—	—	—	6945	970	—	7915	87.7	78.2
1987	—	—	—	7407	508	—	7915	93.6	n.a.
1989	—	—	—	n.a.	n.a.	—	7915	95.5	n.a.
1991*	—	—	—	n.a.	n.a.	—	7915	97.3	n.a.

[1] The data refers to the second half of the years. [2] The numbers in parentheses represent the results of a reclassification of the negative import system to make it comparable with the positive one. However, some authors like Luedde-Neurath (1986:76) argue that the commodities classifications of the two systems were not comparable, and accordingly the results of the reclassification tends to underestimate the number of AA before 1967. The details of the classification of the positive list were not available, while the positive list used 4-digits SITC until 1977, 4-digits BTN until 1980 and 8-digit CCCN since 1983. [3] The category of prohibited items was abolished in 1978. [4] AA items minus the items subjected to special laws, divided by total importable items. Special laws consistent with Gatt regulations were not included.
* Planned.

Sources: Frank *et al.* (1975:45, 59) until 1970, Kim, S. K. (1987:28) for 1970–84 and special law items, and EPB (1989a, 1990) for 1984–91.

Table A.10   Korea's simple and weighted average legal tariff rates,
1952–79

Average rates(%)	1952	1957	1962	1968	1973	1977	1979
Weighted[1]	n.a.	35.4	49.5	56.7	48.1	41.3	34.4
Simple	25.4	30.2	39.9	39.1	31.5	29.7	24.7
Coeff. variation[2]	0.70	0.70	0.77	0.71	0.70	0.61	0.69

[1] Average rate weighted by the value of production in 1975. [2] Standard deviation divided by the mean. Simple average rates only.

Note: special tariffs (1964–73) were not included.

Source: Kim, S. K. (1991:43)

Table A.11 Korea's export promotion measures, 1950 onwards

Type of incentive	Duration	Type of incentive	Duration
1. Tax incentives		Fund for exports of primary products	September 1969–
Commodity tax exemption	April 1950	Foreign currency loans	May 1967–
Business tax exemption	January 1962–	Financing export on credit	October 1969–
Reduction of corporation and income tax by 50% on earnings from exports	January 1961–72	**4 – Other Promotion Schemes**	
Accelerated depreciation on allowance for fixed capital	January 1961–	Foreign exchange deposit system	June 1949– Jan. 1961
Tax credit for foreign market development expenditures	August 1969–	Trading license based on export performance	January 1953
Tax credit for losses due to operations in foreign markets	March 1973–	An export bonus with preferential foreign exch.	1951–May 1961
2. Tariff incentives		Direct export subsidy	1955–56 and 1961–64
Tariff exemptions on capital equipment for export production	March 1964–Dec. 1973	Discount on railroad freight rates	1958–
Tariff payment on an instalment basis for capital used in export promotion	January 1974–	Monopoly rights on exports of specific items to specific areas	April 1960–
Tariff exemptions on raw material and input for export production	April 1959–June 1975	Creation for exporters associations on various export	September 1961–
Tariff drawback on imported raw materials used for export production	July 1975–	Financing Kotra	1962–
Wastage allowance	July 1965–	Export-import link system	1951–55 and 1963–
3. Financial incentives		Discount on electricity rates	1965–76
Financing for collection of export goods	Feb. 1948– July 1955	Waiver insurance for shipping	1965

Continued on page 176

Table A.11   continued

Type of incentive	Duration	Type of incentive	Duration
Export shipment financing	1950–1955	Local letter of credit system	March 1965–
Export promotion fund financed by counterpart fund	November 1959–Jan. 1964	Differential treatment of traders based on export performance	February 1967–
Financing imports of materials to be used in export production	October 1961–	Export insurance	January 1969–
Export credits (trade credit before 1961)	June 1950	General trading companies	May 1965
Financing suppliers of US off-shore military procurement	September 1962–	Eximbank	June 1976–
Fund to promote the export industry	1964–1969	Export targets by industry	1962–
Fund to convert small and medium-sized firms into export industries	February 1964–		

Source: Hong (1979:54) and Frank *et al.* (1975:40).

Table A.12 Estimates of Korea's export subsidies per dollar of export,[1] 1958–83 (%)

Year	Net[2]	Gross[3]
1958	2.4	130.4
1959	2.6	172.0
1960	1.9	137.3
1961	6.7	18.2
1962	8.6	16.6
1963	9.1	45.8
1964	4.5	31.3
1965	3.7	14.8
1966	4.6	19.0
1967	7.4	23.0
1968	6.6	28.1
1969	6.4	27.8
1970	6.7	28.3
1971	6.6	29.6
1972	3.2	26.8
1973	2.2	23.7
1974	2.1	21.2
1975	2.7	16.7
1976	2.5	16.9
1977	1.9	19.2
1978	2.3	19.5
1979	2.3	20.2
1980	3.3	21.3
1981	2.2	n.a.
1982	0.4	n.a.
1983	0.0	n.a.

[1] As a percentage of the official exchange rate.
[2] Equals direct cash interest rates.
(1958–64) + direct tax reduction (1962–73) + interest rate subsidy.
[3] Equals net subsidy + export dollar premium (1958–61, 1963–64) + indirect tax and tariff exemptions (1962–).

Source: Data from Kim, S.K. (1991:33).

Appendix

Table A.13:   Korea's selected interest rates, 1963–86 (end of the period, %)

Year	General loan rate[1]		KDB equipment[2]		Exports		Foreign loans		Curb market		Return to fixed assets in mnf.[3]
	Nom.	Real[4]	Nom.	Real[4]	Nom.	Real[4]	Nom.	Real[5]	Nom.	Real[4]	Real
1963	15.7	−3.9	n.a.	n.a.	n.a.	n.a.	n.a.	n.a.	52.56	32.9	33
1965	14.0	4.1	10.0	0.1	6.5	−3.4	5.5	19.8	58.8	48.9	34
1967	24.0	17.6	10.0	3.6	6.0	−0.4	5.8	−0.5	56.4	50.0	37
1969	24.6	18.2	12.0	5.6	6.0	−0.4	6.1	3.1	51.2	44.8	28
1971	22.0	13.2	12.0	3.2	6.0	−2.6	6.6	9.6	46.3	37.3	23
1973	15.5	8.6	12.0	5.1	6.5	−0.4	7.5	2.3	39.2	32.0	34
1975	15.5	−11.1	12.0	−14.6	8.0	−18.5	7.3	0.0	41.3	15.0	29
1977	16.0	7.0	13.5	4.5	8.0	−1.0	6.0	−3.0	38.1	29.1	33
1979	19.0	0.2	13.5#	−5.3	9.0	−9.8	12.1	−6.7	42.4	23.8	n.a.
1981	17.0	−3.4	16.5	−3.9	15.0	−5.4	16.8	24.1	35.3	14.9	37*
1983	10.0	9.8	10.0	9.8	10.0	9.8	9.7	17.1	25.8	25.6	n.a.
1985	10.0	9.1	10.0	9.1	10.0	9.1	8.4	13.4	24.0	23.1	n.a.
1986	10.0	11.5	10.0	11.5	10.0	11.5	6.9	8.4	24.3	25.8	n.a.

[1] Discount on bills up to one year, non-prime rate. [2] Korea Development Bank loans for equipment. [3] Non-labour share of value-added divided by fixed assets (Hong 1979:171). [4] Deflated by the WPI. [5] Libor (90 days) + Exchange rate depreciation − WPI.* 1980–82 average. Fixed assets include net working capital. #1978.

Source: Bank of Korea, *Economic Statistics Yearbook*, various years; Amsden and Euh (1990:463) and Hong (1979:171).

Table A.14   Korea's total and sectoral import liberalization (AA) ratio in value terms, 1968–87

AA ratios (%)	% AA items in the sector's total imports					% of the sector's AA items in total AA imp.[4]				
	1968	**1976**	**1978**	**1980**	**1987**	**1968**	**1976**	**1978**	**1980**	**1987**
Food and beverages	83.4	67.6	49.0	54.2	70.2	17.8	20.7	8.8	7.9	5.2
Raw material	78.9	63.9	66.2	90.4	73.5	38.1	71.4	62.4	72.6	28.6
Manufactures[1]	40.0	10.6	19.8	28.8	71.8	44.0	14.6	28.9	19.3	57.7
Consumer goods	36.9	5.7	9.8	16.5	67.4	1.6	0.5	0.8	0.6	3.6
Intermediate goods	20.2	12.8	15.6	32.2	65.0	8.4	8.6	9.5	10.2	17.7
Capital goods	53.3	8.9	24.1	27.0	75.2	33.9	5.4	18.6	8.4	36.4
All industries (AI)	55.6	37.1	38.8	61.6	74.2	100	100	100	100	100
AI minus gov. items[2]	40.6	12.1	17.7	25.6	n.a.	—	—	—	—	—
AI in item terms[3]	57.6	51.0	61.3	68.6	93.6	—	—	—	—	—

[1] Manufactures includes capital, consumer and intermediate goods. [2] All industries exclusive of items whose importation is directly or indirectly carried out by the government. [3] AA imports items divided by total imports items, as in the last column of Table IV. [4] Total might not equal 100% because of rounding.

Source: Luedde-Neurath (1986:141 ff.) for 1968–80 and *1988 Statistical Yearbook of Foreign Trade*, 1988 Import-Export Notice for 1987.

Table A.15   Korea's composition of imports by end use (%), 1960–89

	1960	1969	1974	1978	1982	1986	1988	1989
Food and beverages	9.2	17.0	12.2	6.7	7.2	5.3	5.2	5.3
Consumer goods	15.4	4.7	2.9	3.8	2.8	4.3	4.4	4.7
Durables	n.a.	4.0	2.6	3.4	2.5	3.8	3.7	n.a.
Non-durables	n.a.	0.7	0.3	0.4	0.3	0.5	0.7	n.a.
Ind. supplies[1]	49.6	46.5	57.6	55.5	64.1	54.2	53.4	53.6
Capital goods	11.7	31.6	26.9	33.7	25.6	35.9	36.7	36.4
Export use	n.a.	n.a.	n.a.	n.a.	23.9	40.3	41.2	36.4
Domestic use	n.a.	n.a.	n.a.	n.a.	76.1	59.7	58.8	63.6

[1] Includes raw material, fuel and intermediate goods. Note: (a) % ages may not add to 100% because of *non-specified goods.*

Source: Data for 1960 was based on Krueger (1979:72), Korea Foreign Trade Association (1989) for 1969–88 and KDI (1991) for 1989.

Table A.16 Korea's market concentration, 1970–85[1]

	Monopoly			Oligopoly			Competition			Total		
	1970	1977	1985	1970	1977	1985	1970	1977	1985	1970	1977	1985
No. of commodities	442	475	534	774	807	1421	276	264	561	1492	1546	2516
Commodity ratio %[2]	29.6	30.7	21.2	51.4	52.2	56.5	18.5	17.1	22.3	100	100	100
Shipment ratio %[3]	8.7	12.7	9.4	51.4	61.2	52.8	39.8	26.1	37.8	100	100	100

[1] Monopoly = $CR_1 > 80\%$, $S_1/S_2 > 10.0$. Oligopoly = $CR_2 > 80\%$, $S_1 S_2 > 3.0$, $S_3 < 5.0$ or $CR_3 > 60$. Competition = $CR_3 < 60\%$, where CR_1 is the accumulated market concentration of the i leading firms, and S_1 is the market share of the ith firm. [2] Number of items produced in each type of market structure divided by the total number of items. [3] Value of items shipped in each type of market structure divided by the total amount shipped.

Source: Lee Kyu Uck (1988) 'The Current State of Economic Concentration and the Fair Trade Policy', as quoted by Presidential Commission on Economic Restructuring (1988:72).

Table A.17 Net FDI as a share of gross domestic capital formation (GFC) and net capital inflows (NCI) in the East Asian NICs 1966–85

	1966–72	1973–75	1976–78	1979–82	1983–85
Korea					
FDI (US$ 10^6)	28.2	90.5	87.7	53.5	137.2
% of GFC	1.6	1.7	0.8	0.3	0.6
% of NCI	4.3	5.6	10.9	1.1	7.4
Taiwan					
FDI (US$ 10^6)	36.9	59.3	78.7	136.7	229.9
% of GFC	2.9	1.4	1.2	1.1	2.0
% of NCI	25.8[b]	15.4	a	a	a
Singapore					
FDI (US$ 10^6)	83.1[c]	532.0	423.0	1186.6	1158.9
% of GFC	12.7[c]	26.4	17.3	21.7	14.5
% of NCI	23.4[c]	78.1	107.6	104.0	281.3
Hong Kong					
FDI (US$ 10^6)	n.a.	n.a.	183.6	613.9	641.9
% of GFC	n.a.	n.a.	4.4	6.5	8.3
% of NCI	n.a.	n.a.	64.1	50.0	54.5

[a] Net capital outflow. [b] 1966–70. [c] 1967–72.

Note: For Korea, Taiwan and Singapore, total FDI figures are taken from balance-of-payments data, which ideally include equity capital, reinvested earnings, and other capital movements. NCI = −(current account balance) + (unrequited transfers). For Hong Kong, total disbursement of DFI by OECD members only; NCI = total financial flows by OECD, OPEC and multilateral agencies.

Source: Haggard (1990:208) except for b which was taken from Stallings (1990:62).

Table A.18 Trends of Foreign Direct Investment in Korea
1962–89 (US$ million)

Years	Approved	Arrived	Years	Approved	Arrived
1962	0.6	0.6	1976	78.8	105.6
1963	5.6	2.1	1977	83.6	142.9
1964	0.7	3.1	1978	149.4	181.0
1965	21.8	10.7	1979	191.3	195.3
1966	14.1	0.2	1980	143.1	130.9
1967	23.5	12.7	1981	153.2	150.2
1968	25.4	14.7	1982	189.0	128.6
1969	47.1	7.0	1983	269.4	122.5
1970	67.4	25.3	1984	422.4	193.3
1971	43.0	36.7	1985	532.0	235.8
1972	122.4	61.2	1986	353.8	477.4
1973	316.9	158.4	1987	1060.2	624.8
1974	148.5	162.6	1988	1282.7	893.9
1975	203.5	69.2	1989	448.1	433.9

Source: Data from the Ministry of Finance as quoted by Bark (1989:3)

Table A.19 Korea's cumulative ownership distribution of foreign
investment, 1968–83 (%)[1]

Year	Minority owned and co-owned	Majority owned	Wholly owned	Total
1968	67.1	24.7	15.2	100
1972	63.9	16.9	19.2	100
1976	57.0	15.2	27.9	100
1980	62.8	14.3	22.9	100
1980 excl. FEZ*	67.1	14.3	18.5	100
1983	54.0	12.1	33.7	100

[1] Distribution calculated using the amount of investments in US dollars. * Free
Export Zones.

Source: Economic Planning Board as quoted by Koo (1982:46) for 1968–80
and USITC (1985:141) for 1983.

Appendix

Table A.20   Sectoral shares of foreign direct investment in Korea, 1962–
89 (%, approval basis)

	1962–66	1967–71	1972–76	1977–81	1982–86	1987–89
Agriculture	—	0.9	0.9	0.7	0.3	0.5
Mining	—	—	0.5	0.2	0.2	0.1
Services	2.1	14.6	21.7	32.2	46.8	34.8
Manufacturing	97.9	84.5	76.9	66.9	52.7	64.6
Food	6.5	1.0	2.6	7.3	9.1	4.2
Textile and apparel	2.2	11.3	24.7	1.0	1.8	2.2
Chemicals	—	12.9	25.4	29.2	12.7	25.8
Pharmaceuticals	—	1.6	0.3	3.1	7.9	5.1
Petroleum	10.9	20.5	4.7	2.0	0.5	3.6
Metals	—	9.7	6.8	7.5	2.9	2.0
Machineray	6.5	9.7	6.0	12.0	5.8	10.1
Electrical goods and electronics	15.2	21.0	15.3	25.7	27.2	31.5
Transport equipment	—	2.2	5.9	8.1	27.4	10.7
Others	58.7	9.7	7.9	3.9	4.5	4.8
Total US$ million	47	219	878	721	1767	2342.9

Source: Ministry of Finance as quoted by Kim, Il-Hwan (1987:6) and Bark (1989:10).

Table A.21   Share of policy loans in total domestic credit. Korea, 1963–86*

Year	(1) All policy Loans	(1a) Exports	(1b) Earmarked	(1c) Unearmarked
1963	70.3**	3.3	n.a.	n.a.
1965	74.3**	4.0	n.a.	n.a.
1967	65.0**	7.3	n.a.	n.a.
1969	51.0**	9.3	n.a.	n.a.
1971	49.9	6.1	21.2	22.5
1973	54.0	9.5	23.9	20.7
1975	52.8	10.0	20.1	22.6
1977	55.8	10.4	19.8	25.7
1979	59.3	11.0	18.3	29.9
1981	57.0	12.2	16.4	28.4
1983	53.4	12.6	16.5	24.2
1985	49.7	12.8	17.7	21.5
1986	45.0	n.a.	n.a.	n.a.

* Except for 1986, the annual figures are three-year moving averages.** Denominator does not include Bank of Korea's loan.
(1) = (1a) + (1b) + (1c) divided by total domestic credit (TDC = all loans and discounts to the private sector by the Bank of Korea, deposit money banks, Korea Development Bank and Korea Eximbank).
(1a) = loans for foreign trade by deposit money banks and all loans by Korea Eximbank divided by TDC.
(1b) = loans funded by government funds and the loans for agricultural industries, small and medium-sized firms, home building, etc., divided by TDC
(1c) = loans funded by the National Investment Fund (1974), loans in foreign currency, and all loans by the Korea Development Bank, divided by TDC.

Source: Data from Kwack and Chung (1986:130) and Hong (1979:128) for 1963–69 and from Yoo (1990:42) for the rest of the period.

Table A.22   Korea's selected R&D indicators

	1963	1967	1970	1972	1976	1980	1981	1986	1988
R&D/GNP (%)	0.24	0.38	0.48	0.29	0.44	0.86	0.65	1.82	2.0
government	97.0	86.0	77.0	66.0	64.0	68.0	42.0	19.0	20.0
private sector	0.3	14.0	23.0	34.0	36.0	32.0	58.0	81.0	80.9
R&D/Sales (%)	n.a.	n.a.	n.a.	n.a.	0.36	n.a.	0.67	1.63	n.a.
Researchers (10 000 pop.)	n.a.	1.4	n.a.	1.7	3.3	n.a.	5.4	11.3	13.7
Government (%)	n.a.	n.a.	n.a.	46.5	30.8	n.a.	24.4	16.3	n.a.
Universities	n.a.	n.a.	n.a.	36.0	41.2	n.a.	40.9	34.0	n.a.
Private sector	n.a.	n.a.	n.a.	17.4	27.9	n.a.	34.6	48.7	n.a.

* Estimated

Source: MOST (1988) and MOST as quoted in Kim (1989:7) and Lee *et al.* (1991:1432).

Appendix

Table A.23 Overall concentration rate by shipment in Korea, Japan and Taiwan, 1970–82

	Korea		Japan	Taiwan	
	Top 50	Top 100	Top 100	Top 50	Top 100
1970	33.8	44.6	n.a.	n.a.	n.a.
1975	n.a.	n.a.	28.4	15.8	21.7
1977	35.0	44.9	n.a.	15.2	22.4
1980	n.a.	n.a.	27.3	16.4	21.9
1982	37.5	46.8	n.a.	n.a.	n.a.

Source: Lee *et al.* (1986).

Table A.24 Korea's capacity utilization rate by selected industries, 1976–84

ISIC	1970	1972	1976	1978	1980	1982	1984
Manufacturing	65.9	65.1	74.7	83.4	69.5	69.4	80.6
Light industry							
Food, beverage and tobacco	59.2*	70.6*	59.7	81.8	69.2	64.9	74.0
Textile	70.4	66.3	89.7	86.9	80.3	80.2	79.1
Heavy industry							
Industrial chemicals	61.8	62.1	88.7	102.7	85.0	80.0	87.9
Non-metallic mineral	72.5	71.7	85.6	90.6	63.8	68.2	78.1
Iron and steel	60.1	58.9	79.4	89.5	74.5	75.3	87.9
Non-ferrous metal	n.a.	n.a.	70.3	72.6	56.8	69.0	81.7
Fabricated metal			n.a.	n.a.	39.9	43.3	53.8
General machinery	62.2	53.5	71.4	71.1	46.8	52.4	64.8
Electrical machinery			83.3	79.3	65.3	65.2	87.6
Transport equipment	n.a.	n.a.	36.8	40.4	41.9	58.1	78.7

* Excludes tobacco.
Note: data sources did not disclosed the measurement criteria.

Source: For 1970–72, World Bank (1987a:178, vol. I) and for 1976–84, S. Young, and S. Rhee (1986) *Korea's Industrial Adjustment and Import Liberalisation Policies*, KDI and World Bank as cited by Amsden (1987).

Table A.25 Debt-equity ratios in manufacturing for Korea, Japan, USA and Germany, 1965–87*

Year	Korea[1]	Japan[2]	US[2]	Germany[2]
1965	104.0	n.a.	n.a.	n.a.
1967	156.7	n.a.	n.a.	n.a.
1969	266.6	388.3	82.3	155.7
1971	345.3	416.0	87.0	174.7
1973	300.7	444.0	89.3	187.3
1975	340.0	478.3	86.7	206.0
1977	360.7	458.2	89.1	223.0
1979	410.6	404.2	98.0	224.0
1981	441.7	338.1	104.1	239.2
1983	362.9	279.2	016.4	240.7
1985	347.3	239.9	119.5	214.6
1987	329.0	203.9	133.1	221.7

* Three-year moving average. [1] Liabilities divided by net-worth [2] Liabilities divide by net-worth until 1977 and liabilities divided by capital over 1978–87.

Source: BOK, Financial Statement Analysis, various years for Korea. For the other countries, Jones (1987:158) for 1968–78 and Bank of Japan (1990) for 1979–87.

Table A.26 Coverage of Korea's contingent import control, 1981–1989[1]

Measures	1981	1982	1983	1984	1985	1986	1987	1989
Tariffs[2]								
(1) emergency	300	12	104	23	7	2	7	n.a.
(2) adjustment	—	—	—	14	7	5	—	
(1) + (2) / total import. items (%)	4	0.2	1.3	0.5	0.2	0.1	0.1	n.a.
NTBs								
Imp. diversification[3]	205	209	174	168	160	162	n.a.	22
% total imp. items	20.3	20.7	17.2	16.6	15.8	15.0	n.a.	2.2
Surveillance[4]	193	201	161	125	118	106	57	25*
% total imp. items	2.6	2.7	2.1	1.6	1.5	1.0	0.7	0.4*
Special Laws[5]	n.a.	1950	n.a.	n.a.	1875	n.a.	n.a.	n.a.
% total imp. items	n.a.	26.1	n.a.	n.a.	23.6	26.0	n.a.	19.0*

[1] In number of items at the 8-digit level of CCCN. [2] 1981–85 as of July 1 of each year. 1986–87 as of December of each year. Emergency tariffs can be placed in any item. Adjustment tariffs are for newly liberalised items [3] Aimed at reducing bilateral trade imbalances. At the 4-digit level of CCCN. [4] Liberalised items placed under government observation. Eliminated as of January 1, 1989. [5] Import restrictions on 'welfare' and national security grounds *1988

Source: World Bank (1987a, Vol. 1:67), Young (1986:29), EPB (1989a), Kim, S. (1987:21) and IMF (a).

Appendix

Table A.27   Brazil's trade-to-GDP ratios, 1889–1989 (%)*

Periods	Exp./GDP	IMP/GDP	Trade/GDP
1889–1929	16.0	12.6	28.6
1930–39	11.5	9.4	20.9
1940–50	9.9	8.3	18.1
1951–55	7.1	8.1	15.2
1956–64	4.7	6.4	11.1
1965–73	6.0	6.4	12.3
1974–79	6.6	9.1	15.7
1980–85	10.6	8.9	19.5
1986–90	9.4	5.8	15.2

* Current prices.

Source: Data from Goldsmith (1986:11) for the 1889–46 GDP and IBGE (1990) and UN (ITSY).

Table A.28   Brazil GDP structure, 1889–90.

	Agriculture	Industry	Services[1]	Total
1889	56.5	12.0	31.5	100
1929	37.8	20.0	42.2	100
1939	32.7	24.7	42.6	100
1947	33.9	24.5 (18.7)	41.6	100
1955	27.4	30.0 (23.8)	42.6	100
1960	19.7	35.8 (28.3)	44.5	100
1965	17.7	35.7 (27.8)	46.6	100
1970	12.2	37.8 (28.9)	50.0	100
1975	12.0	45.4 (35.2)	42.6	100
1980	11.2	44.6 (34.0)	44.2	100
1985	13.0	51.2 (38.1)	35.8	100
1990	11.7	44.2 (30.0)	44.1	100

[1] It does not include rent, financial institutions and non-specified services. *Note*: figures until 1947 are in constant prices. The rest of the series is on current prices. Numbers in parenthesis are the GDP share of the manufacturing sector.

Source: Goldsmith (1986:11) for 1889 to 1947 and IBGE (1990) for the rest of the period.

Table A.29   Share of the heavy chemical (HCI) and light industry in Brazil's manufactured exports and output, 1919–88 (%)

		1919	1939	1949	1955	1965	1973	1980	1984	1988
Exports[1]	HCI	n.a.	n.a.	3.9	2.0[a]	8.8	18.0	43.3	51.2	60.1*
	Light	n.a.	n.a.	96.1	98.0[a]	90.8	82.0	56.7	48.7	40.0*
Output[2]	HCI	9.8	19.2	24.0	35.2	48.0	51.0	60.0	60.0	59.0
	Light	90.2	80.8	76.0	64.9	52.0	49.0	40.0	40.0	41.0

[1] ISIC. HCI includes chemicals (35), non-metal mineral (36), basic metal (37) and metal manufactures (38). Light industry covers food, beverage and tobacco (31), Textiles (32), wood products (33), paper products (34) and other manufactures (39). [2] HCI is defined according to the IBGE two-digit classification and includes: chemicals, non-metal mineral, metallurgy, machinery, electrical and communications equipment, transport equipment and pharmaceuticals. IBGE data at 1986 prices. Figures for 1955 and 1988 were estimated using two-digit quantum indices.
* 1987 ** includes electronic and communication equipment. [a]1954

Source: UN (ITSY) for export data, and ANESTBR (1990) and IBGE (1990)

Table A.30   Brazil's manufacturing structure by end use, 1919–88 (%)

Goods	1919	1949	1955	1959	1970	1975	1980	1985	1988
Consumer	82.1	69.8	64.2	57.3	54.3	50.1	47.9	49.3	48.9
durables	1.3	2.0	5.5	5.9	9.3	13.3	13.5	11.7	12.4
Non-durables	80.8	67.8	58.7	51.4	45.0	36.8	34.4	37.6	36.5
Intermediate	16.5	25.3	30.4	33.0	34.4	34.6	37.4	40.0	39.5
Capital	1.4	5.1	5.3	9.7	11.3	15.4	14.7	10.6	11.5
Total	100.0	100.0	100.0	100.0	100.0	100.0	100.0	100.0	100.0

Note: Manufacturing output data. For 1919–1970 at current prices. The rest of the period at 1970 cruzeiros.

Source: Bonelli and Façanha (1978:319) for 1919 to 1959 except for 1955 which was taken from Bergsman (1970:92); and Serra (1982) for 1970–1980. For the rest of the period, the structure was estimated by using IBGE (1990) end-use-quantum indices for manufacturing output.

190 *Appendix*

Table A.31   Brazil's export structure by main categories, 1946–87. (US$ Million and % of total exports)

Categories	1946	1950	1955	1964	1974	1980	1987
Total exports	985.3	1355.5	1423.0	1429.8	7950.9	20132.0	26228.6
Primary and	912.6	1339.5	1407.8	1353.5	6030.3	12541.9	13223.1
semi-manuf.[1]	(92.6)	(98.8)	(98.9)	(94.7)	(75.8)	(62.3)	(50.4)
Coffee	(35.3)	(63.9)	(58.9)	(53.1)	(12.3)	(13.7)	(8.3)
Manufactured	72.7	16.0	15.2	76.3	1920.6	7590.1	13005.5
products[2]	(7.4)	(1.2)	(1.1)	(5.3)	(24.1)	(37.7)	(49.6)

[1] STIC divisions 0, 1, 2, 3, 4, 9, 68. [2] STIC divisions 5 to 8 minus 68.

Note: numbers in parentheses are the shares in total exports.
Source: Tyler (1976:123) for 1946 for 1955 and UN (ITSY) for the rest of the period.

Table A.32   Brazil's export and import ratios by manufacturing sector, 1949–84 (%)

Import[1]	1907	1939	1949	1964	1957	1970	1974	1979	1984	1986	1988	1990
Total mnf.	47.0	21.5	13.9	6.1	7.1	8.0 (8.8)	11.9 (12.2)	6.8 (7.4)	(5.1)	(5.7)	(4.4)	(5.7)
HCI	n.a.	n.a.	26.9	9.0	10.2	11.8	15.2	8.4	n.a.	n.a.	n.a.	n.a.
Light	n.a.	n.a.	3.8	1.6	2.2	2.3	5.1	3.4	n.a.	n.a.	n.a.	n.a.
Export[2]												
Total mnf.	9.0	7.6	2.3	2.0	2.6	5.7 (4.5)	6.9 (6.4)	9.1 (8.0)	9.8 (16.0)	(9.8)	(11.5)	(9.3)
HCI	n.a.	n.a.	5.2	1.8	2.0	2.3	3.6	8.2	8.7	n.a.	n.a.	n.a.
Light	n.a.	n.a.	1.5	1.8	2.3	5.8	10.0	8.5	11.4	n.a.	n.a.	n.a.

[1] Imports divided by the total domestic supply. [2] Exports divided by total output. * Estimated by quantum indices.

Notes: (a) see Table A.5 for light and heavy industry definition. (b) Ratios are the weighted average (value-added) for two-digit sectoral data. (IBGE classification).

Source: Villela and Suzigan (1977:39) for 1907–39, Tyler (1976) for the 1949–1967, World Bank (1983a) for 1970–79, ANESTBR (1990) for 1984 data. Numbers in parentheses are from a recent BNDE (1992a) study.

Table A.33 Brazil's composition of imports by end use (%), 1901–87

	1901–07	1924–29	1935–39	1955	1964	1972	1974	1978	1982	1987
Food and bev.	36.9	21.3	17.0	9.7	8.8	7.3	7.1	8.7	8.3	7.4
Consumer goods						4.3	2.5	2.3	1.7	2.9
Durables	n.a.	n.a.	10.3	2.8	2.4	2.4	1.4	1.0	0.5	0.9
Non-durables[1]	n.a.	n.a.	6.7	6.9	6.4	1.9	1.2	1.3	1.1	2.0
Ind. supplies[2]	46.9	52.8	51.1	41.5	47.4	34.0	41.8	29.4	18.8	30.5
Fuel	8.2	11.1	12.2	21.5	20.4	12.6	22.8	32.5	53.4	32.3
Capital goods	7.1	14.8	26.3	27.3	23.4	37.7	22.9	24.2	15.6	22.6

[1] Includes food until 1964. [2] Includes raw material, intermediate goods minus fuel.

Notes: Percentages may not add to 100% because of non specified goods. Definition of the categories among the sources are not strictly comparable.

Source: Data for 1901 to 1930 from Villela and Suzigan (1977:42), for 1935 to 1964 from *Estrutura do Comércio Exterior do Brasil: 1920–1964*, Vol. 2. FGV, Rio de Janeiro, as quoted by Dib (1985:74) and Fishlow (1972:44). For the rest of the period, UN (ITSY)

Table A.34   Brazil's public sector share of gross fixed capital formation,
1947–87[1]

	State firms[2]	Gov. budget	Public sector	Private sector	Total
1947–55	2.9	23.2	26.1	73.9	100
1956–64	9.3	23.8	33.1	66.9	100
1965–73	18.7	23.7	42.4	57.6	100
1974–79	22.1	14.7	36.9	63.1	100
1980–87	19.4	15.2	34.6	65.4	100

[1] Arithmetic average. [2] Over 1966–79, includes only the federal large state firms in steel, mining, petrochemicals, telecommunications, electricity and railroads.

Source: State firms data from Werneck (1969:99) for 1947–65, Trebat (1983:122) for 1966–79, and Dinsmoor (1990:126). Rest of data from IBGE (1990).

Table A.35 Selected Human Capital Indicators, 1940–88

	Illiteracy rate[1]	Primary			Secondary			Tertiary		
	≥10*	≥10*	≥20*	Enr. ratio†	≥10*	≥20*	Enr. ratio†	≥10*	≥20*	Enr. ratio†
1940	65.0	12.1	12.1	n.a.	3.3	3.8	n.a.	0.3	1.3	n.a.
1950	57.0	31.4	31.7	n.a.	6.6	7.0	n.a.	1.6	1.3	n.a.
1960	51.6	33.6	n.a.	108.0**	8.5	n.a.	16.0**	1.9	n.a.	2.0**
1970	39.4	n.a.	32.2	125.0	n.a.	13.0	26	n.a.	1.9	5.6
1980	25.5	n.a.	n.a.	99.0	n.a.	n.a.	34	n.a.	n.a.	11.9
1988	15.3	n.a.	n.a.	104.0	n.a.	n.a.	38.0	n.a.	n.a.	11.1

[1] Aged 10 and over. * Highest school attainment of the literate population aged over 10 and 20.
† Enrolment as a percentage of the age group. ** 1965

Source: IBGE Indicadores Sociais as quoted in World Bank 1979:121, UNESCO Statistical Yearbook and ANESTBR, various issues.

Table A.36   Brazil's effective purchase-power-parity
exchange rates[1] 1954–87 (1980 prices)

Year	Exports[2]	Imports[3]	Official	Year	Exports[2]	Official
1954	23.9	53.7	m.r.[4]	1972	58.7	46.7
1955	29.3	63.8	m.r.	1973	57.8	46.6
1956	29.4	76.0	m.r.	1974	62.0	51.8
1957	31.3	97.3	m.r.	1975	61.0	48.9
1958	34.0	89.2	m.r.	1976	62.6	48.7
1959	41.7	104.3	m.r.	1977	64.5	48.5
1960	44.6	87.6	m.r.	1978	61.5	46.9
1961	49.5	117.9	m.r.	1979	64.1	49.7
1962	49.2	131.7	45.6	1980	56.5	52.7
1963	42.1	120.3	39.6	1981	67.4	52.8
1964	51.7	122.4	41.5	1982	74.3	56.2
1965	53.0	106.9	49.5	1983	83.8	70.4
1966	45.8	75.4	45.8	1984	77.8	68.4
1967	43.1	61.2	42.1	1985	79.0	72.3
1968	46.1	62.5	43.5	1986	n.a.	67.4
1969	53.4	70.8	48.2	1987	n.a.	62.9
1970	56.5	70.9	47.7	1988	n.a.	52.7
1971	58.2	n.a.	47.6	1989	n.a.	32.6

[1] Relevant exchange rate times the ratio of the average WPI of Brazil's major trade partners (EUA, UK, Germany, France, Italy, Netherlands.) to Brazil's WPI [2] Includes export bonuses and net subsidies. [3] Includes legal tariffs and surcharges. Not available for the post-1970 period. [4] Multiple rates.

Source: For 1955–68 nominal effective rates on exports and imports (until 1969) Bergsman (1970:38). Rest of the data own calculation using Baumann (1990:180) estimates for export subsidies and data from BACEN and IMF(b).

Appendix

Table A.37   Trends of net foreign direct investment (FDI) in Brazil, 1948–88.[1]

	US$ million[2]	% mnf. inv.[3]	% net capital inflow[4]
1948	16.5	n.a.	45.9
1952	8.6	n.a.	14.0
1956	84.4	29.6	30.9
1960	104.4	21.7	20.0
1964	47.4	5.9	12.7
1968	99.4	10.3	12.3
1972	486.5	14.5	10.9
1976	1036.3	14.9	12.5
1980	1461.0	22.6	11.3
1984	366.4	n.a.	4.1
1988	95.8	n.a.	5.9

[1] Three-year moving average. [2] Total FDI plus reinvestments minus withdrawals, debt-swaps and Brazilian investment abroad. [3] 1970 prices. [4] Net FDI plus medium and long term loans.

Source: For FDI, BACEN, various issues. For 1955–69 mnf. investment, Serra (1982: 102). For the rest of the data IBGE (1990).

Table A.38   National Development Bank (BNDES) loans by sector (1953–89)[1]

| | sectors (% of total loans) | | | | | % loans to private sector[4] | loans/ GFCF[5] (%) | mnf. loans/mnf. investment (%) | | |
	HCI[2]	light[3]	mnf.	public	private			HCI	light	mnf
1953–55	88.6	11.4	10.3	89.1*	10.9*	n.a.	2.2	n.a.	n.a.	n.a.
1956–64	97.4	2.6	56.0	86.5	13.5	1.1	3.3	n.a.	n.a.	n.a.
1965–73	67.9	32.1	72.9	39.9	60.5	4.8	5.5	n.a.	n.a.	19.3
1974–79	74.2	25.8	66.2	18.9#	81.1#	8.1	13.0	51.4	31.5	43.1(28)
1980–82	72.2	27.8	49.9	n.a.	n.a.	7.2	10.2	50.4†	36.7†	43.9(23)†
1983–89	60.9	39.1	52.9	n.a.	n.a.	3.1	9.1	n.a.	n.a.	n.a.

[1]Arithmetic average of approved loans, except for the figures in parentheses which are disbursed loans. 1981 prices [2]Metallurgy, chemicals, non-metallic, machinery, transport equipment.[3]Textile, footwear and others.[4]BNDE's share of total loans to the private sector. [5]Gross fixed capital formation. *1952–55. #74–77. †1980–81.

Source: Zoninsein (1984) for 1953–81 loans and BNDE (1992a). Investment data from Serra (1982:102) and IBGE (1990).

Appendix

Table A.39   Brazil's real unit labour costs[1], 1949–84

	1949	1959	1962	1963	1964	1967	1968	1969	1970	1972	1973
Total[2]	100	93	99	91	90	90	85	82	82	86	77
Direct[3]	100	81	79	80	78	n.a.	n.a.	n.a.	74	70	66

	1974	1975	1976	1977	1978	1979	1980	1981	1982	1983	1984
Total	76	68	71	74	76	74	62	66	69	61	53
Direct	62	62	65	68	69	69	64	66	64	58	51

[1] Changes in the real manufacturing average wage (deflated by the WPI, 1986=100) adjusted by the changes in labour productivity (Value-addded per employee). [2] All employees [3] Production Workers.

Source: ANESTBR, various issues and IBGE (1990).

Table A.40   Brazil's manufacturing employment elasticities, 1939–84.[1]

(%)	1939–49	1949–59	1959–70	1970–75	1975–80	1970–80	1980–84
	0.6 (4.7)	0.3 (2.9)	0.6 (4.0)	1.0 (11.7)	0.8 (5.2)	0.9 (7.3)	1.2 (−3.5)

[1] Total employment growth divided by real output growth. Compound annual rates until 1970 and ordinary least square rates thereafter. Numbers in parentheses are manufacturing employment growth.

Source: IBGE (1990).

Table A.41   Brazil's legal tariff rate, 1966–77 (%)

	1966	1967	1971	1975	1977
Manufacturing	99	48	67*	n.a	70.0
Capital goods for mnf.	49	36	43.6	41.0	60.6
Capital goods for agric.	32	25	44	38.7	41.3
Interm. goods for mnf	42	30.5	45.6	51.1	75.9
Interm. goods for agric.			26.4	12.8	20.0
Transport equipment	55	42	36.5	47.7	65.2
Consumer durables	80	64	100.7	115.2	140.2
Consumer non-durables	73	54	102.7	105.7	154.4

Note: Data for manufacturing is the sectoral average weighed by the 1970 output. For the rest of the data, simple averages. * 1973.

Source: Doellinger *et al.* (1974:134) for 1966–67, Rosa *et al.* (1979: 12) for 1971–77 and Baumann (1985:230) for the manufacturing average.

Table A.42   Brazil's ICOR, 1948–89[1]

1948–55	2.69
1956–64	2.34
1965–73	1.94
1974–79	4.70
1980–89	9.50

[1] 1980 prices. GDP deflated by the implicit deflator and the gross fixed capital formation by the WPI.

Source: Data from IBGE (1990) and *Conjuntura Econômica*, July 1991.

Table A.43   Share of government, foreign and domestic firms in Brazilian manufacturing, 1971–80 (% of sales)

	1971			1980		
	DF	*FF*	*GF*	*DF*	*FF*	*GF*
Manufacturing	43.6	45.1	11.3	59.0	28.5	12.5
Light industry	67.7	28.5	0.0	77.5	19.3	0.8
Heavy industry	11.6	51.8	36.6	45.5	36.8	17.7
Metallurgy	44.6	27.3	28.1	n.a.	n.a.	n.a.
Machinery	35.8	64.2	0.0	59.0	41.0	0.0
Elec. and comm. equation	35.1	64.9	0.0	56.0	44.0	0.0
Transp. equipment	42.7	57.3	0.0	29.0	68.0	0.0
Chemical	17.8	30.0	52.2	27.0	21.0	52.0
Pharmaceutical	39.5	60.5	0.0	28.0	71.0	0.0

Notes: (a) The figures for the three years are not strictly comparable due to differences in the sample sizes. For 1971, it covered the largest firms accounting for about 60% of manufacturing output, which tends to underestimate the share of the smaller DFs. For 1980, the firms involved accounted for roughly 95% of manufacturing output. (b) data for heavy and light industry (defined as in Table A.29), own calculation using manufacturing value-added as weights. (c) DF stands for domestic firm, MNC for foreign firm and GF for government firm.

Source: Tyler (1976:52) for 1971, and Willmore (1987:165) for 1980.

Table A.44   Share of foreign firms in manufactured, semi-manufactured
and total exports. Brazil, 1967–86 (%)

	(a) Total	(b) Mnf. and semi-mnf.	(c) Equip. and instrum.	(d) Other mnfs
1967	n.a.	33.8*	n.a.	n.a.
1974	n.a.	30.0†	67	17
1978	23.1	44.9(38.8)	64	23
1980	28.4	50.2(38.3)	62	22
1984	26.7	39.4	67	18
1985	27.8	41.7	63	18
1986	28.4	42.2	n.a.	n.a.

* Fanjnzylber (1971:207). Sample includes 1147 firms, but restricted to manufactures, excluding semi-manufactured exports.† Baumann (1985:238).

Notes: (1) In (a) and (b) foreign firm is defined as having non-residents as the major shareholder. Data from a Cacex study whose results were published in BNDES (1988b:111). The results in (b) tend to overestimate the foreign firms' share since it includes firms from agriculture and mining sectors. These two sectors, however, made up for only 3% in average of the total stock of FDI during the period. (2) (c) and (d) is from Fritsch and Franco (1988) using Cacex data (3) The number in parentheses are Cepal's (1985a) and Willmore's (1987) estimates, for 1978 and 1980 respectively. The 1978 figure was drawn from a sample of 12 435 firms, while the 1980 estimate involved 47 769 firms, accounting for more than 95% of manufacturing output.

Table A.45   Share of foreign loans by type and firm ownership
(1966–81)[1]

	1966	1968	1971	1973	1975	1977	1979	1981
Indirect short-term loans (res. 63)				32.8	27.6	25.4	27.7	42.0
Direct long-term loans (law 4131)				67.2	72.4	74.6	72.3	58.1
Total				100	100	100	100	100

	All loans			Direct loans (law 4131)				
Local firms	6.5	13.1	20.9	21.4	7.9	5.0	5.1	4.7
Foreign	44.2	76.3	60	45.3	46.5	40.8	23.7	22.3
Public sec	46.4	6.3	3.9	33.3	45.6	54.3	71.2	73.1
Total	100	100	100	100	100	100	100	100

[1] Three year moving average from 1973 onwards.

Source: For 1966–71 Pereira; J.E. (1974) *Financiamento Externo e Crescimento Econômico no Brasil: 1966:73*, Rio de Janeiro: IPEA/INPES, Coleção Relatórios de Pesquisa n. 27, as quoted in Villela and Baer (1980); and for 1972–81 Cruz (1984:100, 140)

Table A.46   R & D expenditures in selected countries as a proportion of GNP

	1970	1977	1982	Latest year	
Brazil	0.24	0.70	0.59	0.59	(1987)
Argentina	n.a.	1.80	0.20	0.20	(1982)
Mexico	0.20	0.30	0.20	0.60	(1984)
India	n.a.	0.50	0.76	1.00	(1985)
South Korea	0.39	0.60	0.90	1.80	(1986)
Taiwan	n.a.	2.00	0.90	1.06	(1985)
Japan	1.90	2.00	2.40	2.90	(1987)
US	2.60	2.10	2.50	2.60	(1987)

Source: UNESCO, *Statistical Yearbook 1988*, as quoted in Frischtak and Dahman (1990:19)

Table A.47   Brazil's share of exports by economic group and sector, 1950–89

SITC	1950	1960	1970	1975	1980	1984	1987	1989
World	2.2	1.0	0.9	1.0	1.0	1.4	1.1	1.1
LDC manufacturing			0.9	1.5	2.6	3.8	3.9	n.a.
World manufacturing			0.2	0.4	0.7	0.9	0.8	n.a.
Chemicals (5)			0.2	0.3	0.5	1.1	0.8	n.a.
Iron and steel (67)			0.6	0.4	1.2	3.2	2.4	n.a.
Non-ferrous (68)			0.0	0.2	0.2	1.4	1.9	n.a.
Mach. + transp. (7)			0.1	0.4	0.7	0.6	0.6	n.a.
Textile (26+65+84)			0.2	1.0	0.8	1.1	0.7	n.a.
Basic (6+8+68)			0.3	0.6	0.8	1.4	0.9	n.a.

Notes: (a) manufacturing defined as 5 to 8 minus 68. (b) figures for industrial sectors are world shares.

Source: UN (ITSY and HIT).

Appendix

Table A.48   Brazil's basic macro indicators, 1808–1989 (%)

Periods	(a) GDP real growth	(b) Mnf. output Growth	(c) GFCF/GDP	(d) GDP deflator
1908–47	4.4	5.9	n.a.	n.a.
1948–55	6.4	8.4	14.2	14.0
1956–64	7.5	9.2	13.6	40.2
1965–73	9.7	11.4	16.1	28.3
1974–79	6.4	6.2	24.2	41.3
1980–84	−0.7	−2.8	19.3	131.1
1985–89	3.2	2.6	17.3	510.0

Notes: (a) and (b) least square averages. (c) and (d) arithmetic averages.

Source: IBGE (1990) and *Conjuntura Economica*, July 1991.

Table A.49 Brazil's basic foreign trade indicators, 1950–90

Year	Terms of trade (%)	Debt service exports	Mnf. export growth (%)	Real export growth (%)²	Trade balance³ US$10⁶	Current account US$10⁶	Year	Terms of trade (%)	Debt service exports	Mnf. export growth (%)	Real export growth (%)²	Trade balance³ US$10⁶	Current account US$10⁶
1950	66.1	8.3	-47.2	-17.3	421	140	1970	9.9	33.1	62.5	2.8	232	-562
1951	-9.0	2.7	6.9	6.9	66	-403	1971	-6.6	39.7	21.3	5.4	-341	-1307
1952	-8.1	3.9	-58.5	-19.4	-284	-624	1972	0.9	39.1	69.7	28.2	-245	-1489
1953	3.1	5.2	25.3	12.0	423	55	1973	11.0	35.3	77.9	16.0	6	-1688
1954	26.5	11.7	5.6	-10.7	152	-195	1974	-16.7	32.4	42.4	1.7	-4690	-7122.4
1955	-19.3	12.3	61.7	12.0	324	2	1975	-2.6	42.3	15.7	10.2	-3540	-6700.2
1956	0.9	17.1	-13.8	7.1	435	57	1976	12.2	47.4	5.0	0.0	-2255	-6017.1
1957	-1.6	22.2	38.6—	6.7	107	-264	1977	13.0	51.1	30.5	1.5	31	-4037.3
1958	-3.3	30.7	-9.2	-3.6	64	-248	1978	-14.6	62.3	38.4	12.1	-1156	-6990.4
1959	-3.7	36.5	9.9	22.2	72	-311	1979	-7.1	69.3	36.1	9.5	-2840	-10741.6
1960	-5.9	41.9	57.7	3.3	-24	-478	1980	-17.7	64.5	32.4	23.5	-2823	-12807
1961	-0.4	31.4	49.5	9.1	111	-222	1981	-15.4	69.7	20.0	20.0	1589	-11734.3
1962	-6.4	35.3	-13.0	-4.2	-90	-389	1982	-1.8	98.5	-15.2	-8.3	818	-16310.5
1963	-1.1	32.1	12.2	17.4	112	-114	1983	-1.9	54.4	11.7	14.5	6470	-6837.4
1964	22.4	28.5	83.0	-14.8	344	140	1984	9.4	46.9	29.5	22.2	13089	44.8
1965	1.1	28.8	62.4	8.7	654	368	1985	0.0	49.8	0.5	3.2	12486	-241
1966	-8.0	29.0	0.7	16.0	438	54	1986	n.a.	56.2	-4.4	-16.4	8305	-5304
1967	-2.3	38.0	30.8	-3.4	213	-237	1987	n.a.	44.2	21.2	n.a.	11173	-1436
1968	-4.9	33.4	-6.2	14.3	26	-508	1988	n.a.	49.9	29.2†	n.a.	19184*	175*
1969	4.8	29.2	47.9	12.5	318	-281	1989	n.a.	n.a.	-2.8†	n.a.	10990*	1564*

[1] STIC 5 to 8 minus 68. [2] Exports quantum index (1980=1000). [3] Balance-of-payments basis. * Preliminary † CE estimates.

Source: UN (ITSY), IBGE (1990), ANESTBR. Various issues, and Conjuntura Econômica (CE), July 1991.

References

ABREU, M.P. (1990) 'Inflação, Estagnação e Ruptura: 1961-64'. In M. P. ABREU (ed.) *A Ordem do Progresso: Cem Anos de Política Econômica Republicana. 1889–1989.* Rio de Janeiro: Editora Campus.

ALBERT, B. (1983) *'South America and the World Economy from Independence to 1930'.* London: Macmillan.

ALLGEIER, P. F. (1988) 'Korea Trade Policy in the Next Decade: Dealing with Reciprocity', *World Development*, January, Vol. 16, No. 1, pp. 85–97.

ALMEIDA, J. S. (1988) *Instabilidade da Economia e Estrutura Financeira das Empresas no Brasil do Ajustamento Recessivo.* Rio de Janeiro: Discussion Paper No. 178 Institute of Industrial Economics. Federal University of Rio de Janeiro. December.

AMSDEN, A. H. (1987) *Stabilization and Adjustment Policies and Programmes: Republic of Korea.* Geneva: Weider country studies No. 14. United Nations.

—— (1989) *Asia's Next Giant: South Korea and Late Industrialization.* New York: Oxford University Press.

AMSDEN, A. H. and EUH, Y.D. (1990) *Republic of Korea's Financial Reform: What are the Lessons .* Geneva: Discussion Paper No. 30, UNCTAD.

ANUÁRIO ESTATISTICO DO BRASIL (ANESTBR). Various issues. Rio de Janeiro: IBGE.

ARAÚJO Jr., J., HAGUENAUER, L. and MACHADO, J.B. (1990) 'Proteção, Competitividade e Desempenho Exportador da Economia Brasileira nos Anos 80.', *Pensamiento Iberoamericano*, No. 17, pp.13–37.

ARROW, K. (1969) 'Classificatory Notes on the Production and Transmission of Technological Knowledge', *American Economic Review*, 59, 29–35.

BAER, W. (1969) *The Development of Brazil Steel Industry.* Nashville: Vanderbilt University Press.

BAI, M. K. (1982) 'The Turning Point in the Korean Economy', *The Developing Economies*, vol. 20, pp. 117–140.

BAIN, J. S. (1956) *Barriers to New Competition.* Cambridge: Harvard University Press.

BALASSA, B. (1971) (ed.) *Structure of Protection in Developing Countries.* The Johns Hopkins University Press for the World Bank.

—— (1975) 'Reforming the System of Incentives in Developing Countries', *World Development*, vol. 3, pp. 365–382.

—— (1979) 'Incentives Policies in Brazil', *World Development*, Nov/Dec. 7(11/12), pp. 1023–1046.

—— (1981a) 'Export Incentives and Export Performances in Developing Countries : A comparative analysis'. In B. Balassa (ed) *The Newly Industrialising Countries and the World Economy.* New York: Pergamon.

—— (1981b) *A 'Stages' Approach to Comparative Advantage.* In B. Balassa (ed.), *The Newly Industrialising Countries and the World Economy.* New York: Pergamon.

References 205

—— (ed.) (1982) 'Development Strategies in Semi-industrial Countries'. Baltimore Md: Johns Hopkins Univ. Press for the World Bank.

—— (1985) 'The Role of Foreign Trade in Economic Development of Korea'. In W. GALENSON (ed.) *Foreign Trade and Investment: Economic Development in the Asian Newly Industrialising Countries.* Madison, WI: University of Wisconsin Press.

—— (1989) 'Outward Orientation'. In H. Chenery and T.N. Srinivasan (eds) *Handbook of Development Economics, Vol. I.* Amsterdam: Elsevier Science Publishers.

—— (1991) 'Economic Policies in the Pacific Area Developing Countries'. London: Macmillan.

BALDWIN, R. (1969) '*The Case Against Infant-Industry Protection*', *Journal of Political Economy*, 77:295–305.

—— (1988) 'High-Technology Exports and Strategic Trade Policy in Developing Countries: The Case of Brazilian Aircraft'. In G.K. Helleiner (ed.) *Trade Policy Industrialization and Development* Toronto e Helsinki: Wider. UNU.

BANCO CENTRAL DO BRASIL (BACEN), *Boletim Mensal*, various issues.

BANCO NATIONAL DE DESENVOLVIMENTO ECONOMICO E SOCIAL (BNDES) (1988a) 'Coréia do Sul: A Importância de uma Política Industrial'. Rio de Janeiro: Estudos BNDES. April,

—— (1988b) 'Questões Relativas à Competitividade da Indústria Brasileira de Bens de Capital: Bens de Capital de Encomenda e Máquinas-Ferramenta'. Rio de Janeiro. Estudos BNDES. Junho

—— (1988c) 'O Capital Estrangeiro na Indústria Brasileira: Atualidade e Perspectivas'. Rio de Janeiro: Estudos BNDES. Maio.

—— (1992a) 'BNDES 40 anos. Um Agente de Mudanças'. Rio de Janeiro. BNDES.

—— (1992b) 'Indicadores de Competitividade Internacional da Indústria Brasileira 1970/90'. Estudos BNDES No. 21.

BANK OF JAPAN (1990). 'Comparative Economic and Financial Statistics: Japan and other Major Countries'. Tokyo.

BANK OF KOREA (BOK). (a) 'Economic Statistics Yearbook'. Various years. Seoul.

—— (b) 'Financial Statement Analysis'. Various years. Seoul.

—— (c) 'Monthly Bulletin'. Various issues. Seoul.

—— (1985) 'Economic Stabilization and Liberalisation in Korea, 1980-84'. Paper for presentation at the seminar commemorating the 35th anniversary of the Bank of Korea. June 12, Seoul.

BARK, T. (1989) 'Recent Trends, Government Policies and the Economic Impact of Direct Foreign Investment in Korea'. Paper presented at the KDI, Policy Forum on Foreign Direct Investment and Economic Development of LDCs. October, Seoul.

BARROS, J. R.M. and VERSIANI, F. R. (eds) (1977) 'Formação Econômica do Brasil: a Experiência da Industrialização'. São Paulo: Editora Saraiva.

BATISTA, J. C. (1992) 'Debt and Adjustment Policies in Brazil'. San Francisco: Westview Press.

BAUMANN, R. (1985) 'Exportações e Crescimento Industrial no Brasil'. Rio de Janeiro: IPEA/INPES. Série monográfica.

—— (1990) 'Befiex: Efeitos Internos de um Incentivo à Exportação', *Revista Brasileira de Economia*, vol. 44. no. 2, April/ June.

206   *References*

BAUMANN, R and BRAGA, H.C. (1985) *O Sistema Brasileiro de Financiamento as Exportações.* Rio de Janeiro: IPEA/INPES, Série de Estudos de Política Industrial e Comércio Exterior No. 2, March.

BAUMOL, W. P., PANZAR, J. C. and WILLIG, R. D. (1982) *Contestable Markets and the Theory of Industry Structure.* New York: Harcourt Brace Jovanovich.

BECKER, B. K. and EGLER, C. A. (1992) *Brazil: a New Regional Power in the World Economy. A Regional Geography.* Cambridge: Cambridge University Press.

BELL, M., ROSS-LARSON, B. AND WESTPHAL, L. (1984) 'Assessing the Performance of Infant Industries', *Journal of Development Economics,* 16, pp. 101–128. North-Holland.

BELLUZZO, L.G.M. and COUTINHO, L. (1983) *'Política Econômica, Inflexões e Crise: 1974–81'.* In L.G. M. Beluzzo e Coutinho, R. (eds) *Desenvolvimento Capitalista no Brasil: ensaios sobre a crise.* São Paulo: Editora Brasiliense.

BERGSMAN, J. (1970) *Brazil: Industrialization and Trade Policies.* London: Oxford University Press for the OECD.

BERGSMAN, J. and MALAN, P. (1971) *The Structure of Protection in Brazil.* In B. BALASSA *Structure of Protection in Developing Countries.* The Johns Hopkins University Press for the World Bank.

BHAGWATI, J. (1965) 'On the Equivalence of Tariffs and Quotas'. In R. E. Baldwin et al. (eds), *Trade, Growth and the Balance of Payments: Essays in Honour of Gottfried Haberler.* Chicago: Rand McNally.

—— (1982) 'Directly Unproductive, Profit-seeking (DUP) Activities', *Journal of Political Economy,* 90(5) pp. 989–1001.

BIATO, F., GUIMARÃES, E. and FIGUEIREDO, M.H. (1973) *Transferência de Tecnologia no Brasil.* Rio de Janeiro: IPEA/INPES.

BIELSCHOWSKY, R. (1978) 'Notas sobre a Questão da Autonomia Tecnológica na Indústria Brasileira'. In W. Suzigan (ed.) *Indústria: Políticas, Instituições e Desenvolvimento.* Série Monográfica No. 28, IPEA/INPES, Rio de Janeiro.

BLOMSTRÖM, M. (1987) *Transnational Corporations and Manufacturing Exports from Developing Countries.* New York: United Nations Centre on Transnational Corporations.

BONELLI, R. and FAÇANHA, L. O. (1978) 'A Indústria de Bens de Capital no Brasil: Desenvolvimento, Problemas e Perspectivas'. In W. Suzigan (ed.) *Indústria: Políticas, Instituições e Desenvolvimento.* Rio de Janeiro: Série Monográfica No. 28, IPEA/INPES.

BONELLI, R and WERNECK, A. de O. (1978) 'Desempenho Industrial: Auge e Desaceleração nos anos 70'. In W. Suzigan (ed.) *Indústria: Políticas, Instituições e Desenvolvimento.* Rio de Janeiro: Série Monográfica No. 28, IPEA/INPES.

BRAGA, H.C. (1981) 'Aspectos Distributivos do Esquema de Subsídios Fiscais à Exportação de Manufaturados', *Pesquisa e Planejamento Econômico,* 11(3), December.

—— (1988) *Estrutura de Mercado, Tecnologia e Produtividade na Indústria Brasileira: Uma Abordagem Quantitativa.* Universidade Federal do Rio de Janeiro. Mimeo.

BRAGA, H.C. and MATESCO, V. (1986) *Progresso Técnico na Indústria Brasileira: Indicadores e Análise de seus Fatores Determinantes*. Rio de Janeiro: Discussion Paper No. 99 IPEA/INPES.

BRAGA, H.C., SANTIAGO, G. and FERRO, L. (1988) *Proteção Efetiva no Brasil: Uma Estimativa a Partir de Coomparações de Preços*. Rio de Janeiro: Série Épico No. 13, IPEA/INPES.

BRANDER, J. (1986) *'Rationales for Strategic Trade and Industrial Policies'*. In P. Krugman (ed.) *Strategic Trade Policy and The New International Economics*. Cambridge, Mass.: MIT Press.

CARNEIRO, D. D. (1987) *Brazil – Stabilization and Adjustment: Policies and Programs*. Country Study No. 11, Helsinki, WIDER, UNU, 1987a.

CARVALHO, J. S. AND HADDAD, C. L. S. (1981) 'Foreign Trade Strategies and Employment in Brazil'. In A. O. Krueger *et al.* , *Trade and Employment in Developing Countries Vol. 1. Individual studies*. Chicago: Chicago University Press.

CASTRO, A. B. and de SOUZA, F. E. P. (1985) *A Economia Brasileira em Marcha Forçada*. Rio de Janeiro, Ed. Paz e Terra.

CASTRO, C. de M. (1989) 'What is happening in Brazilian Education'. In E. Bacha and H. Klein (eds) *Social Change in Brazil, 1945–85: the Incomplete Transition*. New Mexico: University of New Mexico Press. First published in Portuguese in 1986.

CENÁRIOS. São Paulo. Various Issues.

CEPAL (1985a) 'Market Structure, Firm Size and Brazilian Exports'. *Estudios e Informes de la CEPAL*, No. 44. United Nations.

—— (1985b) *Trade Relations Between Brazil and the United States. Estudios e Informes de la CEPAL*, No. 52. United Nations.

CHAMBERLIN, E.H. (1933) *The Theory of Monopolistic Competition*. Cambridge: Harvard University Press.

CHANG, E. T. (1989) *Barriers to Korea's Manufactured Exports and Negotiating Options*. In J. Whalley (ed.) *Dealing with the North: Developing Countries and the Global Trading System* London, Canada: University of Western Ontario.

CHENERY, H. *et al.* (1986) *Industrialization and Growth: a Comparative Study*. Washington: Oxford University Press for the World Bank.

CHUNG, J. (1986) *Korea*. In F. Rushing and C.G. Brown (eds) *National Policies for Developing High Tech Industries. International Comparison*. Colorado: Westview Special Studies, Westview Press.

CLEMENTS, B. (1988) *Foreign Trade Strategies, Employment, and Income Distribution in Brazil*. New York: Praeger Publishers.

COES, D. V. (1991) 'Brazil'. In P. Demetris, M. Michely and A. Choksi (eds) *Liberalising Free Trade: Brazil, Peru and Colombia*. Vol. 4. Cambridge: Basil Blackwell for the World Bank.

COLCLOUGH, C. (1991) 'Structuralism versus Neo-liberalism: An Introduction'. In C. Colclough and J. Manor (eds) *States or Markets?: Neo-liberalism and the Development Policy Debate*. IDS development Studies Series. New York. Oxford University Press.

COLE, D. and PARK, Y.C. (1983) *Financial Development in Korea, 1945–1978*. London: Harvard University Press.

COLE, D. C. and CHO, Y.J. (1986) 'The Role of the Financial Sector in Korea's Structural Adjustment'. Seoul: KDI Working Paper No. 8607, December.

COLE, D. C. and LYMAN, P. N. (1971) *Korean Development: The Interplay of Politics and Economics*. Cambridge, Mass.: Harvard Univ. Press.

CONJUNTURA ECONÔMICA. Fundação Getulio Vargas. Rio de Janeiro. Various Issues.

CORDEN, M. (1974) *Trade Policy and Economic Welfare*. Oxford: Clarendon Press.

COUNCIL FOR ECONOMIC PLANNING AND DEVELOPMENT (CEPD) (1992) *Taiwan Statistical Databook*. Republic of China.

CRUZ, P.D. (1984) *Dívida Externa e Política Econômica*. São Paulo: Editora Brasiliense.

DEAN, W. (1971) *A Industrialização de São Paulo*. São Paulo. Difusão Européia do livro.

DIB, M. F. S. P. (1985) *Importações Brasileiras: Políticas de Controle e Determinantes da Demanda*. Rio de Janeiro: BNDES.

DINSMOOR, J. (1990) *Brazil: Responses to the Debt Crisis. Impact on Savings, Investment, and Growth*. Washington, D.C.: Johns Hopkins University Press for the Inter-American Development Bank.

DOELLINGER, C., CAVALCANTI, L. and CASTELO BRANCO, F. (1977) 'Política e Estrutura das Importações Brasileiras'. *Relatório de Pesquisa*, No. 38, Rio de Janeiro. IPEA/INPES.

DOELLINGER, C., CAVALCANTI, L. and FARIA, H. (1974) *A Política Brasileira de Comércio Exterior e seus Efeitos: 1967/73*. Rio de Janeiro: IPEA/INPES. Relatório de Pesquisa No. 22.

DOLLAR, D. (1991) Convergence of South Korean Productivity on West German Levels, 1966–78,' *World Development*, 19(2/3), pp. 263–273.

DORNBUSCH, R. AND PARK, Y.C. (1987) '*Korean Growth Policy*', *Brookings Papers on Economic Activity*, 2, pp. 389–453.

ECONOMIC PLANNING BOARD – EPB – (a) *Major Statistics of Korean Economy*. Various years Seoul.

—— (b) *Report on Mining and Manufacturing Survey*. Various years. Seoul.

—— (1989a) *The U.S.–Korea Economic Relationship: Issues and Prospects*. Seoul.

—— (1989b) 'Challenges Facing Korea Today and U.S.-Korea Economic Relations'. A speech delivered at the Institute for International Economics, Washington, D.C. on May 1, 1989.

—— (1990) *The Korean Economy : Past Performance, Current Policies, and Futures Prospects*. Seoul.

EDWARDS, S. (1985) 'Stabilization with Liberalisation: An Evaluation of Ten Years of Chile's Experiment with Free-Market Policies, 1973–1983', *Economic Development and Cultural Change*, vol. 33, No. 2, pp. 223–254.

ENOS, J. L. and PARK, W. H. (1988) *The Adoption and Diffusion of Imported Technology. The Case of Korea*. London: Croom Helm.

ERBER, F. (1985) 'The Development of the Electronic Complex and Government Policies in Brazil', World Development, 13 (3).

ERBER, F. (1992) '*A Política Industrial e de Comércio Exterior: uma Avaliação. In Perspectivas da Economia Brasileira*. Rio de Janeiro, IPEA.

EVANS, P. and TIGRE, P. (1989) 'Going Beyond Clones in Brazil and Korea: A Comparative Analysis of NICs Strategies in the Computer Industry', *World Development*, vol. 17, no. 11, pp. 1751–1768.

FAJNZYLBER, F. (1971) *Sistema Industrial e Exportações de Manufaturados. Análise da Experiência Brasileira.* Rio de Janeiro: IPEA/INPES, Relatório de Pesquisa No. 7.

—— (1981) 'Some Reflections on South-East Asian Export Industrialization', *CEPAL Review*, No. 15, pp. 111–132. December.

FAR EASTERN ECONOMIC REVIEW (FEER). Various issues.

FINANCIAL TIMES (1990) *South Korea Survey.* May 16. London.

FINDLAY, R. (1981) 'Comment to Anne O. Krueger's paper Export-Led Industrial Growth Reconsidered'. In W. HONG, and L. KRAUSE (eds)*Trade and Growth of the Advanced Developing Countries in the Pacific Rim.* Seoul: Korea Development Institute Press.

FISCHER, B., NUNENKAMP, P. *et al.* (1988) 'Capital-Intensive Industries in Newly Industrializing Countries: the case of the Brazilian Automobile and Steel Industries', *Kieler Studien*, No. 221. University of Kiel, Tübingen.

FISHLOW, A. (1972) *Origins and Consequences of Import Substitution in Brazil.* In E. Di Marco (ed.) *Essays in Honor of Raul Prebisch.* New York: Academic Press.

—— (1986) 'A Economia Política do Ajustamento Brasileiro aos Choques do Petróleo: Uma Nota Sobre o Período 1974/84', 19(1) April, 507–550.

—— (1990) 'The Latin American State', *Journal of Economic Perspectives*, vol. 4 , no. 3, pp. 61–74.

FRANK, C., KIM, K.S. and WESTPHAL L. E. (1975) *Foreign Trade Regimes and Economic Development: South Korea.* A Special Conference Series on Foreign Trade Regimes and Economic Development. Vol. III. NBER. New York: Columbia University Press.

FRISCHTAK, C.R. (1990) *Specialisation, Technical Change and Competitiveness in the Brazilian Electronics Industry.* Industry and Energy Department Working Paper. Industry Series Paper No. 15. World Bank. Feb

FRISCHTAK, C.R. and DAHLMAN, C. (1990) *National Systems Supporting Technical Advance in Industry: The Brazilian Experience.* Industry and Energy Department Working Paper. Industry Series Paper No. 32. World Bank.

FRITSCH, W. and FRANCO, G. (1988) 'Foreign Direct Investment and Patterns of Industrialization and Trade in Developing Countries: the Brazilian Experience'. In G.K. Helleiner (ed.) *Trade Policy Industrialization and Development.* Toronto e Helsinki: Wider. UNU.

FUJITA, N. and JAMES, W. (1989) 'Export Promotion and the Heavy Industrialization of Korea', *Developing Economies*, 27(3), pp. 236–50. September.

FURTADO, C (1963) *The Economic Growth of Brazil.* Berkeley: University of California Press.

GOLDSMITH, R. (1986) *Desenvolvimento Financeiro sob um Seculo de Inflação*: São Paulo: Harper and Row.

GONÇALVES, R. (1982) *Características e Evolução do Comércio Exterior de Empresas Transnacionais no Brasil.* Discussion Paper No. 9, Institute of Industrial Economics. Federal University of Rio de Janeiro. December.

GOUVEA NETO, R. (1991) 'How Brazil Competes in the Global Defense Industry', *Latin American Research Review*, Fall.

GRAHAM, E. M. (1991) '*Strategic Trade Policy and the Multinational Enterprise in Developing Countries*'. In P. Buckley and J. Clegg (eds.) *Multinational Enterprise in Less Developed Countries*. Basingstoke: Macmillan.

GUIMARÃES, E.A., MALAN, P.S. and ARAÚJO Jr. (1982). *Changing International Investment Strategies: The 'new forms' of Foreign Investment in Brazil*. Discussion Paper No. 45, IPEA/INPES, Rio de Janeiro.

GUIMARÃES, E. P. (1989) *Recent Trade Policy in Brazil*. Kiel Working Paper No. 389. The Kiel Institute of World Economics.

HAGGARD, S. (1990) *Pathways from the Periphery: The Politics of Growth in the Newly Industrialising Countries*. London: Cornell University Press.

HATTORI, T. (1989) 'Japanese Zaibatsu and Korean Chaebol'. In K.H. Chung and C.H. Lee (eds) *Korea Managerial Dynamics*. New York: Praeger.

HELLEINER, G. K. (1989) 'Transnational Corporations and Direct Foreign Investment'. In H. Chenery and T.N. Srinivasan (eds) *Handbook of Development Economics*, Vol. II. Amsterdam: Elsevier Science Publishers.

HELPMAN, E. (1990) 'The Noncompetitive Theory of International Trade and Trade Policy'. *In Proceedings of the World Bank Annual Conference on Development Economics 1989*.

HELPMAN, E. and KRUGMAN, P. (1985) *Market Structure and Foreign Trade*. Cambridge, M.A.: MIT Press.

—— (1989) *Trade Policy and Market Structure*. Cambridge, M.A.: MIT Press.

HEWITT, T. (1992) 'Employment and Skills in the Brazilian Electronics Industry'. In H. Schmitz and J. Cassiolato. (ed.) *Hi-Tech for Industrial Development. Lessons from the Brazilian Experience in Electronics and Automation*. New York: Routledge.

HIRSCHMAN, A.O. (1958) *The Strategy of Economic Development*. New Haven: Yale University Press.

HOFFMAN, H. (1989) 'Poverty and Prosperity'. In E. Bacha and H. Klein (eds) *Social Change in Brazil, 1945–85: the Incomplete Transition*. New Mexico: University of New Mexico Press.

HONG, W. (1979) *Trade Distortions and Employment Growth in Korea*. Seoul, Korea Development Institute.

—— (1987) 'A Comparative Static Application of the Heckscher-Olhin Model of Factor Proportions: Korea Experience'. *Weltwirtschaftliches Archive*, 123(2).

HONG, W. and KRAUSE, L. (eds.) (1981) *Trade and Growth of the Advanced Developing Countries in the Pacific Rim*. Seoul, Korea Development Institute Press.

HONG, W. AND PARK, Y.C. (1986) 'The Financing of Export-Oriented Growth in Korea'. In A. H. H .Tan and B. Kapuz, *Pacific Growth and Financial Interdependence* London: Allen and Unwin.

HORSTMANN, J. and MARKUNSEN, R. (1986) 'Up the Average Cost Curve: Inefficient Entry and the New Protectionism', *Journal of International Economics*, 20, pp. 225–247.

HORTA, M. H., PIANI, G. and KUME, H. (1991) 'A Política Cambial e Comercial'. In *Perspectivas da Economia Brasileira 1992*. Rio de Janeiro. IPEA.

IBGE (1990) *Estatísticas Históricas do Brasil. Séries Econômicas, Demográficas e Sociais de 1550 a 1988.* Rio de Janeiro.

INSTITUTO de PLANEJAMENTO ECONÔNICO E SOCIAL – IPEA – (1979) Realizações do Governo Geisel. 1974–78. Brasília: March.

INTERNATIONAL MONETARY FUND – IMF – (a) Various years. Annual *Report on Exchange Arrangements and Restrictions.* Washington DC.

—— (b) Various years. *International Financial Statistics.* Washington DC.

JOHNSON, H. (1965a) 'Tariffs and Economic Development, Some Theoretical Issues', *Journal of Development Studies,* 1(1), pp. 25.

—— (1965b) 'Optimal Trade Intervention in the Presence of Domestic Distortions'. In R. E. Baldwin *et al. Trade, Growth and the Balance of Payments.* Chicago: Rand McNally.

JONES, L.P. (1987) 'Jaebul and the Concentration of Economic Power in Korean Development: Issues, Evidence and Alternatives'. In Il Sakong (ed.) *Macroeconomic Policy and Industrial Developments Issues.* Seoul: Korea Development Institute.

JONES, L. P. and SAKONG, I. (1980) *Government, Business and Entrepreneurship in Economic Development: The Korean Case.* Cambridge, Mass.: Harvard University Press.

JUNG, K. H. (1989) 'Business-Government Relations in Korea'. In K. H. Chung and C.H. Lee (eds) *Korea Managerial Dynamics'.* New York: Praeger.

JUNG, W. S. and LEE, G. (1986) 'The Effectiveness of Export Promotion Policies: the case of Korea'. Weltwirtschaftliche Archives, 122(2), pp. 341–357.

JUNG-HO, Y. (1990) *The Industrial Policy of the 1970s and The Evolution of the Manufacturing Sector in Korea* Seoul: Korea Development Institute Working Paper No. 9017, October.

KANG, C.K. (1989) *Industrial Policy in Korea: Review and Perspective.* Seoul: Korea Institute for Economics and Technology (KIET). Occasional Paper.

KEESING, D.B. and LALL, S. (1988) 'Marketing Manufactured Exports from Developing Countries: Learning Sequences and Public Support'. In G.K. Helleiner (ed.) *Trade Policy Industrialization and Development.* Toronto e Helsinki: Wider. UNU.

KIM, Il-HWAN (1987) 'Direct Foreign Investment in Korea'. *Seoul: Korea Exchange Bank Monthly Review,* pp. 3–13. October.

KIM, J. H. (1989) *Korean Industrial Policies for Declining Industries.* Seoul: KDI Working Paper No. 8910, January.

—— (1990a) *The Adjustment of Industrial Policies for Economic Restructuring in Response to Pressure from Foreign Protectionism.* Paper prepared for the Korea Development Institute/ CIER Joint Conference on Industrial Policies. April, Kyongju, Korea.

—— (1990b) *Korean Industrial Policy in the 1970s: The Heavy and Chemical Industry Drive.* Seoul: Korea Development Institute Working Paper No. 9015. July.

KIM, K. D. and LEE, S. H. (1990) 'The Role of the Korean Government in Technology Import'. In C.H. Lee and I. Yamazawa (eds) *The Economic Development of Japan and Korea.*

KIM, L. (1989) 'Technological Transformation in Korea and Its Implications for Other Developing Countries'. Paper presented at the Korea Development

Institute, Policy Forum on *Foreign Direct Investment and Economic Development of LDCs*. Seoul, Korea, October 16–20.

KIM, S. K. (1987) 'The Nature of Trade Protection by Special Laws in Korea'. Seoul: Discussion Paper No. 87-01. Institute of Industrial Relations, Graduate School of Business Administration, Kyung Hee University. October.

—— (1991) 'Korea'. In P. Demetris, M. Michely and A. Choksi, *Liberalising Free Trade: Korea, Philippines and Singapore*, Vol. 4, Washington, D.C. : World Bank Publications.

KIM, Y. B. (1980) 'The Growth and Structural Change of the Textile Industry'. In C. K. Park (ed.) *Macroeconomic and Industrial Development in Korea*. Vol. 3 of *Essays on the Korean Economy*. Seoul: Korea Development Institute.

KOO, BOHN-YOUNG (1982) *New Forms of Foreign Investment in Korea*. Seoul. KDI Working Paper No. 82–02, June.

—— (1984) *The Role of The Government in Korea's Industrial Development*. Seoul: Korea Development Institute Working Paper No. 8407, October.

—— (1985) 'The Role of Direct Foreign Investment in Korea's Recent Economic Growth'. In W. Galenson (ed.) *Foreign Trade and Investment: Economic Development in the Newly Industrialising Asian Countries* Madison: University of Wisconsin Press.

KOO, BON-HO and BARK, T. (1989) 'Recent Macroeconomic Performance and Industrial Structural Adjustment in Korea'. Paper for Foundation for Advanced Information and Research Conference, August, Fukuoka, Japan.

KOREA DEVELOPMENT INSTITUTE – KDI – (1991) *Quarterly Economic Outlook*. Spring, Seoul.

KOREA ECONOMIC JOURNAL. Various Issues. Seoul.

KOREA FOREIGN TRADE ASSOCIATION – KFTA – (1988a) *Import–Export Notice*. Seoul, Korea.

—— (1988b) *Korea's New Import Policies: Expanding Supply Sources, Accelerating Market Liberalisation*. October. Seoul, Korea.

—— (1989) *Major Statistics of Korean Economy*. Seoul.

KOREA TRADE & BUSINESS. Various issues.

KRUEGER, A. O. (1974) 'The Political Economy of the Rent Seeking Society', *American Economic Review*, 64, June, pp. 291–303.

—— (1979) *The Developmental Role of the Foreign Sector and Aid*. Cambridge, Mass.: Harvard Univ. Press.

—— (1981) 'Export-Led Industrial Growth Reconsidered'. In W. Hong, and L. Krause (eds) (1981) *Trade and Growth of the Advanced Developing Countries in the Pacific Rim*. Seoul, Korea Development Institute Press.

—— (1984) 'Trade Policies in Developing Countries'. In R.W. Jones and P.B. Kenen (eds) *Handbook of International Economics. Vol. 1*. Amsterdam: Elsevier Science Publishers.

—— (1985) 'The Experiences and Lessons of Asia's Super Exporters'. In A. O. Krueger, and V. Corbo, *Export Oriented Development Strategies : the Success of Five Newly Industrialising Countries*. Boulder, Colo.: Westview Press.

—— (1990a) 'Asia Trade and Growth Lessons', *American Economic Review*, vol. 80, no. 2, pp. 108–111.

—— (1990b) 'Government Failures in Development', *Journal of Economic Perspectives*, vol. 4, no. 3, pp. 9–23.

—— (1990c) 'Theory and Practice of Commercial Policy: 1945–1990'. National Bureau of Economic Research Working Paper No. 3569.

KRUEGER, A. O. and ORSMOND, D. (1990) 'Impact of Government on Growth and Trade'. National Bureau of Economic Research Working Paper No. 3545, Dec.

KRUGMAN, P. (1984a) 'Import Protection as Export Promotion: International Competition in the Presence of Oligopoly and Economies of Scale'. In H. Kierzkowski (ed.) *Monopolistic Competition and International Trade*. Oxford: Clarendon Press.

—— (1984b) 'The U.S. Response to Foreign Industrial Targeting'. *Brookings Papers on Economic Activity*, vol. 1.

—— (1993) 'Towards a Counter-Counterrevolution in Development Theory', *Proceedings of the World Bank Annual Conference on Development Economics 1992*.

KRUGMAN, P. and OBSTFELD, M. (1988) *International Economics: Theory and Practice*. Boston: Scott, Foresman and Co.

KUME, H. (1988) *A Proteção Efetiva Proposta na Reforma Tarifária*. Rio de Janeiro: Fundação Estudos de Comércio Exterior (FUNCEX), mimeo.

KUZNETS, P. W. (1977) *Economic Growth and Structure in Korea*. New Haven, Yale University Press.

KWACK, S.Y. and CHUNG, U.C. (1986) 'The Role of Financial Policies and Institutions in Korea's Economic Development Process'. In H. S. Cheng (ed.) *Financial Policy and Reform in Pacific Basin Countries* Lexington, Mass.: Lexington Books.

LAGO, L. A. C. (1990) 'A Retomada do Crescimento e as Distorções do "Milagre". 1967–73'. In M. P. Abreu (ed.) *A Ordem do Progresso: Cem Anos de Política Econômica Republicana. 1889–1989*. Rio de Janeiro: Editora Campus.

LALL, S. (1991) 'Explaining Industrial Success in the Developing World'. In S. Lall and V.N. Balasubramaranyan (eds) *Current Issues in Developing Economics*. London: Macmillan.

—— (1992a) *Bank Approach to Industrialization: An OED Study of Three Industrialising Countries*. Washington: World Bank.

—— (1992b) 'Technological Capabilities and Industrialization'. World Development, vol. 20 (2), pp. 165–186.

—— (forthcoming) 'The East Asian Miracle' Study: Does the Bell Toll for Industrial Strategy? World Development.

LALL, S. and KELL, G. (1991) 'Industrial Development in Developing Countries and The Role of Government Interventions'. *Banca Nazionale del Lavoro Quarterly Review*, no. 178, September.

LALL, S. and STREETEN, P. (1977) *Foreign Investment, Transnationals and Developing Countries*. London: Macmilan.

LEE, D. H., BAE, Z. and LEE, J. (1991) 'Performance and Adaptive Roles of the Government-Supported Research Institute in South Korea', *World Development*, 19(10), pp. 1421–1440.

LEE, K-U., URATA, S. and CHOI, I. (1986) 'Recent Development in Industrial Organisation Issues in Korea'. KDI Working Paper No. 8609, December. Seoul.

LEFF, N.H.(1968) *The Brazilian Capital Goods Industry, 1929–1964*. Cambridge. M.A. : Harvard University Press.

LEIBENSTEIN, H. (1981) 'Microeconomics and X-efficiency Theory: If there is no crisis, there ought to be'. In D. Bell and I. Kristel (eds) *The Crisis in Economic Theory*. New York: Basic Books.

LESSA, C. (1982) *Quinze Anos de Política Econômica*. São Paulo, Ed. Brasiliense. Published in English as, *Fifteen Years of Economic Policy in Brazil*. Economic Bulletin for Latin America, November 1964.

LITTLE, I.M.D. (1982) *Economic Development - Theory, Policies and International Relations* . New York: Basic Books.

LITTLE, I. M. D., SCOTT, M. and SCITOVSKY M. S. (1970) *Industry and Trade in Some Developing Countries: A Comparative Study*. London: Oxford University Press.

LUCKE, M. (1990) *Traditional Labour-Intensive Industries in Newly Industrialising Countries. The Case of Brazil*. Kieler Studien, University of Kiel, Tübingen.

LUEDDE-NEURATH, R. (1986) *Import Controls and Exported Oriented Development: A Reassessment of the South Korean Case*. Boulder, Colo: Westview Special Studies on East Asia. Westview Press.

MACHADO, J. B. M. (1990) *Tarifa Aduaneira a Protecionismo no Brasil*. Master thesis submitted to the Institute of Industrial Economics of the Federal University of Rio de Janeiro. Rio de Janeiro: May.

MALAN, P and BONELLI, R. (1990) *Brazil 1950–80: Three Decades of Growth Oriented Policies*. Rio de Janeiro: IPEA/INPES Internal Discussion Paper No. 187.

MALAN, P., BONELLI, R., ABREU, M. and PEREIRA. J. E. C.(1980) *Política Econômica Externa e Industrialização no Brasil. 1939–52*. Rio de Janeiro: IPEA/INPES.

MASON, E. S. *et al.* (1980) *The Economic and Social Modernisation of the Republic of Korea*. Cambridge, Mass. : Harvard Univ. Press.

MATESCO, V. (1988) *As Novas Diretrizes da Política Industrial*. Rio de Janeiro. Relatório do IPEA/INPES Seminário de Política Industrial. July.

McGINN, N.F. *et al.* (1980) *Education and Development in Korea*. Cambridge, MA: Council on East Asian Studies Harvard University. Harvard University Press.

McKINNON, R. (1991) *The Order of Economic Liberalisation: Financial Control in the Transition to a Market Economy*. Baltimore: Johns Hopkins University Press.

MELLO, J.M.C. (1982) *O Capitalismo Tardio*. São Paulo: Editora Brasiliense.

MICHELL, T. (1988) 'From a Developing to a Newly Industrialised Country: The Republic of Korea, 1962–82'. Geneva: International Labour Organisation Publications.

MIHN, K. (1988) 'Industrial Policy for Industrialization of Korea'. Seoul: Korea Institute for Economics and Technology (KIET) Occasional Paper.

MINISTRY OF FINANCE–MOF (1991) 'Direct Foreign Investment System will be Further Liberalised Starting March 1991'. *MOF Monthly Bulletin*, Jan., no 90. Seoul.

MINISTRY OF SCIENCE AND TECHNOLOGY – MOST – (1988) *Introduction to Science and Technology. Republic of Korea*. Seoul.

MINISTRY OF TRADE AND INDUSTRY – MTI – (1990a) *The Korean Economy and U.S.–Korea Trade Relations: A Statistical Profile*. February, Seoul.

—— (1990b) *Partnership in Progress: Korea's Record and Commitment.* February, Seoul.

MODIANO, E. M. (1990) 'A Ópera dos Três Cruzados 1985–1989'. In M. P. ABREU (ed.) *A Ordem do Progresso: Cem Anos de Política Econômica Republicana. 1889–1989.* Rio de Janeiro: Editora Campus.

MOREIRA, H. C. and ARAÚJO, A. B. (1984) *A Política Brasileira de Importações: uma descrição.* Rio de Janeiro: IPEA/INPES, série EPICO No. 1.

MORLEY, S. and SMITH, G. W.(1971) 'Import Substitution and Foreign Investment in Brazil'. *Oxford Economic Papers*, vol. 23, pp. 120–135.

MUSALEM, A. R. (1983) *O Regime de Drawback nas Exportações de Manufaturados e a Balança Comercial no Brasil.* Rio de Janeiro: *Pesquisa e Planejamento Econômico*, 13(3), 745–762.

NAM, C. H. (1981) 'Trade and Industrial Policies, and the Structure of protection in Korea'. In W. Hong and L. Krause, *Trade and Growth of the Advanced Developing Countries in the Pacific Rim.* Seoul: Korea Development Institute Press.

—— (1985) 'Trade Policy and Economic Development in Korea'. Discussion Paper No. 9, Institute of Economic Development, Korea University. Seoul.

NELSON, R. and WINTER, S. (1982) *An Evolutionary Theory of Economic Change.* Cambridge: Harvard University Press.

NEWFARMER, R. (1979) 'TNC Takeovers in Brazil: The Uneven Distribution of Benefits in the Market for Firms'. *World Development*, vol. 7, pp. 25–43.

—— (1983) 'Multinationals and Marketplace Magic'. In C.P. Kindleberger and D. B. Audretsch (eds) *The Multinational Corporation in the 1980s.* Cambridge: MIT Press.

NEWFARMER, R. and MILLER, W. (1975) *Multinationals in Brazil and Mexico: Structural Sources of Economic and non Economic Power.* Washington, U.S. Senate, 1975.

NURKSE, R. (1962) *Patterns of Trade and Development.* Oxford: Blackwell.

OFFICE OF CUSTOMS ADMINISTRATION (1988). *Yearbook of Foreign Trade.* Ministry of Finance, Seoul, Korea.

ORGANIZATION FOR ECONOMIC COOPERATION AND DEVELOPMENT (OECD) (1989) *Main Economic Indicators. Historical Statistics 1969–1988.*

PACK, H. (1989) 'Industrialization and Trade'. In H.B. Chenery and T. N. Srinivasan (eds) *Handbook of Development Economics, vol. 1.* Amsterdam: North-Holland.

PACK, H. and WESTPHAL, L. (1986) 'Industrial Strategy and Technological Change: Theory Versus Reality', *Journal of Development Economics*, 22, 87–128.

PARK, Y. C. (1985) 'Korea's Experience with External Debt Management'. In G. Smith and J. T. Cuddington (eds.) *International Debt and the Developing Countries.* Baltimore, Md.: Johns Hopkins.

PASTORE, A. C., SAVASINI, J. A., ROSA, J. and KUME, H. (1979) *Promoção Efetiva às Exportações no Brasil.* Rio de Janeiro: FUNCEX.

PEREIRA, J. E. de C. (1974) *Financiamento Externo e Crescimento Econômico no Brasil: 1966:73.* Rio de Janeiro: IPEA/INPES, Coleção Relatórios de Pesquisa, no. 27.

PIRAGIBE, C. (1985) *Indústria de Informática: Desenvolvimento Brasileiro e Mundial.* Rio de Janeiro: Editora Campus.

POSNER, M.V. (1961) 'International Trade and Technical Change', *Oxford Economic Papers*, no. 13, pp. 323–41.

PREBISCH, R. (1950) *The Economic Development of Latin America and its Principal Problems.* Lake Success, NY: United Nations Department of Social Affairs.

PRESIDENTIAL COMMISSION REPORT ON ECONOMIC REESTRUC-TURING – PCRER – (1988). Realigning Korea's National Priorities for Economic Advance. Seoul.

QUEM É QUEM. VISÃO. Various Issues.

RAMASWAMI, V. K. and SRINIVASAN, T. N. (1971) 'Tariff Structure and Resource Allocation in the Presence of Factor Substitution'. In *Trade, Balance of Payments and Growth: Papers in International Economics in Honour of Charles P. Kindleberger.* Amsterdam: North-Holland.

RESENDE, A. L. (1990) 'Estabilização e Reforma: 1964–67'. In M. P. Abreu (ed.) *A Ordem do Progresso: Cem Anos de Política Econômica Republicana. 1889–1989.* Rio de Janeiro: Editora Campus.

RHEE, S. (1987) 'Policy Reforms of the Eighties and Industrial Adjustments', KDI Working Paper No. 8708, July. Seoul, Korea.

RHEE, Y.W., ROOS-LARSON, B. and PURSELL, G. (1984) *Korea's Competitive Edge: Managing to Entry Into World Markets.* Baltimore Md: Johns Hopkins Univ. Press for the World Bank.

ROBINSON, J. (1933) *The Economics of Imperfect Competition* London: Macmillan.

RODRIGUES, D.G. (1986) *Empresas Não-Financeiras no Brasil: Evoluçao do Desempenho no Período 1975–84. Rio de Janeiro:* IBMEC.

RODRIK, D. (1988a) 'Closing the Productivity Gap: Does Trade Liberalisation Really Help'? In G.K. Helleiner (ed.) *Trade Policy Industrialization and Development.* Toronto e Helsinki: Wider. UNU.

—— (1988b) 'Imperfect Competition, Scale Economies, and Trade Policy in Developing Countries'. In R. Baldwin (ed.) *Trade Policy Issues and Empirical Analysis.* Chicago: University Chicago Press.

ROMER, P. M. and RIVERA-BATIZ, L. A. (1991) 'International Trade With Endogenous Technological Change', *European Economic Review*, vol. 35 (May 1991), pp. 971–1104.

ROSA, J. *et al.* (1979) Alguns Aspectos da Política Tarifária Recente no Brasil. Rio de Janeiro. FUNCEX, Projeto XXIII (relatório parcial). Outubro. Vol. I.

ROSENSTEIN-RODAN, P. N. (1943) 'Problems of Industrialization of Eastern and South-Eastern Europe', *Economic Journal*, vol. 53, no. 2/3, pp. 202–211.

ROSS, S. A., WESTERFIELD, R. W. and JAFFE, J. (1988) *Corporate Finance.* Boston: Irwin.

SCHERER, F. M. and ROSS (1990) *Industrial Market Structure and Economic Performance.* Boston: Houghton Mifflin Co.

SCHMITZ, H. and HEWITT, T (1992) 'An Assessment of the Market Reserve for the Brazilian Computer Industry'. In H. Schmitz and J. Cassiolato. (eds) *Hi-Tech for Industrial Development. Lessons from the Brazilian Experience in Electronics and Automation.* New York: Routledge.

SCITOVSKY, T. (1963) 'Two Concepts of External Economies'. In A.N.

Agarwala and S.P. Singh (eds.) *The Economic of Underdevelopment.* New York: Oxford University Press.

SERRA, J. (1982) 'Ciclos e Mudanças Estruturais na Economia Brasileira do Pós-Guerra'. In L.G. M. Beluzzo e Coutinho, R. (eds) *Desenvolvimento Capitalista no Brasil: ensaios sobre a crise.* São Paulo: Editora Brasiliense.

SHAPIRO, H. and TAYLOR, L. (1990) The State and the Industrial Strategy. *World Development,* vol. 18, no. 6, pp. 861–878.

SIMONSEN, M.H. (1988) 'Brazil'. In R. Dornbusch and Helmers, F. L.C.H. (eds) *The Open Economy. Tools for Policymakers in Developing Countries.* Washington D.C.: Oxford University Press for the World Bank.

SOCHACZEWSKI, A. C. (1980) 'Financial and Economic Development of Brazil, 1952–68'. Thesis submitted to the University of London for the Degree of Doctor of Philosophy, July.

SOCHACZEWSKI, A. C. and ORENSTEIN, L. (1990) 'Democracia com Desenvolvimento: 1956-1961'. In M. Abreu (ed.) *A Ordem do Progresso: Cem Anos de Política Econômica Republicana. 1889–1989.* Rio de Janeiro: Editora Campus.

SOLOW, R.M. (1957) 'Technical Change and The Aggregate Production Function', *Review of Economics and Statistics,* 39 (August), 312–20.

STALLINGS, B. (1990) 'The Role of Foreign Capital in Economic Development'. In Gary Gereffi and Donald L. Wyman (eds) *Manufacturing Miracles: Paths of Industrialization in Latin America and East Asia.* Princeton: Princeton University Press.

STIGLER, G.J. (1951) 'The Division of Labour is Limited by the Extent of the Market', *Journal of Political Economy,* 59.

STIGLITZ, J. (1988) 'Economic Organisation, Information, and Development'. In H. Chenery and T. N. Srinivasan (eds) *Handbook of Development Economics, Vol. I.* Amsterdam: Elsevier Science Publishers.

—— (1989) 'Markets, Market Failures, and Development', *American Economic Review. Papers and Proceedings,* 79(2), pp. 197–202.

SUH, T. S. (1975) *Import Substitution and Economic Development in Korea.* Seoul: Korea Development Institute Press.

SUZIGAN, W. (1978) 'Política Industrial no Brasil'. In W. Suzigan (ed.) *Indústria: Políticas, Instituições e Desenvolvimento.* Rio de Janeiro: IPEA/ INPES Série Monográfica No. 28.

—— (1980) 'Barreiras não Tarifárias as Importações'. Rio de Janeiro: IPEA/ INPES. Discussion Paper No. 29.

—— (1984) 'Investment in the Manufacturing Industry in Brazil, 1869–1939'. Thesis submitted to the University of London for the Degree of Doctor of Philosophy.

—— (1986) 'A Indústria Brasileira em 1985/86. Desempenho e Política'. In R. Carneiro (ed.) *Política Econômica da Nova República.* São Paulo: Editora Paz e Terra

—— (1988) *Reestruturação Industrial e Competitividade nos Paises Avançados e nos NICs Asiáticos: Lições para o Brasil.* São Paulo: Governo do Estado de São Paulo.

SUZIGAN, W., PEREIRA, J. E. de C. and ALMEIDA, R.A.G.(1972) *Financiamento de Projetos Industriais no Brasil.* Rio de Janeiro: Relatório de Pesquisa No. 9, IPEA/INPES.

SYLOS-LABINI (1962) *Oligopoly and Technical Progress.* Cambridge: Harvard University Press.

TAVARES, C. and LESSA, C. (1985) *O Desenvolvimento e a Política Industrial da Década de 70–Impasses e Alternativas.* Rio de Janeiro: Institute of Industrial Economics. Mimeo.

TAVARES, M. C. (1973) *Da Substituição de Importações ao Capitalismo Financeiro. Ensaios sobre Economia Brasileira.* Rio de Janeiro: Zahar Editores.

TENDLER, J. (1968) *Electric Power in Brazil.* Cambridge, M.A.: Harvard University Press.

TOPIK, S. (1980) 'State Interventionism in a Liberal Regime: Brazil, 1889–1930', *Hispanic American Historical Review*, 60(4), pp. 593–616.

TREBAT, T.J. (1983) *Brazil's State-Owned Enterprises: A Case Study of the State as an Entrepeneur.* Cambridge: Cambridge University Press.

TYLER, W. G. (1976) 'Manufactured Export Expansion and Industrialization in Brazil', *Kieler Studien*, no. 134. University of Kiel.

—— (1981) *The Brazilian Industrial Economy.* Lexington, MA: Lexington Books.

—— (1983) *Incentivos às Exportaçõs e às Vendas no Mercado Interno: Análise da Política Comercial e da Discrimação contra as Exportações – 1980–81.* Rio de Janeiro: Pesquisa e Planejamento Econômico 13(2).

UNCTAD (1990) *Handbook of International Trade and Development Statistics.* Geneva.

UNESCO *Statistical Yearbook* , various years. Paris.

UNITED NATIONS (UN-ITSY) *International Trade Statistical Year-book.* Various years. Geneva.

—— (UN-HIT) *Handbook of International Trade. Various* years. Geneva.

UNITED NATIONS INDUSTRIAL DEVELOPMENT ORGANIZATION (UNIDO). Various years. *Industry and Development– Global Report.* Vienna.

UNITED STATES INTERNATIONAL TRADE COMMISSION (USITC)/(1985) *Foreign Industrial Targeting and its effects on U.S. Industries: Phase III: Brazil, Canada, Korea, Mexico and Taiwan.* Publication no. 1632, January, Washington.

VARIAN, H. R. (1984) *Microeconomic Analysis.* New York: W. W. Norton Company.

VERSIANI, F.R. (1979) 'Industrial Investment in a "Export" Economy: the Brazilian Experience before 1914'. University of London, Institute of Latin American Studies. Working Paper No. 2.

VILLELA, A. V. (1984) *Empresas do Governo como Instrumento de Política Econômica.* Rio de Janeiro: IPEA/INPES Coleção Relatórios de Pesquisa No. 47.

VILLELA, A. V. and BAER, W. (1980) *O Setor Privado Nacional: Problemas e Políticas para o seu Fortalecimento.* Rio de Janeiro: IPEA/INPES Coleção Relatórios de Pesquisa No. 46.

VILLELA, A. V. and SUZIGAN, W. (1977) *Government Policies and Economic Growth.* Rio de Janeiro: IPEA/INPES. Série monografica No. 10.

WADE, R. (1988) 'The Role of Government in Overcoming Market Failure: Taiwan, Republic of Korea and Japan'. In H. Hughes (ed.) *Achieving Industrialization in East Asia.* Cambridge: Cambridge University Press.

—— (1990) *Governing the Market. Economic Theory and the Role of Government in East Asian Industrialization.* Princeton: Princeton University Press.
WEISS, J. (1988) *Industry in Developing Countries: Theory, Policy and Evidence.* London: Routledge.
WELLS, J. (1987) *Empleo en América Latina: Uma Búsqueda de Opciones.* Santiago: PREALC. International Labour Organisation.
WERNECK, A. de O. (1969) 'As Atividades Empresariais do Governo Federal no Brasil', *Revista Brasileira de Economia,* 23(3), pp. 89–110.
WESTPHAL, L. E. (1979) 'Manufacturing'. In P. Hassan and R. C. Rao (eds) *Korea: Policy Issues for Long Term Development.* Baltimore Md: Johns Hopkins Univ. Press for the World Bank.
—— (1982) 'Fostering Technological Mastery by Means of Selective Infant-Industry Protection'. In M. Syrquim and S. Teitel (eds) *Trade, Stability, Technology, and Equity in Latin America.* New York: Academic Press.
—— (1990) 'Industrial Policy in a Export–Propelled Economy: Lessons from the South Korea's Experience', *Journal of Economic Perspectives,* summer, 4, pp. 341–359.
WESTPHAL, L. E. and KIM, K. S. (1982) 'Korea'. In Balassa, B. (Ed) *Development Strategies in Semi– industrial Countries.* Baltimore Md: Johns Hopkins Univ. Press for the World Bank.
WESTPHAL, L. E., KIM, L. and DAHLMAN, C. J. (1985) 'Reflections on the Republic of Korea's Acquisition of Technological Capability'. In N. Rosemberg and C. Frischtak (eds) *International Transfer of Technology: Concepts, Measures, and Comparisons.* New York: Praeger.
WESTPHAL, L. E., RHEE, W.Y. and PURSELL, G. (1979) 'Foreign Influences on Korean Industrial Development', *Oxford Bulletin,* November, pp. 359–388.
WILLMORE, L. (1987) 'Controle Estrangeiro e Concentração na Indústria Brasileira', *Pesquisa e Planejamento Econômico,* 17(1), 161 a 190. Rio de Janeiro.
WOO, K. D. (1978) 'Wages and Labour Productivity in the Cotton Spinning Industries of Japan, Korea, and Taiwan', *Developing Economies,* 16, 182–198.
WORLD BANK (1979) *Brazil. Human Resources Special Report.* A World Bank country study. Washington, D.C. : World Bank.
—— (1983a) *Brazil, Industrial Policies and Manufactured Exports.* A World Bank country study. Washington, D.C. : World Bank.
—— (1983b) *World Development Report* Washington, D.C. : World Bank.
—— (1984a) *Brazil. Financial Systems Review.* A World Bank country study. Washington, D.C. : World Bank.
—— (1984b) *Korea: Development in a Global Context.* Country study. Washington, D.C. : World Bank.
—— (1987a) *Korea: Managing the Industrial Transition.* Vols 1 and 2. Washington, D.C. : World Bank.
—— (1987b) *World Development Report* Washington, D.C. : World Bank.
—— (1991) *World Development Report* Washington, D.C. : World Bank.
—— (1993) *The East Asian Miracle. Economic Growth and Public Policy.* A World Bank Policy Research Report. Washington, D. C.: Oxford University Press.

YOO, JUNG-HO (1990) *The Industrial Policy of the 1970s and The Evolution of the Manufacturing Sector in Korea*. KDI Working Paper no. 9017, October.

YOUNG, S. (1986) 'Import Liberalisation and Industrial Adjustment in Korea'. Seoul: Korea Development Institute Working Paper No. 8613, December.

—— (1987) 'Korea's Trade Policy Problems: a Comprehensive Review'. Seoul: Korea Development Institute Working Paper No. 8720, December.

—— (1988) 'Trade Policy Problems in the Republic of Korea and their Implications for Korea–U.S. Cooperation'. Seoul.: Korea Development Institute Working Paper No. 8824, December.

—— (1989) 'Trade Policy Problems of the Republic of Korea and The Uruguay Round'. Seoul: Korea Development Institute Working Paper No. 8913, April.

ZONINSEIN, J. (1984) 'Atitudes Nacionais e Financiamento da Indústria: A Experiência Brasileira'. Rio de Janeiro: Discussion Paper No. 63 Institute of Industrial Economics. Federal University of Rio de Janeiro. December.

ZYSMAN, J. (1983) *Governments, Markets and Growth: Financial Systems and the Politics of Industrial Change*. Ithaca:, Cornell University Press.

Index

custom-built sector 119–20

debt–equity ratios 123
 Germany 187
 Japan 45, 187
 Korea 45, 187; liberalization 74
 United States of America 45, 187
debts
 Brazil 118, 203
 Korea 63, 172
 newly industrializing countries 2
defence industries 56
direct unproductive profit-seeking 6
domestic resource costs 6
dynamic comparative advantages 39
dynamic economies 16–17

economies of internationalization
 18–19
economies of scale
 Brazil 102
 import substitution 5
 Korea 46
 marginal cost pricing 141n.14
 static economies 18
economies of scope 18
education
 Brazil 52, 92, 96, 107, 117;
  investment 113
 investment 27–8
 Korea 32, 35, 61, 168;
  commitment to 52;
  liberalization 74
effective rates of protection (ERPs)
 Korea 39–40, 58–9
 neoclassicism 4, 5, 7, 13
efficient markets 12
Eletrobras 159n.208
employment
 Brazil 101–2, 198
 Korea 76, 77
entry
 barriers 18
 protectionism 22
exchange rates
 Brazil 99, 109, 114–15, 195;
  auction system 98;
  controls 92–3; orthodox
  adjustment 125
export promotion 9
 Korea 33, 143n.31, 144n.49;
  heavy and chemical
  industries 57; liberalization 72;
  outward-oriented regime 38;

purchase power parity 34, 171
export processing zones (EPZ) 130
export-promotion (EP) policies 1,
 6–9
exports
 from Brazil 88, 189, 190–1, 201,
  203; heterodox stabilization
  129–30; manufacturing 94;
  reforms 106; subsidies 109–11,
  118–19, 126; 'T' plan 97
 from Korea 33–4, 172; financial
  market 51; foreign firms 47,
  48; heavy and chemical
  industries 55, 57, 63–5;
  incentives 143n.32; to
  Japan 32; liberalization 72, 75;
  manufacturing sector 168, 169,
  170; outward-oriented regime
  36–7, 38–9, 41, 43; promotion
  175–6; subsidies 110–11, 177
 newly industrializing countries 2
 protectionism 21

factor markets
 failures 23–9, 35
 imperfections 30
 import substitution 5
 Korea 135; failures 35;
  intervention 48–53, 60–2
 liberalization 73–5, 81–3
Fair Trade Act 80
financial sector
 Brazil 92, 95, 115–16
 and conglomerates 44
 failures 23–7
 import substitution 5
 Korea 48–52, 60–1
 liberalization 73–4
Foreign Capital Inducement Law
 (FCIL) 47, 59–60
foreign direct investment (FDI) 77
 Argentina 149n.114
 Brazil 47, 99, 102, 109, 115–16,
  149n.114, 196, 199–200;
  reforms 106
 Hong Kong 182
 Korea 47–8, 85, 182–4
 Mexico 47, 149n.114
 Singapore 182
 Taiwan 182
free trade 8

Germany
 capital market 25